Food Policy and the Environmental Credit Crunch

The changing economic environment for the consumer that is emerging from the wreckage of the financial credit crunch plays directly into the importance of food spending. This is certainly true from the perspective of food prices in the short run, but also from the perspective of sustainability and reducing the impact of the environmental credit crunch. The economic changes we experience now have a bearing on our ability to manage the environmental credit crunch that looms.

Food Policy and the Environmental Credit Crunch elaborates on the issues addressed in the authors' first book, *From Red to Green?*, and asks whether the financial credit crunch could ameliorate or exacerbate the emergent environmental credit crunch. The conclusion drawn here is that a significant and positive difference could be made by changing some of the ways in which we procure, prepare and consume our food.

Written by an economist and an investment professional, this book addresses the economic and environmental implications of how we treat food. It examines each aspect of the 'food food-chain', from agriculture to production and processing, retail, preparation, consumption and waste.

Julie Hudson, CFA, is a Managing Director at UBS Investment Bank, where she heads up the ESG and Sustainability team established by UBS within its Equity Research division at the end of 2004.

Paul Donovan is a Managing Director and Global Economist at UBS Investment Bank. Paul is responsible for formulating and presenting the UBS Investment Research global economic view.

'Hudson and Donovan provide a fascinating analysis of the environmental and economic costs of modern food. Their conclusion, that food waste must be managed across the entire food-chain, is a lesson humanity must learn if we are to avoid going hungry.' **Ruth Giradet, Stakeholder Engagement Director, Tesco plc**

'A radical change in our relationship with the environment is long overdue. Food is central to that, culturally and economically. Following food from field to waste bin, this book details the power of culture in shaping economics – giving a fresh perspective on tackling the problem of sustainable food supply.' **Bernard Silverman, FRS; Senior Research Fellow, Smith School of Enterprise and the Environment, Oxford; Former President, Royal Statistical Society**

'This book provides a much needed and novel perspective on the global food system and the urgent need to address simultaneously global food and environmental security.' **Charles Godfray, Director, Oxford Martin Programme on the Future of Food, The University of Oxford, UK**

Food Policy and the Environmental Credit Crunch

From soup to nuts

Julie Hudson and Paul Donovan

LONDON AND NEW YORK

First published 2014
by Routledge

2 Park Square, Milton Park, Abingdon, Oxfordshire OX14 4RN
711 Third Avenue, New York, NY 10017

Routledge is an imprint of the Taylor & Francis Group, an informa business

First issued in paperback 2018

© 2014 Julie Hudson and Paul Donovan

The right of Julie Hudson and Paul Donovan to be identified as authors of this work has been asserted by them in accordance with sections 77 and 78 of the Copyright, Designs and Patents Act 1988.

All rights reserved. No part of this book may be reprinted or reproduced or utilised in any form or by any electronic, mechanical, or other means, now known or hereafter invented, including photocopying and recording, or in any information storage or retrieval system, without permission in writing from the publishers.

All reasonable effort has been made to gain permission for the use of recycled material in this book.

The opinions and statements expressed in this book are those of the authors and are not necessarily the opinions of any other person, including UBS AG. UBS AG and its affiliates accept no liability whatsoever for any statements or opinions contained in this book, or for the consequences which may result from any person relying on any such opinions or statements.

Trademark notice: Product or corporate names may be trademarks or registered trademarks, and are used only for identification and explanation without intent to infringe.

British Library Cataloguing in Publication Data
A catalogue record for this book is available from the British Library

Library of Congress Cataloging-in-Publication Data
Hudson, Julie, (Accountant)
Food policy and the environmental credit crunch: from soup to nuts/Julie Hudson and Paul Donovan.
pages cm
Includes bibliographical references and index.
1. Nutrition policy. 2. Environmental policy. 3. Environmental economics. 4. Financial crises.
I. Donovan, Paul, 1972– II. Title.
TX359.H83 2013
363.8'2—dc23
2013013856

ISBN: 978-0-415-64401-3 (hbk)
ISBN: 978-1-138-38306-7 (pbk)

Typeset in Times
by Book Now Ltd, London

Contents

List of illustrations vii
Acknowledgements ix

1 Overview: the great food crunch 1

2 Raw material inputs: mineral 20

3 Raw material inputs: vegetable 42

4 Raw material inputs: animal 63

5 Food processing 83

6 Transport 101

7 Food wholesaling and retailing 120

8 Eating food 139

9 Human health and food 159

10 Food waste 180

11 Conclusion 203

Bibliography 212
Index 222

Illustrations

Figures

3.1	Efficiency: the Hudson–Donovan ecosystem trade-off matrix for grain markets	46
4.1	Life-cycle greenhouse gas emissions, selected food items	72
6.1	Where the orange juice flows	104
6.2	Using transport to reduce environmental footprints: environmental gains from trade	118
7.1	Easy decisions versus trade-offs for food retail: or, why we need this book	125
10.1	The Falstaffian approach to food waste	182

Tables

2.1	A taxonomy of land by land use and how each relates to the ecosystem and the economy	23
2.2	Ecological footprints – distribution by usage, and 'budget'	24
3.1	Food availability in the world's least-developed economies	45
5.1	The tale of three loaves in detail	91
6.1	UK sowing and harvesting seasons for beans, lettuce, tomatoes and apples	115
6.2	The share of selected environmental impacts from transportation, heating and electricity for greenhouse tomato and carrot production (combined)	116
8.1	The tale of three Fisherman's Pies	147
8.2	Breakfast like a king	150
10.1	Summing up – waste in the food food-chain	184

Boxes

1.1	Environmental and economic inequality	17
2.1	Wetlands in history	27
2.2	The tragedy of the commons	31

2.3	The economics of excrement	33
2.4	The Green Revolution	38
3.1	A real-world food shock 2006–8	43
3.2	The economics of the potato famine	51
3.3	Fungal infections	54
3.4	From mud-bath to Bath	56
4.1	The silver darlings	64
4.2	Milk and efficiency	74
4.3	The economics of disease control	76
5.1	Chips with everything	87
5.2	Waste case study: coffee	97
6.1	How green are African green beans?	109
8.1	School dinners	154
9.1	Fasting oneself clever	164
9.2	Adding variety to the diet with the mealworm	173
11.1	Raw material inputs – mineral	204
11.2	Raw material inputs – vegetable	205
11.3	Raw material inputs – animal	205
11.4	Transport	206
11.5	Food processing	207
11.6	Retailing and wholesaling	208
11.7	Cooking pot and table	209
11.8	Health	209
11.9	Waste	210

Acknowledgements

The subtitle of this book, *From Soup to Nuts,* is an Anglo-American phrase that means 'from start to finish'. A formal English dinner would begin with the soup course and conclude with nuts being cracked (often as the port wine circulated around the table). The idea of food as a metaphor for a complete process in life is old – the Romans used *'ab ovo usque ad mala'*[1] ('eggs to apples') as reflecting the same thing. Romans began their meals with eggs and ended with fruit.

The 'soup' part of this project came from our previous book *From Red to Green? How the financial credit crunch could bankrupt the environment*[2] – a thrilling tale packed full of drama and excitement, which is still available to purchase from all good booksellers. The opening chapter of *From Red to Green?* was about food, and such was the wealth of background material that we accumulated it seemed that we had another book just waiting to be written without any effort on our part.

Of course, such hopes are always an illusion. No book appears on the scene without a great deal of support, and we have relied on many, many people for their contributions, words of encouragement, and gentle hints. Larry Hatheway, UBS Chief Economist; Nick Pink, UBS Global Director of Research; and Tom Daula, UBS Head of Global Research and Analytics gave us their permission to write the book and offered support for the project – which is a personal undertaking. The research department at UBS encourages rigorous analysis in many forms, and we know that we are lucky to work for an entity where such rigour is regarded as a necessity and not a luxury. Erika Karp, UBS Head of Global Sector Research, along with Larry, read the book in advance of publication and we have profited greatly from their comments. Erika has also been a particularly enthusiastic and tireless supporter of the topics covered in this book.

Patrick O'Bryan and Ruth Ridout provided editorial oversight, added coherence, and were eternally patient with our repeated grammatical errors. Michael Butterworth also provided a very useful pair of eyes, catching errors he was not even supposed to be looking for. As authors we write separately (generally speaking we are not even on the same continent at the same time), and this can present a challenge in preparing an integrated piece of work. The process of turning the raw ingredients into what is hopefully a digestible whole was made a great deal easier with the help of these people.

As we progressed through the various stages of the food food-chain we relied on the expertise and wisdom of a great number of people. Sometimes it was a snatched conversation, sometimes more detailed assistance, but special thanks are owed to many.

George Magnus has been invaluable in offering advice on writing books, and as an economic sparring partner and sounding board over the years. Mona Sutphen, former US White House Deputy Chief of Staff, and Danny Alexander, Chief Secretary to the Treasury in the UK gave help on the political and policy side. Professor Charles Godfray, who is not only one of the only people able to identify certain tiny wasps (which does not appear in any of the recipes discussed within) but also a fount of knowledge on the subject of sustainable food, was kind enough to read the book and comment. Dr Nicolette Ray, Honorary Assistant Professor at Hong Kong University, helped direct some of the nutritional aspects of the book by freely passing on her expertise and knowledge. Ruth Giradet, Stakeholder Engagement Director of Tesco, has shared her background knowledge over the years, shared a debating platform with one of the authors and a spotted ceramic pig called Humpty Dumpty without any qualms, and also took time to comment on the text. Paul Schneider took time to read and comment on an early draft.

Contributions to the book are not always directly related to it, but there are many subtle ways in which people have helped shape the final outcome. Therefore Paul would like to thank: Rachel Baird for being an early, gentle voice of environmental conscience; Becca James for having enough faith to commission a wedding cake; Maria Donovan for commissioning a second wedding cake; David Wareham and Bhauna Patel for being the only two people who can share a kitchen with me without committing acts of violence; Ciara Wells for her vast experience of and years of helping with direct research into wine; countless other friends who have resolutely endured my attempts at cooking; Chris and Judith Trimming for providing a refuge from the stresses of editing, as well as offering (with Graham Seviour) agricultural expertise.

Julie would like to thank colleagues within or associated with UBS who have knowingly or unknowingly stimulated ideas – Hubert Jeaneau, Eva Zlotnicka, Joe Dewhurst and Wayne Gordon, to name just four. The many inspiring Earthwatch scientists and project leaders must also not be forgotten. In particular, for this book: those involved in the Costa Rica Coffee expedition (Sebastián Castro Tanzi and Natalia Ureña Retana); and in the 'Edge of the Arctic' Climate Change expeditions (especially Pete Kershaw for useful reading on the subject of snow geese). Also the Smith School (and the many people connected with it) for the rich seam of sustainability-related knowledge, experience and expertise it brings to the table. She would also like to thank her family for devouring anything she cooked and put on the table as a youngster, for continuing to do so when the opportunity arises, and also for having discovered when not to offer to do things like peeling and washing up. (Afterwards, for anyone wondering when this is.)

Both of us attended – at different times, and quite coincidentally – St Anne's College at Oxford University. We both feel that we owe a great deal to the way in which the fellows of St Anne's pushed (and still push) their students to question, investigate and rigorously tackle intellectual challenges. The way the college encourages independent thinking and research has undoubtedly played an important part in how we have subsequently approached problems. The author royalties from this book are being donated to the college, which appropriately enough is engaged in rebuilding its kitchens.

And so, looking back on the process of writing this book, the contributors and assistance provided has been as complicated as the food food-chain we are trying to describe. Like the food we eat, lots of people have added their efforts to generate the final result. Of course, like any caterer, this fact does not absolve us from responsibility for the final product. The blame for any errors or omissions must lie with us. The quality of the ingredients was first rate; if you think the final dish is half-baked, it is the fault of the authors.

Notes

1 Horace, *Satire* 1.3.
2 Donovan and Hudson (2011).

To our mothers:

Patricia Hudson – for asking my singularly unimpressed cookery teacher if she had actually ever tasted any of my cooking

Sheila Donovan – who taught me to cook at an early age, and has tirelessly criticised my eating habits ever since

1 Overview

The great food crunch

> If there is a real scarcity of an article of prime necessity to life, the result will be more widespread and will act injuriously, for the consumer will pinch and deny himself in other ways to be able to obtain what is necessary to his existence.
>
> (Worthington C. Ford, 1882)

The importance of food

Even the most casual reader of the works of Charles Dickens cannot have failed to notice the importance of food in almost every novel. The Dickensian pauper wages a daily battle against a calorific deficit and often loses the war, ending up in an early grave. The Bumbles and Squeerses of Dickens' world keep their charges on the brink of starvation, in the name of the profit that enables them to feast in private. Character and culture shine through the manner in which Dickens' cast of characters nibble, guzzle and bolt their food in wedges, or most infamously ask for 'more'. The ideas of food insecurity, inequity, financial power games, and the culture of food consumption and what it says about people and society pervade Dickens' work.

If there is a difference between the life and times as observed by Dickens and the present day, it is that modern markets mean these ideas of food insecurity and inequality *must* be viewed from a more global perspective. Modern media means that we *can* view these issues from a more global perspective. Global trade means that something like a pineapple is hardly regarded as exotic. Two centuries ago the pineapple was so exotic as to be immortalised in stone on gateposts. Food has also become steadily more commercialised, distributed by large global companies with fingers in many pies. The trends of globalisation and corporatisation have resulted in significant changes, both good and bad, to the economics and culture of food provisioning and food consumption. Perhaps one of the most significant changes is that the food in the consumer's supermarket trolley is no longer entirely food.

Food is not food

In the developed world, most of what we eat is *not* food. This is not a critique of the nutritional content of a modern fast food diet, nor yet a comment on chemicals and adulteration. It simply means that the *economic* content of food is not food at all as usually understood.

From childhood onwards we tend to have a romanticised notion of a 'food food-chain' that takes us from agriculture to the food on our plate – the farmer taking grain to the miller, who makes the flour for the baker, who makes the bread that we buy. This image of a simplistic supply chain is reinforced by everything from nursery rhymes, to advertising campaigns by food producers and retailers, to media reports that imply a direct link between agricultural commodity prices and the food that we buy.

Supermarkets put pictures of farmers on their packaging, to foster the belief that what we are buying is food. Bread producers show us waving fields of wheat in the television advertisements, as if wheat was in some way important to the price we pay for the bread we consume. Wine producers show us pictures of grapes being gathered to promote the agricultural tie. It is all about as relevant to reality as was Marie Antoinette's farm of Petit Hameau. Simple 'nursery rhyme' supply chains do still exist in a number of less developed economies. In the developed world this simplified and shortened supply chain disappeared around 1850 and had been in decline for centuries before that. As consumers we delude ourselves into thinking that some pastoral idyll still exists to produce the food that we eat – indeed, we delude ourselves into thinking that a pastoral idyll existed at all. Humanity has been manipulating, adjusting and interfering with the production and consumption of food for ten millennia or so.

Food is economically complex. *This economic complexity creates environmental complexity, and the combination of the economic and environmental complexity of food is what forms the foundation of this book.*

What can economics tell us about food?

What can economics tell us about food and agriculture? In the twenty-first century, an understanding of links in every dimension – geographic, political, social and environmental – is what matters for the economist at the cutting-edge. Similarly, while the field of agricultural economics once confined its focus to farm management and commodity markets, today it deals far more in food, of course, but also the trade that supplies the food, the resources available for food processing, and links between agriculture and the economy, and, of course, the environment.[1] Economists, it seems, have to know everything about everything. Fortunately, economists have absolutely no problem with claiming to know everything about everything.

To understand the environmental and economic complexity of food we need to understand four basic ingredients. First, there is the complexity of food – the fact that food has come to be removed from agriculture. Second, there is the challenge of what we term the environmental credit crunch, and how that might hit across the food food-chain (from agricultural production to waste). Third, there is the financial credit crunch, which is the most significant economic event for at least a generation, and what that means for consumer behaviour. Finally, there is the problem of irrationality amongst consumers, and how that affects our economic and ultimately our environmental reactions to food.

The complexity of food

All economic activity has environmental consequences. Any assessment of the environmental impact of food cannot, and must not, stop at the farm gate. We need to focus on the economic and environmental consequences of what happens to get the agricultural commodity to the farm gate. We also need to focus on the economic and environmental processes that happen after the farm gate, as they turn an agricultural commodity into a food form that we can recognise, purchase, occasionally cook and sometimes consume. Each stage of the economic process has an environmental consequence, and the full environmental cost of that process may or may not be reflected in the economic price of the food that we ultimately purchase.

These processes also create feedback loops. The way consumers react adversely to increases in food pricing may put pressure on farmers, encouraging them to raise the yield on their fields. Should the farmer respond by applying more fertiliser, this would have environmental implications. It also has economic implications, in that a new cost variable has to be added to the already complex supply chain.

Milk is not milk – the importance of life after the farm

Before 1866, all milk in the UK came from local cows. Even in cities, milk came from 'town cows' housed in urban dairies – because how else would fresh milk be delivered to city dwellers, when transporting anything from rural districts by horse-drawn cart took so much time? In 1866 there was a cattle 'plague' which killed off most urban bovines. That, combined with the rise of the railways, led to milk being whisked around the country by train – the eponymous 'milk train', the first train of the day, now caught by economists on their way to work, was born.

What we can see here is the transition of milk from being essentially a local, dairy-based product to one that is more complex. From 1866, milk (at least in major metropolitan areas) had to take into account not just the dairy's costs, and the costs of feeding the cow, but also the costs of coal (used to power steam trains), the costs of packaging (galvanised steel churns, for the most part), and the associated labour costs. These costs were economic, clearly, but they were also environmental. What is a steam train if not the embodiment of an economic and environmental cost packaged together? A steam train must be one of the world's most visible manifestations of a carbon footprint, and coal is very definitely a constrained environmental resource. By adding in stages of distribution, we are increasing the economic and environmental consequences of food consumption until eventually we wind up at today's point, where milk (economically speaking) is not milk at all.

When we purchase milk in a developed economy today less than half the money that we hand over at the checkout (or nowadays insert into the automatic checkout's coin slot) finds its way into the hands of a dairy farmer. Most of what we are paying for is what happens to the milk after it leaves the farm gate. What we are paying for is the labour involved in transporting, pasteurising, quality-checking, packaging, marketing and selling that milk. Part of what we are paying for is the supermarket checkout operator's wages (or the wages of the workers manufacturing and maintaining the automatic checkout), the wages of the builder who built the supermarket, the salary of the marketing executive who launched the latest promotional campaign for the supermarket, and even a very small amount of money to the economist who advises everyone on the economic climate. The dairy farmer is almost incidental to the whole process.

Food is 20 per cent food

When a shopper spends money on a basket of food items in a developed economy, on average only around a fifth to a quarter of what is spent actually finds its way to a farmer. Just under four-fifths of what we spend our food money on is nothing to do with food (in the form of agricultural commodities) at all. Purchasing fast food has even less agricultural content. Spending three pounds on a hamburger meal from a fast-food outlet will mean only a tiny amount on agricultural food. Perhaps fifty or sixty pence of the three pounds spent by the consumer ever finds its way to a farmer. Persuading shoppers to buy bread by showing pictures of fields of wheat, advertising milk chocolate with pictures of milk, or putting pictures of pastoral scenes on the side of lorries distributing fast food components to hamburger chains is pure fantasy in terms of the (economic) content of these products.

One of the best ways of demonstrating this is to reflect on a somewhat extreme form of food consumption. Consider a can of cola, or any carbonated drink. A quick glance at the ingredients list will reveal that (secret formula or no) it is basically a combination of carbonated water, sweeteners, food colorants and flavourings. And yet, a can of cola purchased in a restaurant at a ski resort is worth its weight in, if not gold, then at least tin (a can of cola retails for around six euros in a French ski resort, which works out as being around 24,000 dollars per tonne). This cannot be because processed carbonated water, coloured, is valued as much as tin. The reason cola costs so much in a mountain restaurant is because the carbonated water, coloured brown, is subsequently packaged, branded, marketed, transported, chilled and sold to the thirsty skier through the whole mechanism of intermediaries, wholesalers and retailers. The price at the end of the purchase is not of the agricultural components of cola – it is mainly the price required to cover the economic costs of all of those different intermediate stages.

How China's food consumption rises 3 per cent and 30 per cent at the same time

China is now the world's largest food retailer (that is to say, the value of the Chinese food retail industry is greater than the value of food retail in any other country). This is not just a function of China's population size; it is a function of its economic development and urbanisation. Urbanisation means that populations are moving further and further away from the sources of agriculture, and so food must be purchased through the intermediation services of a food retailer. Chinese food spending (the value of food retail) has been rising by between 20 and 30 per cent per year in the recent past. However, Chinese calorie consumption is going up by only 2–3 per cent each year. The difference between these two numbers is largely the fact that consumers in China are increasingly likely to buy their food from a more elaborate supply chain, with more labour costs, more packaging and more advertising.

The difference between buying rice loose by the sack from a farmer and buying it in a brightly coloured, branded cardboard box in a supermarket is not that great in nutritional terms. In economic terms, these two purchases are a lifestyle apart. Again, every cardboard box made, every advertising hoarding created, every supermarket constructed has an economic and an environmental consequence. If we are to understand the environmental implications of how humanity gets its calories, we have to understand all parts of this complex process.

Writing on the development of the British diet in the 1850s, the economist John Burnett commented 'Man's most basic need was at last becoming the nation's biggest business'.[2] This is why the economic and environmental consequences of the food that we eat are so important. The fact that the price we pay for food, or for ubiquitous beverages such as milk and cola, has so many components demonstrates what a very complex supply chain we face. To focus either an economic or an environmental analysis of food on the farming industry is to miss out 80 per cent of what matters, because agriculture is only 20 per cent of food.

The challenge of the environmental credit crunch

A crunch in economic credit, environmental credit or financial credit terms occurs when what was previously plentiful is no longer plentiful (or, in extremis, is no longer available). A food crunch arises when there is not enough food to go round for today's consumption. The basic problem of a food crunch is the same as any other crunch (i.e. shortage). The consequences of a food crunch are more significant, however. Periodically, drought or other disasters in developing countries provide a stark reminder of why and how. At the extreme, a food crunch saturates the media with images of starving people struggling to stay alive. Experience suggests that the food crunch that follows from drought, warfare, or other extreme events, is not equally shared. It hits poor countries, and poor people, the hardest. In less extreme forms, a food crunch of the future could leave many human beings in a permanent state of under-nourishment. Insufficient nutrition brings many ills in its wake, for individuals and society alike.

The geopolitical risks associated with food make one of the conclusions in our book *From Red to Green?*[3] surprising. As food is one of life's necessities, one might think that humanity would be especially careful to avoid wasting food and the resources that produce food. Not so. Critical though food is to human survival, the issue of wasted resources is one of the most important challenges that must be addressed. As we shall see, there may be perfectly good reasons why controlling food waste is less easy than it looks.

Putting this another way, the question is whether it is possible to use existing food supplies better, or whether there are good reasons why this has not been tried. It is a question worth asking, for, if the food waste problem can be solved, it may offer the potential to kill at least two birds with one stone. Needing lower levels of food provisioning in volume terms could only be helpful in the context of food security. Further, the environmental credit crunch, which we define below, might be significantly offset. Is the reduction of waste in the food sector the low-hanging fruit it seems to be at first sight?

Food supply can be described as inordinately wasteful. First, raw materials that go into food provisioning, such as water and agrochemicals, are used wastefully. Second, the typical developed-economy diet, with its emphasis on meat, is structured in a way that is wasteful of water, energy and land; from an environmental perspective, meat is an extremely inefficient way of providing calories for the human diet. Third, a shocking proportion of food is often thrown away uneaten because of an inadequate storage and transport infrastructure (often a problem in developing countries) or because of the 'pile it high, sell it cheap' marketing practices that can be typical in some developed economies. Fourth, in developed countries in particular, but increasingly in developing countries too, eating habits are wasteful through the over-consumption of unnecessary calories. This problem wastes not only food, but other resources (such as healthcare, and human productivity and wellbeing) too. Large swathes of the human population are eating as if there is no tomorrow, without reflecting on the irony that, if they continue to do so, there may be a rather uncomfortable tomorrow for their descendants.

What is an environmental credit crunch?

Eating as if there is no tomorrow is unsustainable in the face of an environmental credit crunch. To understand what this means in practical terms it is time to define in further detail what credit is. Credit is the ability to use tomorrow's standard of living to raise today's standard of living. In financial terms, this is well understood. If a consumer wants to buy a television, but has no savings, she can seek to borrow money against future income by purchasing the television by credit card. Such a consumer raises her standard of living today, working on the perhaps moot assumption that purchasing a television raises one's standard of living. In exchange, she accepts a lower future standard of living by having a lower future disposable income as she repays the credit card debt. Willy, the eponymous salesman in Arthur Miller's *Death of a Salesman* was the embodiment of this concept. Willy had a high standard of living early in his life, enjoying the material benefits of the 1950s American Dream. He had a car, a refrigerator and so forth, but lacking the immediate disposable income he bought the goods using hire purchase or instalment credit. As a result, his subsequent standard of living was lowered, as his income was absorbed in meeting the payments for the goods he had already purchased. The goods inevitably became obsolete or broke around the time that Willy had finished paying for their purchase.

Credit also applies in environmental terms. Human beings have a choice in how they use the world's resources. They can choose to consume finite resources like oil, to produce energy, to manufacture fertilisers, to raise their current standard of living. Using energy-intensive fertilisers undoubtedly increases the yield of agricultural production. This makes the production of agricultural commodities cheaper, which improves the standard of living for the general population. In using energy-intensive fertilisers, however, there is an acceptance that the future standard of living will be lower. Finite resources are, well, finite. Of course, the lower standard of living may apply to future generations, rather than the current generation, but that is the nature of environmental credit. (It is a concept that can apply to financial credit – the Japanese property boom of the 1980s saw mortgages that were designed to last for two or three generations.)

A credit crunch, as should be obvious from the recent global financial crisis, is when this process of borrowing from the future becomes more difficult. In extremis, it might become impossible. If your bank refuses to extend your overdraft, will not issue you with another credit card, or baulks at any attempt to remortgage your house, you experience the full force of a financial credit crunch. In just the same way, if there is not enough oil to power the production of a modern fertiliser, this is an environmental credit crunch. If aquifers run dry, and no longer provide the water to irrigate crops, then there is an environmental credit crunch.

One of the clearest instances of environmental credit being consumed is the guano boom of the late nineteenth century, which will be explored in more detail in the chapter on land. Guano (sea-bird excrement from Peru) was a vitally important fertiliser, which was used substantially in the United Kingdom in the years after the repeal of the Corn Laws, in order to raise the productivity of domestic agriculture and fend off the threat of cheap imports from overseas. However, the stockpiles of guano had taken years to build, and the surge in consumption ultimately exhausted their supply. An essentially finite resource was consumed, and when the guano supply was exhausted it could no longer enhance agricultural production and raise standards of living.

Clearly, an environmental credit crunch is going to matter. A proverb from ancient Byzantium says 'He who has food has many problems; he who has no food has only one problem'. The environmental credit crunch threatens our ability to produce agricultural commodities, and with it creates a strain on economic resources and policy decision.

Food, environmental feedback loops and technology

Although this book tends to focus on developed markets, the global nature of food markets suggests that the indirect impacts of developed-economy consumers' eating patterns on the developing-country environment may be significant. Rivers in developing countries are said to be reduced to a trickle to feed export markets, and rainforest is cut down to grow crops like palm oil that are used elsewhere in the world. It is unlikely that this is news to readers of this book, given the frequency with which such issues appear in the press. None of us want

8 Overview: the great food crunch

the destruction of sensitive ecosystems to be laid at our door. So why do human beings behave in this irrational manner? The answer may lie in some of the structural changes that have taken place in food-provisioning systems in recent decades. Consumers are just less personally aware of the consequences of their consumption today; the feedback loops that used to give warnings of problems with food supply are simply too remote to have a direct impact on the personal experiences of a developed-economy consumer.

Human history contains many examples of the short-run credit crunches that seem to be a feature of agricultural systems. The biblical idea of seven years of fat, seven years of lean can be thought of as an agricultural credit cycle. Uncomfortable as seven years of lean no doubt were, they were helpful in a very important respect. They were a salutary reminder of resource limits and human vulnerability to extremes in food availability, and they happened often enough to regulate human behaviour.

Over time, human ingenuity has allowed human beings to moderate the volatility of food supplies. This has been achieved in a number of ways, some of which entail working with natural forces. So, soil can be allowed to rest, or nutrients restored through crop rotation, to maintain productivity. For thousands of years, farmers have selected plant varieties for their ability to thrive in different conditions. Modern technology has furnished other means to the same ends at lower cost. So, fertilisers are used to restore the fertility of soil without the need for down time; agrochemicals deal with pests, thereby avoiding the need to rotate. In short, in recent decades, human beings have done such a good job of protecting themselves from the agricultural credit cycle through global trade and technological innovation that the existence of the agricultural cycle tends to be forgotten, along with the very existence of environmental limits.

The ups and downs of prices in agricultural commodity markets do provide an echo of the agricultural cycles. There are even occasionally significant human reactions – the tortilla riots in Mexico or rice riots in Asia. However, this is not the same thing as facing the reality of not knowing where the next meal is coming from. Thus, in normal conditions, the risk of wide swings inherent in food-supply systems tends to be forgotten in wealthy countries. Better-off social groups where food is a small part of the weekly budget are likely to forget the risks of food supply. It is the poorest people in developed nations or those in the least developed nations, for whom food accounts for a significant percentage of the household budget, who are most exposed to the food consequences of the vagaries of the weather and other changes in the environment.

The possibility that technology advances may not be able to protect people from the natural limits to the productivity of ecosystems reared its ugly head (albeit with hindsight) in the context of the so-called Green Revolution. Here, a carefully engineered combination of three inputs – variety selection, fertiliser and irrigation – produced significant improvements in agricultural productivity. However, technologically driven efficiency improvements came at a price. The large amounts of water needed for this system turned out to be its Achilles heel. In effect, the risk of resource constraints had not actually been resolved. As risk tends to do, it had simply moved somewhere else.

It seems very hard to justify a food system which takes thirty-three calories of energy inputs to produce each single calorie of meat required for that ubiquitous symbol of fast-food nationhood, the hamburger. The same food item requires no less than thirty-five bathtubs of water in its production.[4] The advances in agricultural technology of the Green Revolution were undertaken with two ideas in mind: to improve productivity from year to year, but also to improve the resilience of the sector to shocks – in other words, to reduce volatility in productivity from year to year. Superficially speaking, it is clear that improved efficiency translates to increased productivity. However, what happens if the efficiency and productivity gains come with a hidden cost of reduced system resilience? When such costs are significant, then any gains in productivity can be described as illusory.

Why worry about food now? In many ways, food should not be a major concern. For perhaps the first time in human civilisation, famine seems to be preventable. The world is capable of producing sufficient calories to feed the global population. Global trade in food, which is of course an economic action, and the regional variations of the global climate mean that we should always be able to export sufficient calories from areas of plenty to areas of want. Moreover, we can export the food quickly. Food can be airlifted into a starving region within twenty-four hours if needed. When famines occur today it is the consequence of human action or inaction. Wars (as in parts of Africa) or mistaken ideology can create a famine, but it is preventable under a system of enlightened economic government.

In spite of this state of affairs, there is a growing problem for global food. The issue that is coming to the fore is how to manage food in the face of an environmental credit crunch. The environmental credit crunch is building. It may not have quite the same immediately global abruptness as the recent financial credit crunch, but ecosystem degradation is happening globally, and parts of the ecosystem are capable of sudden collapse. This brings us to the important concept of resilience. A lack of resilience in the context of the banking system was bad enough. In the context of the ecosystem, its consequences are potentially more potent.

The importance of bouncing back

What is resilience? In the context of materials it means an ability to return to their former shape after a shock (think of rubber resuming its shape after being stretched). For humans, it describes the ability to bounce back from illness or other adversity. For systems in general it refers to their ability to keep functioning under pressure, whether short-lived or long-lasting. Thus, for the food system, it refers, in the narrowest definition, to the ability of food crops to survive weather volatility. More broadly, resilience here denotes the ability of the food system to continue to supply food to consumers in the face of environmental pressures or climate shocks.

It is hard to say whether poverty is a consequence of a lack of resilience in social systems, or whether poverty results in systems that are not resilient. Whichever way causality runs, a lack of resilience in the overall food provisioning system in developing countries is one reason why the consequences of a global food 'crunch' would be unequally distributed. The ability of a system to bounce back is reduced when systems are stressed by over-use (much the same as over-stretching rubber, or repeated attacks of the 'flu in a person). Thus, although waste reduction is certainly not the only thing that should be done to improve system resilience, it is likely that improved resilience might be one of the benefits of a successful programme of food-waste reduction.

International trade is important to global and regional food security and promotes resilience. On balance, it is likely that it is a good thing, but *how* trade is done is likely to matter as much as *what* is done. In the context of our energy-hungry and water-thirsty hamburger, trade can (markets permitting) allow the meat for the hamburger to come from countries well-endowed with cheap energy and plenty of water. Thus, in the short run, system resilience can be maintained by following the economic law of comparative advantage.

However, if the pastureland used to farm the livestock that furnish the exported raw ingredients for the hamburger were made available by chopping down virgin forest, international trade could be blamed for damaging system resilience. In the short run, globalisation may appear to allow everyone to have their cake and eat it, quite literally. Globalisation leads to more efficient food production in both an economic and an environmental sense. Globalisation makes for a more resilient global agriculture sector at the same time. But, to use a food metaphor, globalisation may be placing all one's eggs in one basket. Could global food providers in the corporate sector ultimately become 'too big to fail'?

Agriculture was, once upon a time, a very fragmented industry, and one of the benefits of fragmentation is risk diversification – the eggs are in several baskets. As farms have grown in size, diversification is reduced. Single crops over large areas have become the order of the day. In parallel, the providers of other agricultural raw inputs, and the owners of food distribution networks, have grown in scale, driving out smaller players. Does this matter? The answer may depend on positioning in the food food-chain. If a critical piece of the global agricultural system were to be hit by an adverse shock, and global trade should prove to be incapable of plugging the supply gap (meaning that the system could not bounce back), then clearly this does matter.

Firms based in the banking industry use a concept known as Value at Risk in order to assess the potential market risk an institution might be exposed to, under certain extreme scenarios. For food a similar measure might at the extreme be called Civilisation at Risk, for it communicates the importance of resilience in human food supplies in the face of environmental change. It is time to think about the system that helps facilitate a stable environment – the ecosystem.

Using and abusing the ecosystem

Food production depends entirely for its existence upon so-called ecosystem services. In other words, it is wholly dependent upon 'nature'. Without soil, micronutrients, water, sunshine, flora and fauna, we would have nothing to eat or drink, therefore would not exist. In the context of this book the term 'ecosystem services' thus describes the natural resources that allow us to eat. The same ecosystem services that support the human diet also happen to support other aspects of civilisation.

One problem with the term ecosystem services is the implication that useful things like soil, water and plant life are here purely for the benefit of human beings – the instrumental view of natural resources. To describe something as a 'service' implies a contractual arrangement in which something is offered in exchange for some other benefit. 'Service' also introduces the idea of power, one thing over another. The worst thing about the term is that it perpetuates some unsustainable myths, suggesting that human beings are the most important thing on the planet, that they control it, and that the earth system can be explained by economics.

The polar opposite of the concept of 'service' is James Lovelock's Gaian metaphor for the earth as a fully interconnected self-regulating entity – the earth as a system that exists for its own sake.[5] In the play *Wastwater*, playwright Simon Stephens compares the earth system to a brain – another self-regulating entity full of connections.[6] When we talk about the brain we do not describe the hippocampus as providing short-term memory services to the rest of the brain, nor the eyes as providing communications services to the frontal lobes. All of these functions are recognised for the role they play in the overall structure.

The argument in favour of the terms like ecosystem services is that, without them, we tend to forget just how dependent we are upon the many self-regulating functions of the planet. Terms borrowed from economics are a reminder that the earth system has an intrinsic value, and could potentially be protected by a contract setting out terms of use, notwithstanding the reservations expressed above. Economics has its uses after all. There are of course dangers inherent in this idea. As Oscar Wilde pointed out, people tend to know the price of everything and the value of nothing. Putting a price on something is no guarantee that it will be here for the next generation. Sometimes, putting a price on something can be a sure-fire way of wiping it out as it creates an incentive to consume. Think of the animals hunted to extinction in the name of human beauty, fertility or longevity. Leaving aside such extremes, and thinking of the larger problem of feeding nine or ten billion people on an equitable and sustainable basis – what matters is the practical impact of terms like 'services'. Therefore, bear with us as we continue to use the term ecosystem services in considering the potential food crunch.

A clean, healthy, well-balanced ecosystem is required to supply human beings with the nutrients they need for a productive life, in all senses of the phrase. The Millennium Ecosystem Assessment, produced between 2001 and 2005, describes the many linkages between ecosystems and human health. The services provided by the ecosystem and the biodiversity it is made up of underpin a number of aspects of civilised society: security, basic materials needed for a good life, health and good social relations. Food is a particularly sensitive issue in this system. When something goes wrong with food supplies, civil unrest can compromise security, the idea of the good life goes out of the window as the fight to survive dominates, and health and good relations are compromised.

The usefulness of this World Resources Institute (WRI)[7] framework lies in its ability to capture a complex system of dependencies. It makes it clear that food is not just food, but much more than that (which is what economics has already told us). Getting to grips with the impact of human food procurement upon the environment and civilised society is no simple matter. The food food-chain discussed within this book is woven through every aspect of this framework. When it comes to the provisioning, regulation and cultural functions of the ecosystem it tends to be the case that, in developed economies, no one part of ecosystem services dominates any other from a human perspective. A different perspective might be required for developing economies, where food, water and shelter would dominate.

The ecosystem is far more complex than the financial system. Nevertheless, insofar as it has provided the most significant experience of system collapse in the life-times of most developed-economy citizens, the financial credit crunch can provide insight into the potential impact of an environmental credit crunch on the flow of ecosystem services we rely on daily.

The financial credit crunch

The financial credit crunch that started (depending on the economy examined and the economist you read) somewhere between 2005 and 2008 has led to some fairly significant changes in consumer and financial behaviour. At its most simple, the reduction in financial credit availability that is the defining characteristic of a financial credit crunch means that we have reduced our ability to raise our standard of living today.

From this basic starting point, we can find four key traits that have arisen as a result of the financial credit crunch, all of which will have implications for the environment, and for food and agriculture.

First, there is the immediate impact on consumption levels (and economic growth levels). If we are less able to borrow money, we are less able to consume beyond our means. Therefore, consumption today is likely to be constrained by our income growth (whereas in the halcyon days of credit availability, no one was seemingly troubled by so unimportant a thing as their income when determining whether or not to consume). This suggests a slower level of consumption and economic growth.

A consumption level that is income constrained (or more income constrained) implies a slower increase in one's standard of living. This is never popular, of course. The general unpopularity of not raising one's standard of living in the old, pre-financial-credit-crunch manner leads to the second consequence of the financial credit crunch: consumers try to maintain their standard of living (or their standard of living growth) in spite of the reduction in resources. There are two ways of doing this. First one can 'trade down' and accept economically cheaper products. The collapse in the sales of organic eggs in the UK that coincided with the financial credit crunch is one instance of this. Consumers still bought eggs, but they substituted cheaper eggs (generally free-range eggs, the sales of which increased) in order to make their money go further. Reduced spending on eating out is another instance of this – people still consume calories, but they substitute consumption at home for consumption at a pub or restaurant.

If trading down is not practical, if there are no cheaper substitutes for instance, the alternative method of maintaining one's standard of living is to be more efficient in consumption. This can be brought about by reducing unnecessary waste. The classic instance of that is wartime rationing, when wasting food was (literally) a criminal offence. It might also be about making products last longer – for instance, keeping a cooker for another year or two rather than purchasing a more efficient model, in order to avoid the expense of a capital outlay (though of course incurring the economic and indeed environmental expense of being less energy efficient in the meantime).

Third, we will be more constrained in our ability to upgrade our infrastructure. This is similar to the frugality of delaying a new cooker purchase. Investing in something (farming equipment, catering equipment or whatever) involves an initial expense that generates a return (or efficiencies) over a number of years. In other words, the money is needed up front but the benefit accrues over time. As a result, infrastructure investment is the ideal candidate for financial credit funding, because financial credit gives cash in a lump sum up front and then requires repayment in instalments over time. Financial credit is the mirror image of the cost and returns earned from infrastructure investment. If financial credit is constrained then infrastructure investment is also likely to become more constrained.

The fourth consequence of the global financial credit crunch is not a direct consequence, but it is potentially the most important for food and agriculture. In a world where consumption is more constrained and where economic growth is slower, there is likely to be an inclination towards trade protectionism. The precedent for this is of course the 1930s, when autarky (self-sufficiency taken to an unhealthy extreme) became the stated policy of many. The environmental credit crunch is likely to make this process worse as far as food and agriculture are concerned. Faced with rising food prices, food-producing countries can, will (indeed, already have) prioritise their own populations' needs over the global need for food. The issue from an optimal environmental and economic outcome is that food autarky in this manner may prioritise low food prices at home over malnutrition (or even potentially starvation) abroad.

This raises the related issue of food security. Countries that have hitherto been comfortable importers of food from the rest of the world may become concerned about the security of those food sources. If trade protectionism is more frequent, depending on imported food may become an issue of national security, and the threat of the loss of imports a source of disruption to economic and environmental policies. The threat of food security can thus prompt domestic agricultural change. In 1914, two-thirds of all sugar consumed in the United Kingdom was imported from the Austro-Hungarian empire. The First World War obviously stopped those supplies, and led to the development of a domestic sugar-beet industry to create a secure supply. Whether this was either economically or environmentally an optimal policy is debatable.

The inherent irrationality of consumers

The final economic consideration with regard to food is that food assumes a disproportionate importance in the minds of most consumers. That food is important is not in question – food is essential for human existence after all. But for the developed world at least, most people passed the calorific threshold for survival several burgers ago, hence the populist media's reference to 'obesity epidemics'. Increasingly, the calorific threshold for survival has been exceeded in the emerging world as well – as noted earlier, famine is now a function of human action and not of economic or environmental necessity.

Typically, a developed-economy household will spend somewhere between 10 and 15 per cent of their income on food and drink. This is reflected in the calculations of consumer price inflation. Of course, there are considerable variations in any society. The growth of income inequality amongst developed economies means that there have been increased variations in the proportion of a household budget spent on food. The poorest fifth of the American population spends, on average, 36 per cent of their income on food. The richest fifth of the American population spends, on average, 7 per cent of their income on food. Unless contemplating the sort of orgy of excess that is popularly associated with the rise and fall of the Roman Empire, there is a natural limit to spending on food.[8]

Even allowing for variations according to income, food is not a major part of the developed-economy consumer's budget. However, food has one key characteristic that means it 'punches above its weight' in terms of consumer perceptions.

Food is something we purchase frequently

Food is generally something that is purchased on a daily basis. Even if it is only a chocolate bar from a vending machine, food is purchased with very high frequency. Indeed, as we argue in Chapter 7 on food retailing, the likelihood is that the financial credit crunch will increase the frequency with which we purchase food.

Herein lies the problem. Economists are perfectly rational human beings who calculate the importance of something like food consumption according to quantifiable measures of spending habits. Food is weighted at 10 per cent in the UK consumer price inflation calculation because that is, on average, the proportion of a UK household's spending that goes on food. Consumers, however, lack the rationality of economists. Consumers, to be blunt, are irrational beings that do not behave in the way economic models say that they should. Consumers do not think about their household budget according to weighted averages of their spending over a period of time. Consumers notice the price of things that they buy frequently, because the price is presented to them on a frequent basis.

Constantly being reminded of the price of a high-frequency purchase attaches a disproportionate importance to that item in the mind of the irrational consumer. In most developed societies the things consumers purchase with greatest frequency are food and fuel for the car. If the price of food or fuel undergoes a change, the consumer will ascribe a disproportionate weight to that change. A 10-percentage-point increase in the price of a bar of chocolate is evidence of rampant inflation across the country. The weekly shopping basket of food items that costs 7 per cent more is obviously a signal that one's standard of living is collapsing. It is not rational. It is not accurate. But it persists.

The fact that food assumes an importance out of proportion to its economic significance generates political and social consequences, which in turn may generate environmental consequences. To follow through the steps: food as a high-frequency purchase means that consumers are sensitive to its price. This disproportionate sensitivity to price gives politicians an incentive to manage food prices in the short term, and particularly to manage prices in such a way as to coincide with the electoral cycle. That desire to contain food prices will increase the political incentive to use environmental credit by consuming finite resources to increase agricultural yields and keep the price of food down, even if the consequence (post an environmental credit crunch) is higher prices in the future. If the consequence of the policy is sufficiently far in the future, beyond the next election at least, political expediency may well triumph over environmental and long-term economic good sense.

The politics of food pricing should not be understated. The nineteenth-century political focus on the size of the harvests (as a leading indicator of social unrest); the UK general election of 1906 that was essentially about the impact of free trade on the price of food; the importance of food availability and pricing for morale in both the World Wars; the US price controls of 1972 that can be directly linked to President Nixon's obsession with the price of a hamburger; the bread rationing in the UK in November 1979; food riots in newly industrialised economies' urban areas in recent years. All of these examples show the intimate relationship of food and politics.

The nursery-rhyme-inspired vision of a pastoral idyll, combined with an irrational and disproportionate weighting to the economic importance of food in developed economies, has created a powerful force. It is a force that is economically suboptimal, and potentially environmentally dangerous.

Feeding nine to ten billion – the crunchy quality of food and finance

As the global human population continues to increase, the challenge is to furnish people with a good-quality, nutritious diet on an equitable basis with constrained animal, mineral and vegetable resources. As the Millennium Ecosystem Assessment report points out, ecosystems have historically done a good job of meeting the rising global demand for food. In recent years, the supply of many key agricultural products has grown faster than the global population. However, this has been achieved at the price of trade-offs. To slip into economic language, human beings have leveraged their technology to 'sweat' the environmental assets of the planet. This has resulted in major impacts on how we grow (chemical fertilisers, increased carbon dioxide emissions) and what we grow (dominance of single crops).

As the Millennium Ecosystem Assessment Full Report puts it:

> Over the long term, declines in supporting and regulating ecosystem services, such as soil fertility, water cycling, and genetic resources, potentially undermine the ability of food production to keep pace with population growth in the absence of new, major technological advancements in agriculture.[9]

Who is hurting?

Who is likely to suffer most in an environmental credit crunch? If financial credit was used to furnish middle- and lower-income families with necessities, then it is these groups that would suffer disproportionately in a financial credit crunch. Similarly, the benefits of cheap food that have arisen from the use of environmental credit have tended to accrue to lower-income groups. An environmental credit crunch means higher food prices (relative to wages, or relative to the price of other goods). As such, it is the lower-income groups who again are likely to suffer from the environmental credit crunch. In a financial *or* an environmental credit crunch, it tends to be the least wealthy who are hit hardest in the short run. The least wealthy also tend to be least able to adapt to the new post-crisis world.

Generalising, markets have a tendency to concentrate wealth. Global agricultural markets are no different. From the perspective of economic efficiency this may be helpful. However, such concentration may have social consequences. Food and water are necessities of life; access to both is a human right. Processed food and beverages (in developed economies) are also discretionary goods – luxuries one chooses to buy. It seems reasonable to suggest that discretionary items on which life does not depend can be fairly subjected to market forces.

Food can therefore be described as a hybrid, in market terms. The hybrid nature of food and water means that an environmental credit crunch, in the context of food, will not be equal in its effects throughout society: for some, it will simply mean a little belt-tightening, for others, it will mean starvation rations. Moreover, those most likely to be impacted by insufficient access to food and water in an environmental credit crunch are also unlikely to be furnished with the means of digging themselves out of the hole they find themselves in. In normal operating conditions they are also unlikely to be furnished with the means of investing in technology or infrastructure that might improve their lot in the medium term. Those who most need stable, resilient food-provisioning systems are unlikely to have the means of attaining them.

> **Box 1.1 Environmental and economic inequality**
>
> The Green Revolution is an example of unequal wealth distribution. This advance in agricultural technology conferred a significant increase in agricultural productivity, but only to those with access to the right technology. At first sight, the enhancement in agricultural productivity and efficiency looks like good news for all – cheaper food should follow from higher volumes of production delivered at a lower cost. However, in general terms, any new technology that causes production costs to collapse and volumes to rise will have the effect of pushing the highest-cost producers (those without technology access) out of the market. The social costs of this can be considerable – it is just too bad if they happen to be subsistence farmers, for instance.
>
> At least in the transition period, moving to more efficient but more technological agriculture may hinder the fight against hunger,[10] because the collision between global economic forces and local conditions inevitably puts the small developing-country farmer out of business. If this problem is not offset (through welfare policies, perhaps) the consequences could be dire. A key question that drops out of this is what the drive for greater efficiency means for the resilience of food-provisioning systems, and how balance can be attained in such a way to arrive at secure and sustainable food supplies.

The economics of food and agriculture

Clearly, in economic terms, food is much, much more than what happens in agriculture. The economics of food take agricultural commodities and put them through a whole series of economic actions that result in the food we recognise. We must move away from the simplistic notion that what we eat has much to do with agricultural commodities, and recognise the complexity of the economics of food. That complexity, with its myriad layers of processing, packaging, transport, advertising, retailing and so on, creates an equivalent environmental complexity. With an environmental and a financial credit crunch taking place at the same time, and with some consumers predisposed to be irrationally sensitive to issues of food pricing, this is a critical issue.

Economic plenty has given those in developed economies a degree of complacency about food availability and cost that is remarkable. That complacency would not have existed seventy years ago. It may not exist in the future. The two credit crunches the world is facing up to are about to shake us up.

Changing food consumption patterns does tend to require big events. Seismic shifts in consumer behaviour occurred in the UK as a result of the Second World War, when over half of all food spending was subject to some form of additional rationing control. Prior to that, arguably the biggest change in food consumption was wrought by the Great Depression of the later 1870s and the 1880s. This was an agricultural depression, brought about by the import of cheap grain and meat from overseas, and led to a shift in the affordability of food. In economic terms, these were huge events – the Second World War was a move towards a command economy, the Great Depression of the later nineteenth century was economically and socially disruptive.

The global financial credit crunch can easily be considered a comparable economic event, if one that is not so costly in humanitarian terms. Surveys indicate people are worried that today's children (in developed economies) may have a lower standard of living than their parents or be unable to exceed the standard of living of their parents. This sentiment has not been experienced in recent economic history – at least, not in so widespread a fashion.

Feeding billions better

The overall aim of a perfectly designed food system should be to support a good quality of life for current *and* future generations of human beings, within reasonable constraints. This book seeks to map out the means by which billions can be 'better' fed; whether this is defined as having enough to eat (for the millions living on a dollar a day or less) or not consuming too many empty calories (for many in developed economies). Key concepts, from an environmental perspective, include inequality and resilience. From an economic perspective, the central issues are innovation and more efficient allocation of resources. These issues are important to providing food in a sustainable manner, as we look to move away from a world that survives by running up an environmental credit card bill (without any idea of how to repay the outstanding amount). If we begin to live within our environmental means in the short term, and to restructure so as to repay some of the environmental debt in the medium term, we may be able to avert or at least soften the impact of the pressures on food supply that come from population growth and the environmental credit crunch.

The rest of the book

The chapters of this book have been placed more or less in the same order as the food food-chain, running from the physical to the intangible. Hence, the next three chapters explore mineral, vegetable and animal resources. Throughout, we endeavour to explore how each link in the food food-chain will impact the other links. The web of connections and feedback loops has at times made ordering this book difficult. At the other end of the food food-chain, we seek to understand ways in which the culture of food drives aspects of food consumption patterns, promoting or indeed impeding change. Culture and social structure may turn out to be the central drivers of food in economic and environmental terms.

Notes

1 Bruce and Rausser (2002), p. xi. This volume is Part 3 of the *Handbook of Agricultural Economics,* and its four chapters look at Agriculture, Natural Resources and the Environment.

2 Burnett (1966), p. 112.
3 Donovan and Hudson (2011).
4 Authors' calculations based on numbers in McWilliams (2009), p. 141.
5 Lovelock (2006).
6 Stephens (2011).
7 Millennium Ecosystem Assessment (2005a), p. vi. For a guide to the full range of Millennium Ecosystem Assessment reports see www.unep.org/maweb/en/index.aspx. See also www.wri.org
8 Data calculated from the weightings of the US Consumer Expenditure Survey, www.bls.gov
9 Millennium Ecosystem Assessment (2005b), Section 5.1, p. 832.
10 Cf. Mazoyer and Roudart (2006), p. 15.

2 Raw material inputs
Mineral

> Land and water resources and the way they are used are central to the challenge of improving food security across the world. Demographic pressures, climate change, and the increased competition for land and water are likely to increase vulnerability to food security, particularly in Africa and Asia.
> (Food and Agriculture Organization of the United Nations)[1]

This chapter and the two that follow review the earliest stage of food production, namely the production and procurement of the key raw materials that go into food. Owing to the scope covered, we break the topic of raw material inputs into three sections – mineral, vegetable and animal. For each in turn we consider the interaction between the environment and society, and economics. These three chapters touch on everything from geopolitics to genetics. This chapter, however, is primarily about land – what is on it, the economics and ecosystem issues relating to it, and how all of these shape how we get what we eat.

The pull of the land

Land has a powerful economic resonance throughout history. From the moment mankind got tired of hunting and gathering, and decided to settle down in a nice quiet neighbourhood, with good transport links and decent schools, land became one of the most potent symbols of economic wealth. Medieval manors symbolised the dominance of the aristocracy (and when land changed hands, the ownership of the people on the land – serfs – changed with it). The *nouveau riche* of the British Industrial Revolution aspired to the legitimising power of land ownership – nothing diluted the pollution of being in trade like owning a country estate.

The desire for land could lead to changes on a monumental scale. The early Renaissance papacy parcelled out ownership of continents to favoured kings. The Highland Clearances of Scotland pushed families from their traditional clan lands with many knock-on effects, one of which is briefly mentioned in Box 4.1. The 'rush for Africa' of the nineteenth-century European colonists pushed entire peoples from their lands. The race for land in the Midwest of the United States (to say nothing of the Louisiana Purchase or the acquisition of Alaska) showed a frantic desire to own territory. Even in the twentieth century, Germany's National Socialist regime obsessed about land with its desire for *Lebensraum*. It is hardly an exaggeration to say that human history can be told as a story of the struggle to acquire land.

This naturally raises the question – why struggle at all? What is it that makes land ownership inspire legal wrangles, bloodshed and envy? The answer is that land has an economic value. People wish to own land, and that very powerful desire generates a price.

In economic terms there are two intertwined strands to the issues of land. First, there are the competing demands for land use. Do we want to own land to build a house, construct a factory, or grow food? Or, indeed, do we wish to own land for leisure purposes? Second, what economic return does that use of land generate? The economic return can of course inform the use of land – humanity will tend to exhibit a certain degree of greed, so human beings will tend to want to put their land to the most profitable use possible, and thus will choose between the competing forms of land use on the basis of the economic return each form can generate. As economic returns shift, so the attractions of different sorts of land use will change.

The famous landscape gardener Humphrey Repton declared 'the beauty of pleasure-ground, and the profit of a farm, are incompatible', and of course they are. (The other writer, who is, naturally enough, not an economist, begs to differ.) While Repton may not have wanted the view from his drawing room window to be sullied by the sights and smells of farmyard animals or, indeed, the sights and smells of the farming peasantry, not everyone was sensitive to aesthetics when there was a profit to be had. Eighteenth- and nineteenth-century ornamental parks (used essentially for leisure with perhaps a vague pretence of hunting) were quickly adapted into coal mines (clearly industrial use) if minerals were found beneath the surface. Discovering a coal mine on one's property was a useful means of settling gaming debts acquired in the clubs of Regency London, and consequently considered to be superior to owning a deer park. Shifts in technology and economic structures can change the relative returns to land over time. Until the twentieth century no one was especially interested in acquiring the land of the Arabian Peninsula. The fact that a rather smelly, occasionally flammable, liquid naturally oozed out of the ground was something even the most roseate-visioned real-estate agent would have had difficulty selling. Then along came the internal combustion engine, and the value changed.

As soon as a society becomes settled, and occupies a physical space, the land around the village or town or city is required to provide food for it. However, if that food is to be fresh its production needs to be proximate to where people live. One reason that toast is widespread in the United Kingdom but an almost alien culinary concept in continental Europe is that the United Kingdom was the first to urbanise its population on a massive scale. Food storage is an urban problem, and toast is an admirable method of making stale bread palatable. In the UK, the battle between housing demand for land and agricultural demand for land resolved itself in favour of the former, and the price was food that was not entirely fresh.

Businesses also want to be located close to their source of workers, so they too are likely to demand land in the neighbourhood of urban centres. So agriculture must fend off not only the encroachment of suburbia, but also the demands of factories and offices.

The competing uses of land

In English, the single word 'earth' has many different associations. Leaving aside the aesthetic ideas the word evokes, earth is used to denote everything from the entire planet, to the soil in which we grow our food, to the clays and other minerals we extract to make the culinary utensils we use to process and consume our food, to the earth in which we are finally, seemingly, recycled back from whence we came. Without the earth we till to grow food, dig up to extract minerals to fertilise the soil, and dig into to recycle organic leftovers, planet Earth would be much harder to live on.

If we simplify by dispensing with the use of land for leisure purposes, an economist would categorise land as being required for housing, business use, or agriculture. For the purposes of this book, it is agriculture that matters – but as economics is all relative that means that the position of agriculture relative to business and housing use is important. Moreover, all three demands are often to be found jostling for the same physical space. The enlightened economist would add that agricultural, housing and business needs compete with the needs of the environment, without which agriculture, housing and business could not exist.

The economist, looking at economic returns, looks at business and housing as distinct entities, and lumps agriculture into a single category. The environmentalist has different priorities, amalgamating business and housing use, and distinguishing agricultural land into different categories. Simplifying the environmental approach into six broad categories, we have: forest, cropland, grassland, settlement land, wetland, and other land, as shown in Table 2.1.[2]

Some of these environmental classifications have economic consequences and all have ecosystem consequences. In some cases, ecosystem services compete with economic needs – hence, economics sometimes demands the clearing of forest land when the importance of forest land to the ecosystem indicates that forest land should not be cleared. In some cases they are complementary to each other – hence, the use of the English moorland to graze animals in Lancashire and Yorkshire has helped to maintain these areas while also feeding livestock in a sustainable economic manner.

According to the United Nations, over the last half-century, the world's cultivated land area has grown by 12 per cent, yet over the same period agricultural production has far outstripped the supply of agricultural land (production having grown between 250 per cent and 300 per cent).[3] On the face of it, this is a positive story, with human ingenuity triumphing over the constraints of physical land supply. Unfortunately, these headline numbers mask a significant problem. The increase in food production has been financed by credit – environmental credit

Table 2.1 A taxonomy of land by land use and how each relates to the ecosystem and the economy

Land type	Definition	Ecosystem services	Conventional economy
Forest	All land with woody vegetation	Nutrient recycling; water storage recycling and flood control; safe harbour for biodiversity; carbon and methane sequestration; structural support (natural infrastructure); cultural and aesthetic focal point; provisioning	Managed plantations Fibre, fuel, food, conservation
Cropland	Arable/tilled land other than forestry	Nutrient recycling; water delivery (may need human help); provisioning Ecosystem services diminished by tillage: flood control; biodiversity protection; carbon and methane sequestration; culture	Agricultural commodities Fibre, fuel, feed, food
Grassland	All grassland, from wild grassland to pasture to silvi-pastural land, not considered as cropland	Nutrient recycling; water storage and recycling; flood control; biodiversity safe harbour; greenhouse-gas sequestration; culture and aesthetics	Agricultural produce Fuel, feed, conservation
Wetlands	Land covered by water for all or part of the year	Nutrient recycling; water storage and recycling; flood control; biodiversity safe harbour; greenhouse-gas sequestration; culture and aesthetics	Likely to be marginal to the economy, with the exception of the tourism and environmental conservation sectors
Settlements	All developed land including land under infrastructure	Support/foundation for built infrastructure; natural infrastructure transports provisions to urban environment Ecosystem services constrained by build environment	All sectors of the economy, with the exception of agriculture
Other land	Unmanaged land including bare soil, rock, and ice	Ecosystem services such as nutrient recycling, and provisioning may be limited Uninhabitable land may play a structural role in the wider ecosystem (e.g. ice caps, or aquifers beneath desert land)	Conservation and culture (e.g. tourism)

Sources: Authors and the Intergovernmental Panel on Climate Change.

(in many cases also by financial credit). The scale of this seems quite alarming, and it is where we must first turn our attention.

Land and the environmental credit crunch

Consider Table 2.2. This shows the ratio of human environmental resource use against the availability of those environmental resources. In other words, if the ratio is 1.0, then we are sustaining our lifestyle without draining the resources of the environment. In economic terms, we are living within our environmental income. If the ratio is greater than 1.0 then we are drawing down resources at an unsustainable pace, and taking resources from future generations. We are effectively borrowing on our environmental credit card to achieve the standard of living we want today. We have only to think of Charles Dickens' Mr. Micawber to recall the cost of continuing to borrow in that manner.

What Table 2.2 is telling us is that the world as a whole is consuming the environmental resources of one-and-a-half planets to meet the demands of a single planet. What it is also telling us, of course, is that it is the high-income economies of the world that are running up the bills. The low- and middle-income countries are living within their environmental means.

What we can also see from Table 2.2 is why this might matter. Enter geopolitics. Some regions are so well-endowed with environmental resources that they have capacity to spare. Latin America currently requires only half of its environmental capacity to meet the needs of its population. This suggests that other less well-endowed countries may need to borrow environmental output from the better-endowed. Unfortunately, it is not easy to control such borrowing.

We are already racking up an environmental credit-card bill with the global population we have. Imagine the borrowing required to feed nine or ten billion people. The United Nations' Food and Agriculture Organization estimates that we will need 70 per cent more food production than we did in 2005–7, in order to feed the world population of 2050. The challenge for the world is to balance the competing demands for land so as to make sure that there is enough land available

Table 2.2 Ecological footprints – distribution by usage, and 'budget'

		Cropland land	Grazing land	Forest ground	Fishing	Carbon	Built-up land	Global hectares/ person	Footprint/ biocapacity
World		22%	8%	10%	4%	55%	2%	2.7	1.5
High-income		18%	6%	10%	3%	60%	2%	5.6	1.8
Middle-income		28%	9%	10%	5%	45%	4%	1.9	1.1
Low-income		42%	11%	20%	5%	16%	6%	1.1	1.0
Africa		35%	16%	20%	5%	20%	4%	1.5	1.0
Middle East/ Central Asia		24%	8%	5%	2%	59%	2%	2.5	2.7
Asia Pacific		28%	4%	9%	7%	47%	4%	1.6	1.9
Latin America		24%	25%	14%	4%	30%	3%	2.7	0.5
North America		16%	3%	12%	1%	67%	1%	7.1	1.4
EU		24%	7%	11%	3%	51%	3%	4.7	2.1

Source: Adapted from World Wildlife Fund for Nature (2012), Table 2, Ecological Footprint Data Tables.

to produce food – but also to provide housing and sites for businesses, and to do all of this in a manner that is environmentally sustainable.

The question is how to meet the growing needs of a growing population with a planet that cannot grow in surface area. We need to find half a planet today, maybe more than half a planet in the future, or accept a lower standard of living. This search for land is the focus of the remainder of this chapter.

For food, we have basically two choices. Either we increase the amount of cultivated land, or we increase the agricultural output of existing agricultural land (in a sustainable manner). The former is the quick economic solution, but an undesirable environmental solution. The latter is an economic and an environmental solution. Let us consider the two options in turn.

We need another planet

The surface of the planet is essentially finite. Yes, reclamation from the sea is technically possible and indeed important if you are living in the Netherlands or Hong Kong, but for economically practical purposes on a global scale, land is a finite resource. Agricultural land is in more flexible supply. One could chop down forests to provide cropland, for instance. The risk here is that one then damages the ecosystem in such a way as to reduce the supply of agricultural land in the future (losing forests leads to soil erosion and floods, washing away crops).

There is a further problem with finding our additional half-planet by increasing the supply of agricultural land at the expense of other uses. A growing population means a growing demand for housing. It also means a growing demand for employment. So both business and housing demand for land is going to rise as the global population moves onwards and upwards towards nine billion by 2050. But there is clearly a problem if we need more land for housing, more land for business, and more land for agriculture.

The limit to changing land use

In recent decades, concerns have grown over the rate at which forestland, grassland and even former wetland have been converted to other uses such as housing and agriculture. It is not the conversion itself that is the cause for concern, but the speed at which this is taking place. As we shall see, improvements in technology rendered the job of agriculture less and less back-breaking, but have also tended to bring more land under cultivation (increasing agricultural land and reducing non-agricultural land). For the most part, once land is converted to housing, business or agricultural use, it is unlikely that there will ever be a reversion to the forest or wilderness that was there before.

The surge in demand for food and other consumer products magnified by population growth entails the conversion of more and more land to new uses, and specifically to agriculture. Increasing food supply by converting land into agricultural use also has very significant environmental impacts. These environmental impacts have consequences for human survival. This means that the limits to land conversion are more restrictive than the physical limits alone suggest.

When we talk about changing land use what we really mean is reducing forest and wetlands and increasing residential and crop use. Each of these four changes has an environmental impact; the environmental impact may then change the future supply of land.

Changing land use by cutting forests

Forestland is an important component of the environment. By providing habitat and uncultivated land, wild forest helps to support biodiversity. Forests play a key role in water regulation and nutrient recycling. They are also an important carbon sink. It is estimated that halving the rate of deforestation by 2030 would reduce greenhouse-gas emissions by the equivalent of the carbon dioxide emissions of the entire US power industry.[4] It follows, therefore, that felling forests has environmental consequences. Deforestation could foster climate change or encourage flooding, and through that lead to the destruction of agricultural land. The problem is that the loss of agricultural land is likely to occur some distance away from the newly created agricultural land of deforestation.

Latin America is an area in which the leading cause of deforestation is the conversion of forestland to agriculture. Forestry in Europe and Latin America is superficially similar: about half the land in each region is forestland, and each accounts for a significant portion of global forestland – Europe is 25 per cent of the world's forest, Latin America is 21 per cent. Importantly, however, Brazilian forestry sequesters three times as much carbon per hectare as Russian forestry. Given the size of Brazil's forests, that means Brazilian forests absorb twice the carbon of Russian forests in absolute amounts.

Before trade became truly global, decisions about leaving land as forest or using it for agriculture were entirely local (an idea we will return to in a subsequent discussion on slash-and-burn agriculture). In a world dominated by global trade, consumption patterns in one country or region may drive the decisions about land use trade-offs in another country or region. As Table 2.2 shows, Latin America lives within its ecological footprint, but forestland is still being lost. The motives behind felling forests in Brazil must lie in a combination of local governance and shifts in global trading patterns in agriculture.

With food, a key risk is that Western consumption patterns might put ecosystems at risk in Latin America and Asia. Piecemeal solutions like consumer boycotts of produce grown on land converted from forest could do as much harm as good, economically. In 2011, a battle played out in Brazil over a law that has successfully slowed deforestation. In April 2012, the Brazilian Chamber of Commerce passed a new forest code that would allow farmers to set aside smaller areas of forestland. Some environmentalists described this as a 'disaster',[5] while the farmers felt this relaxation of the limits on changes to land use would support sustainable food production.

Changing land use by draining wetlands

From an environmental perspective, wetlands are probably one of the most valuable resources in terms of ecosystem services per square foot. From an economics perspective, wetlands are generally viewed as having limited economic value (thus presenting an economic case for their change of use). It is in the swamps and bogs that the battle lines of economists and environmentalists are to be set.

Wetlands play a range of functions in the ecosystem, ranging from flood protection to biodiversity protection. As less economically productive land it is likely that wetlands will tend to be vulnerable to conversion to other uses. Mangrove swamps are a good example – in Ecuador, the removal of the mangroves forced the (economically expensive) building of sea-walls to replace the flood protection once furnished by the plants. The trade-off between food provisioning and the coastal protection 'services' provided by mangroves may turn out to be extremely costly should salt-water floods be able to encroach more easily upon land used for habitation or agriculture. Living in harmony with the land may turn out to be the cheaper option in economic and ecological terms in the long run.

Box 2.1 Wetlands in history

The seventeenth-century residents of the Isle of Axholme, an area of North Lincolnshire in the United Kingdom, lived in ecological harmony with the fenland.[6] In winter, the Fenlands flooded, which restored fertility to the land. In summer, lower water levels permitted modest cropping and animal husbandry which, alongside fish and fowl, provided the community with dietary sufficiency and balance. All changed when the land was drained, having been expropriated by one Cornelius Vermuyden and the Crown.

The seventeenth-century drainage schemes rolled out by Vermuyden and his associates in the name of profit did (eventually) turn fenland into rich arable land. However, from the perspective of the residents of the time, an equitable, balanced way of life based (in modern parlance) on a 'permaculture'[7] approach to agriculture was wiped out. Whether Vermuyden's belief that the fens of Axholme could be more profitable drained than undrained was correct depends on the point of view. From an economic perspective what happened looks like a forced redistribution of 'profit' rather than a bigger pie. From an environmental perspective the harmonious, productive permaculture was industrialised out of existence. Thus, the political economy was allowed to over-ride political ecology.

In some countries, wetland banking has been used to allow firms to build on wetland as long as they restore an equivalent wetland elsewhere. This presents many challenges, not the least of which is measuring and policing the 'equivalent' wetland. It may be even harder to understand what systems-wide changes are triggered by such changes.

Changing land use by going urban

One of the more extreme forms of land-use change is to convert it to residential land. Land hidden beneath settlements can do very little other than physically support what sits on top of it, although the best of the land, the top soil, might be conserved for use in agriculture elsewhere before building commences. From both ecosystem services and food production perspectives such land is severely constrained, and it seems reasonable to describe such a change as permanent. At the same time, economic development has tended to mean a steady shift off rural land into urban cities. Once land is built on, it is (stating the obvious) of limited use in agriculture. As urbanisation should result in more intensive occupancy rates, it is helpful from an ecosystems perspective. Urbanisation helps reduce the conversion of rural land to residential use. The flipside of this is that large urban populations tend to be a pollution source, with that pollution sometimes rendering the surrounding agricultural land less productive.

There is the potential for some mitigation. The attentive reader may recall the mention of the urban cow in the opening chapter. The husbandry of livestock in the backyard presents obvious challenges in the modern urban environment, but technology may be able to deliver other forms of urban agriculture. Hence, bee-hives have appeared on the flat roof space of some buildings, restaurants grow some green produce via hydroponics, and allotments appear to be growing in popularity in the United Kingdom and elsewhere.

Changing land use by planting crops

Agricultural land is something of an economic and an environmental hybrid when it comes to land use. Increasing land for crops may be a less permanent change from the perspective of the ecosystem (one form of plant life is being replaced with another). In choosing to convert land to agriculture, the sort of land to be converted is important. If the land is suitable for conversion it will be productive, and thus provide a food supply that should reduce the pressure to cut down forests or drain wetlands elsewhere. Unfortunately, the tendency is for the land that is least suited to agricultural conversion to be located in those countries that have most need of increased agricultural output.

The soil is the largest biological sink for methane, a potent greenhouse gas, but what the soil is used for makes a difference to the environment. Scientific work in the area of microbiology[8] has found that changing land to agricultural use can reduce the effectiveness of soil as methane sink. It has been argued that the conversion of forestland to agricultural land causes a 60 per cent fall in the soil's methane oxidisation capacity,[9] and the conversion of fallow land or the addition of fertilisers is also said to diminish the effectiveness of soil as methane sink.

Crop production uses approximately 11 per cent of the world's land surface and 70 per cent of usable water. Moreover, 40 per cent of irrigated land relies on groundwater – rivers and aquifers rather than rain. Increasing the amount of agricultural land suggests that there will be a greater distortion of the water cycle, which may affect agricultural land in the future (aquifers run out) or in other geographic areas (rivers run dry). A further important environmental cost of the conversion of land to agricultural land is the reduction in biodiversity. Wheat fields contain wheat, and not much else.

The struggle between the needs of the environment and the demands of food production are more easily balanced when considering grassland. As grassland, the land is closer to a state of nature in terms of its function. However, natural grassland may be economically inefficient. The role played by grasslands in the economics of meat production is explored in Chapter 4, where we discuss the possible move towards large-scale factory farming. Mother Nature is, it seems, not productive enough for market systems. The stomach of the cow is the most efficient way of converting calories in grass into calories the human stomach can cope with (as meat or milk). However, grazing land cannot provide sufficiently concentrated nutrition for large milk herds to hit maximum productivity.

The consequences of changing land use

In some parts of the world – for instance, the tropics, where ecosystems are prone to hit tipping points – any short-run environmental damage from converting land to agriculture could become permanent. It is no exaggeration to say that if we go on in this way, there may be no tomorrow, or only a very uncomfortable tomorrow, for some members of future generations, even if current generations manage to escape the worst effects of the food crunch.

If the world is to avoid some kind of *Hunger Games* style dystopia,[10] then we need to find some way of breaking the environmental credit crunch and making land a less finite resource. But we need to do this in a way that is environmentally sustainable – otherwise we are just transferring the problem to future generations (and racking up a larger environmental credit card bill today). This brings us onto the concept that will set any economist's pulse racing: the concept of yield.

The value of land – yields

The concept of land as a finite resource is true in a physical sense. However, it is not necessarily true in an economic sense. Economists treat land as having very little intrinsic value – that is to say land is not much use as land. Land's value comes from what land can produce. That means that, at the very least, the finite boundaries of land can be stretched in a relatively elastic way if we can improve the yield that land generates.

Yield on land comes in various forms. In housing terms it can be thought of as the rental income from a property. As slum landlords have discovered the world over, if you increase the number of people living in any specific space, there is a chance that you can increase the yield from that land by charging them all rent. Tower blocks in modern society are an obvious way of increasing the yield on land used for housing.

When we come to agricultural land we start to get into far more fertile territory. The yield on agricultural land is basically how much food the land can produce. The agricultural yield of land is a mix of weather conditions, access to water and fertility. If farmers can double the productivity of the field by doubling the amount of food produced on that field, they can effectively double the amount of agricultural land supply – at least in the way that agricultural land supply matters, namely the production of food.

How realistic is it to suggest that land supply can be doubled by doubling yields? It has happened globally in the last half-century, as we have already noted. If we wish to find another half a planet, it could be done by increasing agricultural yields by a further 50 per cent over the next quarter-century.

Increasing the yield on agricultural land is, indeed, the very foundation of modern urban society. Towns and cities cannot exist unless the land around them generates a surplus of food beyond the farmer's own subsistence levels. Artisans, rulers and priests require food just as much as a farmer, but they cannot be expected to produce their own food when their available time is spent being artistic, lording it over their fellow citizens, or conducting rituals to intercede with the deity. It is also frequently remarked upon that the Industrial Revolution of the eighteenth century accompanied, indeed had to accompany, the Agricultural Revolution that increased the yield of existing farmland. Modern economic structures and urban lifestyles absolutely require an increase in agricultural yield to exist. Economics relies upon getting more calories out of an acre of land.

The earliest attempts to increase agricultural yields came from what is formally known as 'swidden agriculture', and rather more familiarly known as 'slash-and-burn' agriculture. This is converting forestland into agricultural land, but the concept of yield is central to this process. The aspiring suburbanite finds a convenient patch of forest or brushland, burns whatever is there, runs over it with a plough, and plants crops. For the early years, this process is fine, but over time the crop yields will decline, and fewer calories will be produced per acre cultivated. Eventually, the urban lifestyle can no longer be supported by the agricultural yield on the land available. The choice is then to find another patch of land, to move (which is a pain to have to do if you have just established a city, not to mention recently refurbished your kitchen), or to find some way of increasing the output of the land. The exhausted land typically takes two decades to recover its fertility, if left to its own devices.

Thus, if humans want to avoid the inconvenience attendant on a nomadic lifestyle, urban areas require an agricultural hinterland that can reliably feed the urban population, without having to wait twenty years for fertility to be restored. Fertility and irrigation serve as the cornerstones of agricultural yield, and both are supplemented by the application of technology to increase efficiency of fertility and water use. The question is whether technology can deliver on the economist's desire for an infinitely available resource, and if not, where the limits to productivity might be.

> **Box 2.2 The tragedy of the commons**
>
> Garrett Hardin, writing in the 1960s, described the economics of exhaustible resources through the example of herdsmen putting their goats on the common to graze.[11] For each individual farmer the incentive is to put as many goats as possible on the land. When everyone does this, the land is grazed to exhaustion and the herd and its human owners must starve or move on. The tragedy is so described because, left to themselves, human beings happily join the race to use up the most of any limited resource until there is none left, and then must face the unpleasant consequences.

So, let us examine the drivers of yield. We can identify four key aspects. Fertility is the driver of yield, as even the owner of the humblest pot plant can testify. Water is critical, and the source of much human conflict. After that we have energy (which is involved in both fertility and water use), and technology, which is the area of focus.

Fertility and yield

The most innocent of amateur gardeners knows that soil matters. Soil can fairly be described as organic gold. So, what is soil? Soil starts out when the first few hardy plants – perhaps mosses and lichens – establish a toe-hold on bare rock. As these plants die off, their remains produce a thin layer of organic matter. This forms a support for other flora and fauna. Eventually, mineral and organic matter combine to form a top soil whose qualities will depend on the characteristics of three key ingredients – the minerals held in the rock broken down by the plants, the humus (organic matter) the plants kindly provide as a side-effect of life, and the chemicals that the plants themselves have injected into the soil (principally nitrogen, which is transferred from air to soil by some plants).

From the very earliest societies, the necessity of maintaining fertility in land was understood. The technicalities were not understood, but for the most part the issue was maintaining sufficient nitrogen in the soil to allow plants to flourish (either because plants were consumed for their own sake, or because plants were used as fodder for animals, which were in turn consumed). Other minerals are also important, but nitrogen is generally the limiting factor on fertility, and thus the limiting factor on agricultural yield, and thus (critically) the limiting factor for economic profit.

There are three ways that farmers can improve the nitrogen content of their land. First, there is 'fallowing' – leaving the land alone and not growing any crop for a period of time will allow nitrogen to be restored. This is how the slash-and-burn agriculturalists eventually restore fertility to their plots of land – but as noted earlier, this is a two-decade process. Second, there is crop rotation. This simply swaps crops that consume nitrogen with crops that restore nitrogen to the soil (the latter are typically legumes – clover is a big giver of nitrogen, but turnips have their place). Finally, nitrogen can be increased through the application of fertiliser.

Leaving land fallow is the least economically attractive option. The economic asset (land) is not earning any income for the fallow period, and this is a state of affairs that economists abhor. Roman farmers originally left their fields fallow every other year. As the Roman population grew, land supply became a constraint on food supply. Shifting from one fallow year in every two, to one fallow year in every three increased food production significantly – although not by 50 per cent, as working the fields more frequently would have reduced fertility (and thus the agricultural yield, and therefore the economic profit).

Fallow periods could be thought of as accumulations of environmental credit. There was a huge surge in agricultural output in Britain during the Second World War. Bedford Franklin, writing in 1948, described British agriculture over that period in the following terms: 'In an emergency the ordinary man draws heavily on his savings in the Bank; in war the farmer draws on his accumulated savings of fertility under well stocked grassland.'[12] In other words, fallow ground was ploughed up, and the fertility it had acquired was drawn down to allow for a staggering increase in British agricultural production. Franklin is talking about environmental credit before the concept was articulated – and his analogy is a fairly decent stab at presenting the concept in conventional credit terms (all the more impressive as he was not, poor man, an economist).

Fallow periods were all very well when the land available per head of the population was reasonable. However, by the late nineteenth century, China was estimated to have just one acre of cultivatable land per person (compared with twenty acres per person in the United States). Having an acre stand idle for a fallow period was simply not compatible with the survival of the Chinese population.

Fortunately, ancient Chinese civilisation had already hit on a solution to this crisis: cannabis. Chinese farmers found that by rotating their crops, they could ensure that the fertility (yield, profit) of their fields was maintained. Complex crop-rotation schemes over five years or more were devised, with cannabis playing a role in putting nitrogen back into the soil. Much later, a similar plan was promoted for English agriculture by Charles, Second Viscount Townshend in the early eighteenth century. This enlightened agriculturalist also advocated the use of crop rotation to maintain fertility. For some reason, Lord Townshend preferred using turnips to cannabis as his nitrogen-replenishing crop, earning the alliterative nickname 'Turnip Townshend' for his trouble.

While the turnip has many worthy attributes,[13] it is possible that the general population is not as appreciative of a diet of turnips as it might be. Crop rotation with legumes does encourage the production of meat. A field of clover or crop of turnips can be eaten by cattle. It is one reason why a wholly vegetarian diet, with no cattle grazing on grassland during a fallow period, could be considered economically and even environmentally wasteful. (If this sounds odd, remember that human beings are not well equipped to digest grass.)

The economic problem with rotation is that it limits what the farmer can grow at any time. Whether the market wants legumes or not, legumes are what they will get if that is what the land requires under a crop-rotation regime. If the farmer is not supplying what the population wants, then the profit will be lessened. This is not a good development economically. As a result, the application of fertiliser has become the main mechanism by which soil fertility, agricultural yield and economic profit are maintained.

The economic importance of fertilising the fields has long been recognised. The Incas used to bury sardine heads to fertilise their crops. From the thirteenth century on, the tenant peasantry of Crawley in England were required, each year, to move manure from the gate of the manor farm to the surrounding fields (they got out of this presumably onerous and odorous task in 1690 by paying a shilling each for an exemption). An English Act of Parliament in 1812[14] specifically exempted carts of manure from road tolls, recognising the value to agriculture of moving the manure around. With population growth, however, by the late eighteenth century the global conventional supply of fertiliser was starting to prove insufficient.

***Box 2.3* The economics of excrement**

Bird droppings, politely referred to as guano, demonstrate the vital economic importance of fertility to the industrialised world. It is also a classic case of an environmental credit crunch. Economically, guano was big business. The efficacy of bird droppings as a form of fertiliser was first noted in European texts in 1609, but somehow this was overlooked by contemporaries. As late as 1813, the UK agriculturalist Davy wrote 'the dung of sea birds has, I believe, never been used as a manure in this country'.[15] Over the coming decades, however, agriculture in the UK disappeared below a mountain of bird dung.

Guano began to be exported from Latin America to the United Kingdom around 1820. By 1885, it was all over. Over the half-century that guano was exploited, fortunes were made. The British firm Anthony Gibbs and Sons bought the stuff at 15 dollars per ton, and sold it to farmers for 50 dollars per ton – a respectable mark-up, which enabled that family to finance a large proportion of the foundation of Keble College, Oxford.[16] Those who have seen the architecture of Keble College may perhaps be unsurprised to learn what its foundations rest upon.

Peru, as supplier of guano to the world, profited. In 1860, almost 15 million dollars was paid for guano rights. In 1869, the French company Dreyfus gave the Peruvian government enough money in exchange for guano that the government was able to restore its credit rating on the international markets. Guano meant increased agricultural yield, which meant more calories and profits per acre of cultivation. Exploitation of fertiliser allowed existing stocks of land to feed increasing populations.

(Continued)

> *(Continued)*
>
> The desire for economic profit ignored the looming environmental credit crunch. This was a real-life tragedy of the commons; profit was there to be made, and to be made as quickly as possible. By the late 1880s the stocks of guano, accumulated over centuries, were exhausted. The environmental credit card reached its limit, and no more credit was available. Once again, agriculturalists contemplated the possibility of a dark, Malthusian future – a future darkened by reckless procreation during the period of agricultural plenty that had been financed by the environmental credit of guano.

Today, fertilisers are produced on an industrial scale. This is what has enabled the world to sustain the global population that it has today. It is estimated that 40 per cent of the global population depends on industrial fertilisers to survive at all, and that half the world depends on industrial fertiliser to receive adequate nutrition.

Natasha Gilbert, writing in the science magazine *Nature*, describes soil enrichment as the key to tackling hunger in Africa. While the application of industrially manufactured fertilisers is not the only means of avoiding soil depletion, it helps to value the losses currently incurred through poor agricultural management. Failing to put nutrients back into the African soil is calculated as being the equivalent of almost four billion dollars' worth of industrially manufactured fertiliser per year.[17]

So, does the environmental credit crunch apply to fertiliser? Nitrogen, like water (as we shall see), is an infinite resource. There is a nitrogen cycle, just as there is a water cycle. In a world where nitrogen is around 80 per cent of the atmosphere, there seems little prospect of the demand outstripping the supply. The problem is that nitrogen in the air is not the same thing as nitrogen in the land, and it is the land part that matters.

Organic nitrogen – derived from planting nitrogen-replenishing crops or from the application of animal manure – is a renewable resource. However, it is industrially produced fertiliser that is critical to sustaining the global population today. This is particularly true in emerging economies – over half the world's supply of nitrogen-based fertiliser is both produced and consumed in Asia. Industrially produced fertiliser is very much subject to the ravages of the environmental credit crunch. Industrially produced fertiliser is the end result of an energy-intensive production chain (it is this that leads to 'oil-based' fertilisers as a concept. The fertiliser is not generally an oil by-product. It is produced by burning oil to generate energy). Constraints on energy supply engendered by the environmental credit crunch are therefore central to the economics of land productivity.

Before leaving fertiliser, it is worth touching on how it is applied. Fertiliser, just like anything else, can be wasted. Applying fertiliser to the soil which is not absorbed by the plant (but washed away) is a waste, in both economic and environmental terms. Economically, this is money that is literally ending up down the drain (as the fertiliser enters the water system and not the plant). Environmentally, the fertiliser represents wasted energy, and may generate pollution.

The world has become more efficient in its consumption of fertiliser. Total nitrogen fertiliser consumption peaked at over five million tonnes of nutrients a year, in the 1980s. Total nitrogen fertiliser consumption is now running at around 60–70 per cent of its peak (consumption still fluctuates from year to year).[18] This reduction in fertiliser consumption is not, of course, due to a reduction in food production – quite the reverse. The first decade of this century saw crop production rise 1.2 per cent per person per year.

This means that the world is getting more crop production out of less fertiliser applied. In the late 1880s, wheat at the Broadbalk Experiment at the Rothamsted Research experimental centre in England absorbed about 30 per cent of the nitrogen applied to it – 70 per cent was wasted in both the environmental and the economic sense. In 1979, the situation had completely reversed and wheat absorbed 70 per cent of applied nitrogen. During the next decade around 80 per cent was absorbed. Thereafter, further efficiency led to absolute consumption of fertiliser falling, even as more crops were produced.

There is still room for dramatic efficiency improvement. Only 26–28 per cent of the nitrogen applied to Chinese rice production actually goes to the plant. Almost three-quarters is lost (washed away, in effect). For vegetables, less than 20 per cent of Chinese fertiliser is absorbed by the plant. Nitrogen that is washed into the water supply is not only a potential environmental pollutant it is also an economic waste. Anything that can be done to minimise the loss of fertiliser will extend the financial and economic credit available for food production. The idea of 100 per cent efficiency in fertiliser application is undoubtedly a pipedream, but surely the world can do better than having its most populous nation wasting up to 80 per cent of applied fertiliser, and thus up to 80 per cent of the energy used to produce that fertiliser?

Efficiency here refers to applied fertilisers. There are risks if fertility is drawn from the soil and shipped elsewhere. Simon Fairlie[19] describes the role of phosphorous in the typical wheat crop: 96 per cent of the phosphorous removed from the land is 'in the crop', and the remaining 4 per cent is lost through leaching and soil erosion. If the phosphorous is in the soil naturally, that soil loses fertility through selling the crop. With manure and sewerage ploughed back in, most of the phosphorous 'lost' in the crop can be relatively easily returned to the land. If the crop is sent elsewhere and manure or fertiliser is not imported to replace the phosphorous packaged 'in the crop' an environmental credit crunch will result.

Energy and yield

Nature has worked out a way of transferring nitrogen from air to soil at atmospheric pressure, and with very little energy required, through the use of legume plants. Humans can transfer nitrogen into a form that can be applied to the land but only through a process that requires intense pressure and heat – and both of these processes require energy.

A superficial glance at the energy consumption of fertiliser production seems to be alarming. Temperatures of 400°C and a pressure of up to 350 atmospheres are required to produce the right conditions for generating fertiliser. This requires a serious amount of energy, ordinarily speaking. Recall that around 40 per cent of humanity depends on the fertiliser that produces the crops that provide the calories necessary for survival – which means that 40 per cent of humanity depends on the energy that is required to produce that fertiliser in the first place. Energy is one of those resources that are subject to the environmental credit crunch. The potential for an economic and an environmental crisis on the land is therefore juxtaposed in this relationship.

The economics of this are obvious. If the price of energy goes up, the price of producing fertiliser will go up. If the price of producing fertiliser goes up, the price of producing food will go up – either because the higher cost of fertiliser is passed on in the form of higher prices, or because less fertiliser is used and therefore the agricultural yield on land goes down, and thus the supply of food falls relative to the level of demand. Thus, if a shortage of energy supply (a form of environmental credit crunch) creates higher energy prices, the economic mechanism will produce a price impact for food.

However, before we become too concerned about the role of energy in the agricultural yield of land, we should consider how important energy is to the process. At the moment, somewhat less than 2 per cent of the world's energy supply is used to produce fertiliser. This is why getting food to the farm gate (a process that includes the energy required to drive a tractor) is only around 17.5 per cent of the energy content of the food that is consumed in a developed economy, and 30 per cent of the energy content of food at a global level.[20] This means that a rise in energy prices, because of the environmental credit crunch or any other reason, should not have a huge impact on the agricultural productivity of land (nor, indeed, is it likely to moderate their environmental impacts). The environmental credit crunch matters, and in a really extreme way it is potentially a limiting factor on yields, but economics do not drive it much of the time, explaining why it is not seen as a dominant force.

Of course, there are two factors that could reduce the threat of an energy credit crunch to land yields. First, there is the possibility of using renewable energy sources rather than finite energy sources to generate the power that produces fertiliser. An 'oil-based' fertiliser is an identical product to a 'hydroelectric-based' fertiliser in all respects other than in its environmental footprint. Of course, it is worth reflecting that there are many competing energy demands in modern society – and as the economic standard of living increases, the demand for energy is likely to continue to rise.

Second, there is the possibility of learning the secrets of nature. If scientists are able to find a way of converting nitrogen from the air into a usable form without the high temperatures and pressure of the industrial fertiliser production process, then the threat of an environmental credit crunch impacting the productivity of agricultural land will recede rapidly into the history books. A turnip has the secret of converting nitrogen into a fixed form at low temperatures and normal atmospheric pressure. Sadly, what comes naturally to a turnip still appears to elude the global scientific community. That does not mean that the secret will remain elusive indefinitely. If the challenges of an environmental credit crunch do start to impede the productivity of land and through that raise food prices, an economic impulse to research and innovate will increase. As the current industrial fertiliser production technique originated around a century ago, it might be time to think about upgrading the process.

Water and yield

In economic terms, water is an infinite resource. Water is the ultimate recycled product. The ice glacier of millennia past winds up in today's cup of tea, or of course irrigates the tea plant that supplies the tea leaf. The human kidney is, not to put too fine a point on it, admirably designed for recycling water. Given this state of affairs, what can economists say about something that is in infinite supply, and is infinitely recyclable? Economics is about finite resources and infinite desires. If water is abundant, surely economics is redundant?

The heretical notion that economics is redundant can be dismissed at once. Water is theoretically in infinite supply, but in practical terms (and in particular for agriculture) there are constraints that call for economic solutions. The problem for agriculture, and humanity, is twofold. First, water needs to be in the right form. The heady cocktail of minerals that is seawater is not much use for agricultural purposes (not for nothing is the phrase 'salt the earth' synonymous with ruin and devastation). Water needs to be potable, or near potable for agricultural purposes. Second, water needs to be in the right place. Humanity has an unfortunate habit of occupying areas without sufficient water supplies to meet their needs.

The economics of water is rapidly becoming a high priority in parts of the world. China has water disputes with every one of its land neighbours. The states of the Colorado Basin in the United States engage in protracted disputes over water. Ethiopia and Egypt have come close to war over the water resources of the Nile. And, of course, water supply has the potential to change. One of the consequences of climate change in the coming decades is that sub Saharan Africa is likely to become wetter (also warmer). Land use therefore can and doubtless will change as the climate changes.

To talk of water is to talk of agriculture. Around 70 per cent of global water use is agricultural (20 per cent is industry and 10 per cent is household use). Around 40 per cent of the world's grain harvest (for all forms of grain) comes from irrigated land. Here is the economics. Irrigation water requires infrastructure (by definition), which requires investment. If the farmer is no longer relying on rainfall, then money must be spent to bring water to the crops. That money spent on the irrigation infrastructure will reduce the profit on agricultural land. Thus, either the price of food must rise to make irrigation worthwhile, or the yield per acre must rise so as to justify the expense of irrigation.

> *Box 2.4* **The Green Revolution**
>
> The Yaqui Valley, in Mexico, is widely regarded as the home of the well-known Green Revolution. It is one of the largest agricultural areas in Mexico, covering some 31,000 hectares (76,600 acres). What is less often discussed is the cultural shift that was a consequence of the Green Revolution. Farmers who wanted to stick with Mayan land husbandry traditions moved to the foothills, and the rest moved into the valley. This divide permitted Dr Elizabeth Guillette to undertake a review of the impacts on human health of intensive agrochemical use,[21] but of course the divide goes much further than that. Agriculture is, ultimately, about the relationship between human beings and the land they live on.
>
> The term Green Revolution refers to the use of high-yielding crop varieties, deployed along with a bundle of other inputs – agrochemicals (fertilisers and pest control), irrigation, and mechanisation with the overall goal of agricultural intensification.[22] The upside of this system was a dramatic increase in productivity (a 118 per cent increase in yield in developing countries, 67 per cent in high-income countries, and (up to a point) an avoidance of changes to land use). The downside was threefold. Water draw-down for irrigation changed local hydrology; fertilisers polluted ecosystems, degrading water and air quality, thereby also posing a threat to human health; and changes to land ownership brought with it profound changes to stewardship, as well as pushing previous incumbents off the land.

Technology and yield

Agriculture was an important technological development in its own right when it first arrived, supplanting the hunter–gatherer approach because it allowed human beings to provide their food more reliably and efficiently. Since then, human ingenuity has produced many other new ideas, transforming the field. Given the back-breaking nature of traditional agriculture, the ability of technology to improve productivity has been absolutely critical to human and economic development. Without agricultural technology, civilisation would not be where it is today – this important positive must be borne in mind as we explore the question of resource limits.

The most obvious consequence of improved efficiency through the use of technology should be less need to increase the amount of land converted to agriculture, and this does indeed seem to have happened. It is worth remembering, however, that even as productive efficiency rises, use of the relevant resource can also continue to rise in absolute volume terms. The problem is that the arrival of the new technology also tends to bring with it increased access to the key resource; new technology is like a car with an accelerator and no brakes, transferring the tragedy of the commons from one resource to another.

Technology also requires certain levels of education and infrastructure. Timing fertiliser application correctly (taking into account plant needs and soil type) to avoid waste depends on good technique, which requires education.[23] In developed countries, as the efficiency of nitrogen take-up suggests, technology has astounding implications. Satellite navigation systems can allow the precise application of precise amounts of fertiliser, adjusting square metre by square metre to best meet the known conditions of the soil. Avoiding waste through this sort of technology brings the co-benefits of better economic yields, and lower environmental impact. It is also far beyond the means of most emerging-economy farmers.

This suggests technology can be both good and bad news. In some poorer countries, there seems little doubt that a judicious application of modern technology would help, if it could be applied. In irrigated wheat production, nitrogen deficiency is the commonest nutritional problem, often because applying the right amount of fertiliser at the right time and in the right weather conditions poses challenges.

A further problem with fertilisers is that when they are applied over a long period of time, soil structures can eventually degrade, suggesting that there is no substitute for some of the things Mother Nature does naturally. Hence, no-till farming that preserves soil structures and using plants that naturally restore nutrients (we are back to turnips) might turn out to be more efficient approaches to soil stewardship in the long run – although no-till farming has implications for weed control, as we shall come to in the next chapter. Newer ideas such as micro-dosing might reduce costs for farmers by reducing the volumes of chemical fertiliser required, with lower environmental impacts to boot.

Technology advances in water delivery have played a crucial role in facilitating agriculture throughout history. This is illustrated nowhere better than in Egypt, where fluctuation between feast and famine can be directly associated with ecological limits, which could be pushed back for a while with the help of technology but then inevitably reasserted themselves as the population continued to grow.

The answer to the tragedy of the commons is generally believed to be land ownership, which brings with it an incentive to exercise good stewardship over the land, thereby maintaining its productivity. It may not be, however, the final answer. Access to land, however achieved, gives access to other 'commons' not contained within the confines of specific land plots such as water; the unintended consequences of the Green Revolution are nothing more than a reassertion of the tragedy.

Food security

As the above paragraphs suggest, one of the issues which complicates the economics and environmental implications of land use is the issue of *whose* land is in use. In a perfect world where economists run everything, national food security would be of limited concern. International trade would be unhindered, and food could be produced wherever it was most efficient (from both an economic and an environmental perspective). Trade, unhampered by political complications, would ensure the effective distribution of that food. However, we are not in a perfect world, and issues around agricultural efficiency can create complications for land management.

Governments, generally speaking, are reluctant to become too dependent on overseas suppliers of food. In the event of political disputes, food supplies could be disrupted (the use of food as a 'weapon' was a notable feature of both the World Wars, of course). In the event of economic problems, food could become more difficult to obtain, and certainly more expensive.

This concern about food security leads to two consequences – short of seeking to acquire more land by conquest. First, there is an attempt to increase the efficiency of food production. Economically speaking, this is generally a positive development (the yield on land is being raised), and with the right economic incentives this can be done in an environmentally efficient manner. It is noticeable that the great advances in food efficiency have tended to coincide with periods of conflict. Generally speaking, if a country is seeking food security it will also have an incentive to maximise environmental efficiency, as waste of all imported goods is likely to be resisted.

The second consequence is less obviously a positive development. Attempts at food security may lead to attempts to produce foodstuff in an economically inefficient manner. In order to encourage food production of foods that would otherwise be imported, governments may seek to incentivise through subsidies (which are generally economically inefficient). Thus, we end up with greenhouses of tomatoes in climates that are ill-suited to their cultivation, in order to ensure a secure supply of tomatoes and to avoid the insecurity of depending on imports.

The combination of a financial and an environmental credit crunch is likely to increase the role of food security in our economic and political lives. Already we have had countries (like the Ukraine) imposing export bans on foodstuffs in order to keep domestic food prices low. The financial credit crunch makes people sensitive to prices. If people are voters, then politicians become sensitive to food prices. Foreigners do not vote in domestic elections, and farmers (who would benefit from being able to sell to the world market) are normally a minority of the electorate. The result is inevitably a skewed economic policy which creates perverse economic outcomes. The consequence of this is likely to be a global move towards autarky – food self-sufficiency. This can only go some way in that direction, but even a small move that undermines the free trade in foodstuffs is likely to be economically damaging, with unpredictable environmental consequences.

So where is our half a planet, then?

The main points to take away from this chapter are as follows. First, agricultural efficiency can be good news, but if changes made in the name of efficiency are not carefully piloted they can simply lead to even more usage, defeating the purpose of efficiency. Second, ecological and economic considerations can run counter to each other; this can be extremely difficult to manage in the context of important global 'commons' residing on, in or under land in a few countries. Geopolitics very quickly comes into the picture (stating the obvious) when food-related land use decisions are made, and global institutions may be needed to maintain the balance between the rich and powerful, the less powerful, and the ecosystem. Third, overall ecosystem resilience is absolutely crucial for sustainable food provisioning in the future. This aspect of risk management appears to be seriously neglected in the context of conventional economics.

Notes

1. Food and Agriculture Organization of the United Nations (2011a).
2. Based on Penman *et al.* (2003), who describe 'top-level' land-use categories for greenhouse-gas reporting in Section 2.2.
3. Food and Agriculture Organization of the United Nations (2011a).
4. Authors' calculations.
5. BBC (2012).
6. Thirsk (1984), p. 162.
7. See Mollison (1988) for a detailed discussion of the permaculture, or 'cultivated ecology', concept.
8. Nedwell *et al.* (2003).
9. Ibid., p. 150.
10. Collins (2008).
11. Hardin (1968).
12. From Franklin (1948), p. 206.
13. Mrs Beeton's *Family Cookery* (n.d.) offers turnips in the form of soup, salad, greens, au gratin, boiled and mashed.
14. 'A Bill to explain the exemption from toll, in several Acts of Parliament, for Carriages carrying Dung or any other Manure', 8 May 1812.
15. Leigh (2004), p. 104.
16. Leigh (2004), p. 81.
17. Gilbert (2012).
18. Data from the International Fertilizer Association at www.fertilizer.org.
19. Fairlie (2010).
20. Developed-economy data drawn from University of Wisconsin–Madison Centre, cited in Leigh (2004). Total data comes from the Food and Agriculture Organization of the United Nations (2012).
21. Guillette (1998).
22. Matson (2012).
23. Ortiz-Monasterio (2002).

3 Raw material inputs
Vegetable

Season of mists and mellow fruitfulness,
Close bosom-friend of the maturing sun;
Conspiring with him how to load and bless
With fruit the vines that round the thatch-eves run;
To bend with apples the moss'd cottage-trees,
And fill all fruit with ripeness to the core.

(John Keats, *To Autumn*, 1819)

We proceed to the next step in the agricultural food-chain, from mineral to vegetable, and from ecosystem support to ecosystem output. This chapter focuses primarily on things that grow in the ground – cereals, pulses, fruits and vegetables, and of course the important food ingredients that are produced from them such as food oils. Formally, this is known as vegetal matter, what the British call 'veg', the Australians 'veggies' and some cultures describe as 'basic pizza topping'. We start by considering the importance of vegetables as a source of food, and then examine the way we grow our crops.

Eat up your greens

Conventional wisdom suggests that as wealth increases, the lowly vegetable is less appreciated, to be replaced by more meat (to the detriment of the environment). The point that must not be lost is that the diet becomes more varied in *all* its dimensions as wealth increases, and this is a good thing. Greater variation in developing-country diets in particular should be seen as beneficial, for when it comes to diet, two and two are decidedly greater than four. Consider three hypothetical diets, each containing an identical number of grams of protein: a diet entirely based on wheat; a diet entirely based on legumes; and a diet that is some happy combination of the two. The combined diet, naturally enough, contains a combination of *different* proteins, *all* of which are required for good health. This makes it far more nutritious in terms of protein delivery than the diets that are superficially sufficient but nutritionally deficient (i.e. the diets based exclusively on wheat or exclusively on legumes). Not for nothing do we have the proverb that 'man cannot live by bread alone'.

In a similar vein, the full range of vitamins needed for human health are more likely to be absorbed through a varied diet, while micronutrient deficiency is a likely consequence of a restricted diet. As the range of food groups within the purview of this chapter – cereals, pulses, fruits and vegetables – suggests, planet Earth produces a veritable cornucopia of vegetable-based foods. There are enough different sorts of vegetables out there to provide for healthy humans, and indeed a healthy environment, if properly managed. That humanity is aware of this is not in question. There are estimates that humans use 45 per cent of all plant growth on the planet. Of course, some of this is for fuel or construction, and some of it is fodder for animals (in turn consumed), but a lot of plant growth is basically about food.

Of course, the range of vegetable-based foods is widest when considered globally. Bananas do not naturally occur in Europe, for instance, so if we want to add the diversity of bananas to the diet of a European, we need to trade to get them to Europe. Banana boats create an essential variety in one's diet.

Where do the fruits of trade fall?

It is generally accepted that trade increases economic wellbeing in total. However, the benefits of trade do not have to be equally distributed (the wellbeing improvement is aggregate). If the fruits of free trade fall unevenly, this can have implications for the environment. Although this book focuses primarily on food systems in developed economies, the food of developed economies is almost inextricably linked to the environment of developing countries through global trade.

Developing economies tend to be more sensitive to change. Very often the social institutions are less stable than in developed economies, putting social order at risk from external shocks. As many developing economies are in relatively warm climes, the environment is also sensitive to change. An environmental shock is far more likely to be catastrophic in developing countries, while a similar shock would be difficult but manageable for a developed economy. What this means, of course, is that a shock in a developed market's food food-chain could pose unmanageable difficulties for a developing economy.

Box 3.1 A real-world food shock 2006–8

A study undertaken by the United Nations[1] found that the impact of a food price shock on individual countries depended on two conditions: the preparedness for crisis management (our old friend *resilience*) and the net food trade balance. The more resilient countries had in place the institutions, resources (in the broadest sense) and systems required to apply export restrictions, to suppress domestic prices by releasing food from stockpiles and to provide the safety net of food support. Countries dependent on food imports suffered the most from price rises. Food exporters, on the contrary, could choose to control domestic prices and benefited financially from the price shock.

(Continued)

> (Continued)
>
> In the context of an environmental food shock, exactly the same would apply. The resilient countries would also be those with institutions, resources and systems needed to protect the domestic population from the immediate impacts of the shock and to invest in food provisioning. Countries over-endowed with natural capital would be likely to carry on regardless; countries without would potentially be in great difficulty.

A working global food system is great at introducing variety into one's diet. However, a working global food system must avoid putting pressure on the environment of developing countries: the risk is too high. If a European economy depends on bananas for variety in its diet, but the supply of bananas stops because the environment of the Caribbean producer has been over-exploited, then the European country loses variety and health in the medium term.

Meat and five veg

In any debate over food, before too long the idea that we are eating too much meat rises to the surface. Meat is the subject of the next chapter, but from a global vantage point it is vegetables that still dominate. The British 'meat and two veg' concept of a meal considerably underestimates the vegetable. In 2007, 2,796 calories-worth of food per day were available per person at a global level, of which only 17 per cent came from meat while 83 per cent came from cereals and vegetables. Globally, it is 'meat and five veg'.

If we look at the data, there has been a steady rise in the number of calories available to the world over the past half-century. But, more importantly, the conventional wisdom about the meat we eat is wrong. *The proportion of calories available from meat and from veg is unchanged.* The 'meat and five veg' ratio holds over time. From a nutritional perspective this looks like very good news. From the perspective of economics and equality, the news may be less good.

Table 3.1 shows a simple nutritional breakdown of the food intake for the world's least-developed countries (which account for 12 per cent of the global population).[2] The calories available are not enough to keep a working adult in good health, indicating malnutrition in the population at large. The growth in available calories has been about half that achieved in the developed economies over roughly half a century.

The difference between the available food-mix for developed economies and the least-developed economies is explained by a complex mix of environmental, political, sociological, geographic and economic influences.

Table 3.1 Food availability in the world's least-developed economies

	2009 food supply (kcal/capita/day)	2009 protein-supply quantity (g/capita/day)	2009 fat-supply quantity (g/capita/day)	Food-supply shares	Protein-supply shares	Fat-supply shares
Grand total	2298	60.0	42.6			
Vegetal products	2120	47.2	32.8	92%	79%	72%
Animal products	178	12.8	11.8	8%	21%	28%

Source: United Nations' Food and Agriculture Organization Food Balance Sheets.

The value of veg

The broad category of 'veg' therefore has a considerable importance to food. With variety it creates a healthy diet, and it is the dominant part of our diet. We produce enough veg to sustain us at the moment, but the distribution of that food is not necessarily optimal. However, as we move on to a larger and larger global population, it is important that we continue to produce enough food and that we do so in a way that does not prejudice the ability of future generations to produce enough food. This is not going to be as easy as it sounds, and it is this problem that is the topic for the rest of this chapter.

Getting enough to eat

The economics of growing crops are not especially complicated. The process is simply about how to get the most out of the crop cycle. As we saw in Chapter 2 on land, the economic value of land is about its yield – and the question there is what can be done to the land to make it more efficient. For crops, it is pretty much the same thing, except that now we are talking about what can be done to the crops themselves to make them more productive. This basically comes into two categories: the aspects of the crop cycle that relate to preparing the ground, planting and harvesting; and then ensuring that what is planted remains as healthy as possible, and gives the greatest yield it can.

Economic theory is simple enough, but we have a specific constraint. There is no point in maximising the yield today if by doing so we reduce the yield tomorrow. There are techniques that can deliver higher volumes of crops in the present, but the use of these techniques may create havoc with our ability to grow crops in the future.

Writer Cormac McCarthy, in his Pulitzer Prize-winning novel *The Road*, described a world in which the biosphere is dead and nothing grows on the blackened land, cauterised by an unnamed disaster of cataclysmic proportions. The remaining humans are forced to wander the earth, scavenging for the dwindling remains of preserved food still lying forgotten in the larders and silent refrigerators. Human society was so depleted that the wherewithal to undertake research to reverse the damage was simply not present. It is an extreme, and hopefully fictional vision of the future, but it does emphasise the conflict between food now and food in the future.

46 *Raw material inputs: vegetable*

Ecosystem collapse means no food crops, full stop. The production of food crops of any kind needs to be done in such a way that the particular ecosystem flows that provide them are maintained *indefinitely*. Thus, food production must always involve a trade-off between the need to maintain environmental health, and the need to produce food efficiently. We can summarise this by looking at the battleground of economists and environmentalists, and the four possible scenarios this can produce (Figure 3.1).

In the 'profit at any cost' scenario, everything is about the production of the largest possible volume of crops at the lowest cost. In the 'treehugger' scenario, it is the environment that is the dominant concern and the need to feed the population is subordinated. The ideal is the Hudson–Donovan 'optimal' scenario, which describes a good balance between the environment and economics. Under this scenario there is effectively a trinity of sustainability: the population is sustained with enough food today; the environment is sustained for the medium term; because the environment is sustained, food supplies are sustainable in the medium term.

The 'Doomsday' scenario is the least optimal of the possibilities shown (the hint to that is given in the scenario's name). 'Doomsday' could arise because over time the 'profit at any cost' scenario may prove unsustainable. The long-term risk inherent in large-scale chemical-driven approaches to farming is the potential for a fall-off in economic efficiency as a consequence of the degradation of the environment.

So, what we need to do is find a way of living in the nirvana of the Hudson–Donovan 'optimal' scenario. As we have already noted, that means achieving the right yield in the right way through the mechanics of preparing and planting and harvesting, and through keeping the plants healthy when they are in the ground.

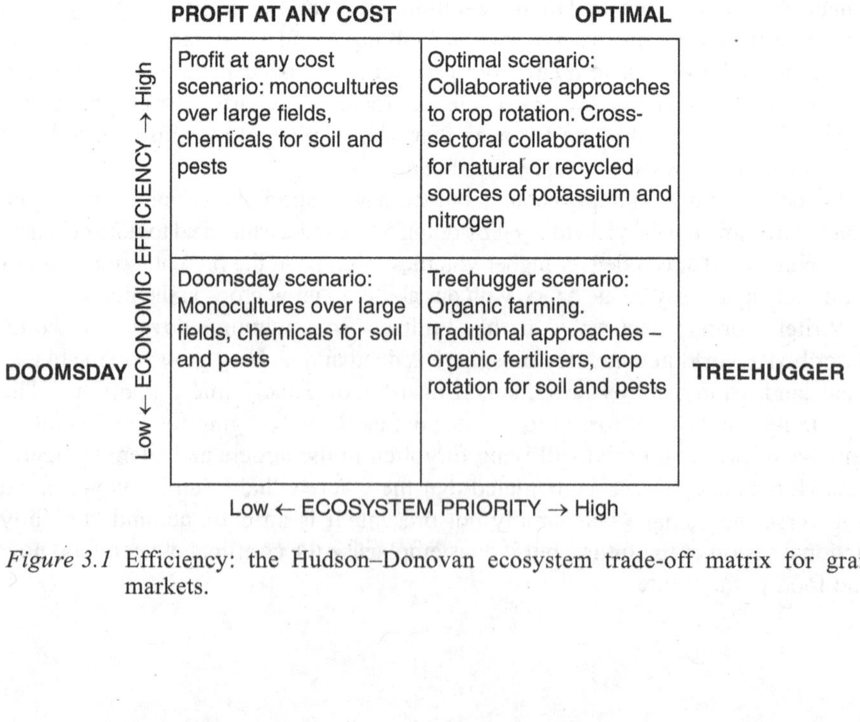

	PROFIT AT ANY COST	**OPTIMAL**
High ECONOMIC EFFICIENCY	Profit at any cost scenario: monocultures over large fields, chemicals for soil and pests	Optimal scenario: Collaborative approaches to crop rotation. Cross-sectoral collaboration for natural or recycled sources of potassium and nitrogen
Low ECONOMIC EFFICIENCY	Doomsday scenario: Monocultures over large fields, chemicals for soil and pests	Treehugger scenario: Organic farming. Traditional approaches – organic fertilisers, crop rotation for soil and pests
	DOOMSDAY	**TREEHUGGER**

Low ← ECOSYSTEM PRIORITY → High

Figure 3.1 Efficiency: the Hudson–Donovan ecosystem trade-off matrix for grain markets.

Veg mechanics

In 1947, British agriculture faced a huge challenge, which was causing great concern amongst those in power. Every year, 16,000 horses were born in the United Kingdom. Of those 16,000 foals, a meat-deprived British population ate 2,500. Of course in 2013 the British population was also eating horsemeat. The difference was that in 1947, horse was knowingly consumed, and eating 2,500 foals a year was creating a crisis. The best minds that British agriculture had to offer knew with absolute certainty that farming in the UK had to have 45,000 live (unconsumed) foals every year simply to supply the horses necessary for the farm work. In the 1940s, British agriculture was being described as the most mechanised agriculture in the world. There were 175,000 tractors working the British fields. And yet, in spite of that, in 1949 the UK still had over half a million horses working on the land and the stock had to be replenished. The shortage threatened by low equine birth rates and consumption of meat could lead to the collapse in arable farming because of course there would be nothing to draw the plough or the seed drill if this disastrous erosion of horsepower was to carry on much longer.

What followed seems logical to those looking back from the comfortable vantage point of the twenty-first century, but was not readily predicted by the agriculturalists of two generations ago. Horse-drawn ploughs were replaced by tractors. By the mid-1950s, horses were outnumbered by tractors. Scythe-wielding harvest workers who had dominated the landscape and provided suitable subjects for the artwork of John Constable were gone from most of the developed world within a matter of years. They still exist in parts of Eastern Europe, but in Western Europe their sole appearance is generally as extras in television period dramas.

The capital revolution in agriculture can fairly be described as a second Agricultural Revolution. The fall in the numbers of agricultural labourers over the past century does not mean that the remaining farmers are Stakhanovite supermen or superwomen. It means that capital has replaced labour – one of the most basic processes in economics. This has changed the economics of agriculture, not through increasing the yield per acre (although that has happened too), but by increasing the yield per agricultural labourer employed. Traditional farming spent money on labour. A breakdown of the costs of cultivation in the late eighteenth century shows that. The costs in bringing in eight acres worth of carrots in the Mendips area of England in the 1780s were roughly 83 per cent labour, broadly defined (ploughing, harrowing, sewing with hand drills, hoeing, digging and carting). Even allowing for the fact that outsourcing carting, ploughing and harrowing costs must have had a certain amount of consideration for the horses, this is still an extraordinarily labour-intensive business.

The dramatic shift to capital-based arable farming in the 1940s was driven by economics (of course). In 1947, at the point that the lamentable lack of new horses was causing so much concern, labour cost was around fifteen shillings per horsepower hour. Throw in a couple of horses, and the running costs (labour and horses) fell to two shillings and sixpence per horsepower hour (or one-sixth of the running cost of an agricultural labourer acting alone, for the benefit of international and younger readers). One agricultural labourer with a tractor cost sixpence per horsepower hour to run (one-thirtieth the cost of the man without the machine). The dramatic difference in the running costs meant that tractors became the obvious economic choice. Within forty years the nigh-on half a million horses in British agriculture had been replaced by half a million tractors. However, these tractors had the power of twenty-five million horses.

There are tractors, and there are tractors

Substituting the horse for the tractor is not, by any means, the end of the story. Tractors are cheap to run and therefore the cost of producing grain and vegetables is reduced. Less labour is necessary down on the farm, which means less labour cost. But tractors are subject to continuous improvement. Twenty years ago, tractors and combine harvesters drove up and down fields more efficiently (in an economic sense) than the horse-drawn plough had done, but the tractor or harvester had less intelligence than the horse had. One could certainly question that today. The combine harvester of today 'knows' precisely where it is, thanks to satellite technology. As a result, the machine knows what sort of soil it is dealing with, what sort of water content it is facing up to in the crop that it is harvesting, what the weed problems are, while all the while keeping an eye on what the yield is.

Precision in arable farming is an important, but often overlooked, aspect of the efficiency gains that ultimately must be used to avert the environmental credit crunch (and bring economic benefits). The harvest hymn 'We plough the fields and scatter, the good seed on the land' is all very well, but scattering good seed is a very bad waste of effort and money. Much of any seed that was broadcast (thrown out by hand) was wasted – hence the medieval farming saying 'one for the pigeon, one for the crow, one for the harrow and one to grow'. A quarter of what was sown could, on this evidence at least, be relied upon to grow into a harvestable crop. The invention of the seed drill changed that, of course. Jethro Tull, the mid-eighteenth century agricultural pioneer, calculated that by placing the seed precisely in the ground through the use of a seed drill, the yield on seed could quadruple. This aligns neatly with the country saying already cited, by suggesting that precision planting saves three-quarters of the seed from waste. Today, over a million tonnes of seed is planted in Britain, and over fifty million tonnes is harvested.

Clearly, few farmers in the developed world today wander their fields with baskets of seed, flinging out handfuls at random. But the technological advances of modern times are no less important to economic and to agricultural efficiency. The technology that goes into agricultural equipment is truly staggering. All of this increases the yield of the crop being grown and harvested. It increases the efficiency of fertiliser applied, which, as we saw in Chapter 2, amounts to both an economic and an environmental saving. But a problem persists. Efficiency still comes at a price. First, there is an economic price. Second, there is an environmental price.

The economic price of veg mechanics

Tractors are not cheap. Combine harvesters and crop sprayers cost money. Spending a quarter of a million pounds on a single piece of equipment is easily achieved. Indeed, modern farm machinery is so expensive that some farmers share equipment, or subcontract specific tasks to contractors who own one or two pieces of machinery as their sole capital.

With financial credit less readily available, and potentially more expensive, the risk is that improvements in the efficiency (economic or environmental) of farm equipment will take many years to be embraced by a majority of the farming community. No farmer is going to scrap a quarter of a million pounds' worth of combine harvester that is only five years old, just because a more fuel-efficient model has come onto the market. It is unlikely that the fuel savings could ever compensate for so rapid a depreciation of an extremely expensive piece of equipment. Even when yields can be enhanced by more accurate planting and harvesting, the insurmountable obstacle of upfront capital being required is a deterrent to acquiring the more efficient capital stock.

What the financial credit crunch has done, therefore, is not aggravate the environmental credit crunch – at least not particularly. As far as vegetables and crops are concerned, things are not getting worse. It is true that the fuel consumption of agricultural equipment is not going to improve if existing capital equipment is used, and in that sense the environmental credit of finite fossil fuels is being consumed. But the fuel consumption is not the main environmental credit constraint. Rather, what the financial credit crunch has done is to make it more difficult to upgrade agricultural capital stock and further improve the amount of environmental credit. We could farm in a way that is less damaging to the environment, which uses less fertiliser and increases yield still further. But replacing the capital equipment of agriculture overnight is not possible, and the tightening of financial credit means that it will take longer to upgrade today.

The slow pace with which new technology can disperse through the modern farming community is nothing new. In the eighteenth century it was estimated that new farming techniques were spread at the rate of a mile a year from their point of origin. Technology costs money, it must be seen to be working, and even then there is inertia in its adoption. However, the timing of the financial credit crunch is certainly unfortunate in slowing the dispersion of technology, and the economic and environmental efficiency gains that trail in its wake.

The environmental costs of veg mechanics

'Have you ever considered that the cereal you eat is brought to you each morning by the wind?'[3] This is more than just poetry. Wind pollination drives the production of three crops – maize, rice and wheat – that accounted for 87 per cent of world grain production and 43 per cent of calories consumed in 2003. Given the numbers of people involved now (seven billion souls) and in the future (nine or ten billion by 2050) the immediate challenge is sustainable production in high volume of food commodities that are dependent on multiple aspects of the environment described in Chapter 1. Moreover, enough of these three crops must be delivered to allow billions of people to obtain their daily bread on an affordable basis.

Economics suggest that the affordability comes from efficiency, and the modern mechanisation process helps that. However, efficiency, and in particular mechanisation-based efficiency, comes from economies of scale. Bigger is better, in economic terms (up to a point). Clearly, no one is going to spend a quarter of a million pounds on a combine harvester to harvest the crop from ten acres of land. The question is whether the economies of scale that are associated with mechanisation are compatible with the environmentally sustainable agriculture that will be needed to feed the world over the medium term. What we are talking about is larger farms concentrating resources to be efficient. Such shifts can have unwanted consequences for the environment and indeed human communities. This can happen in any market in the right conditions. Although it is a cash crop and not a source of nutrition, coffee happens to provide a good example of the environmental risks that arise from mechanisation and economies of scale.

The coffee crisis and the potato parallel

For the hapless individual forced to start work at the crack of dawn – the Spanish lorry driver in need of the first *cortado* of the day, or the poor economist with shining morning face going once more into the unending breach of the financial credit crunch – a coffee crisis is what happens in the event of a caffeine deficit. In the context of this book, their predicament pales against the effect on some human beings of the *real* coffee crisis. The coffee crisis that began in 1999 provides a convenient case study for the consequences of the collision between global markets and local suppliers so frequently encountered in the context of food commodity markets.

After the 1999 break-down of the International Coffee Agreement, coffee prices collapsed. This was a big enough problem on its own. For small producers, a structural change in the coffee market – a swing in the balance of power towards the consumer away from the farmer – made things worse. Some observers take the view that whereas in the 1980s the share of value-added across the value chain was reasonably equitably divided between coffee-producing and coffee-consuming countries, by the early to mid-1990s little more than 10 per cent of value-added was left for coffee producers.[4] The fall in the price of 'green' (environmentally friendly) coffee between the 1990s and 2000s did not help matters.

These events were also negative for the environment. If the main goal is to keep production costs low, by definition there is no elbow-room for niceties like environmentally friendly farming practices. This point is hard to prove because (by definition) no one has the resources to keep environmental data in a crisis, but Eve Rickert documented the negative impacts of land-use change on biodiversity, as coffee farmers converted to pasture, other crops or just left.[5] The small-scale farmer is no match for the demands for efficiency in the global market. Thus, an opportunity is lost for those who know most about the local ecosystem to have a hand in protecting it.

The power of market forces in creating environmental risks is not just for cash crops like coffee. The Irish potato famine was an environmental crisis that derived from economic circumstances. In this case it is true that small farmers were the problem, but the devastating nature of the famine was the consequence of small farmers acting effectively in concert (a single crop dominating agriculture in the name of efficiency). So, although nineteenth-century Ireland is different in appearance from twentieth-century coffee production, the lesson is that *any* economic circumstance that forces a reduction in diversity is likely to be environmentally detrimental.

Box 3.2 **The economics of the potato famine**

The causes of the Irish famine were complex, and generally economic. To blame politicians of the day for their inaction, or to attribute it to the fungal disease that caused potatoes to putrefy is conventional, but misses the background. The utter dependence of the Irish population on the potato was at least part of the problem.

The potato was dominant as a crop in Ireland because it is a high-yielding crop (calories per amount of effort, or per amount of land). Land ownership structures in nineteenth century Ireland created very small plots of land, with limited tenure rights – so farmers had little incentive to improve their land and every incentive to maximise their return from it in the short term. There was no money for capital equipment, and the structure of small plots of land made capital equipment impractical anyway – and the potato can handily be cultivated with a spade and nothing else. So the potato became dominant. Then it became diseased. This is hardly surprising. The potato is attacked by forty different types of fungus, around twenty-four viruses and six different bacteria. It is also, of course, attacked by insects. Disease is the norm for the potato. The dominance of potato consumption made the disease dominate the economy as the crop failed. Because the economic structures (land ownership, capital equipment available, etc.) did not change, the focus on potatoes as a crop did not change, and so the disease persisted as potatoes were replanted in the years after the blight was first discovered.

The famine itself was a function of the diseased crop, of course. But the economics of agriculture before the famine was what seemingly allowed the damage to become so devastating.

It might be imagined that there is a natural limit to scale farming. One could not convert all of the United Kingdom into a wheat prairie because, quite simply, large swathes of the United Kingdom are not suited by climate or soil or geography to growing wheat. However, this natural limit does not necessarily apply to the supply chain. As industrial farming has become the order of the day in many food commodities, market concentration is apparent in several of the key inputs (seed provision, fertilisers, crop protection) as well as in the outputs themselves. This potentially gives some participants market power. If these participants are not focused on environmental concerns, and these participants have sufficient power in the market, market forces can potentially override environmental considerations.

Veg health

The issues of preparing and planting crops are an area where economics and environmentalists can readily agree on much – at least as to the broad direction of policy. Increasing efficiency is what is desired, and economic and environmental efficiency now tend to go hand in hand. The economist does not want to waste energy unnecessarily by wasting fertiliser through careless or inefficient application. Similarly, the environmentalist will seek to minimise the use of fertiliser to minimise the environmental damage.

However, when it comes to the issues of keeping crops healthy, there is greater provision for disagreement between economists and environmentalists. Plant health inevitably brings up the questions of weed and pest control. For the economist, looking to maximise economic efficiency, whatever weapons in the armoury can be mobilised, should be mobilised. For the environmentalist, the environmental externalities may need to be considered. Plant health is one of the key divisions between the 'profit at any cost' and 'treehugger' scenarios we introduced earlier.

The economics of weeds

Weeds are economically inefficient, and have always been a challenge for crop production. The virulence of weeds meant that Roman farmers often harvested them along with their crops, leading them to be consumed and eventually cultivated as food sources in their own right. Oats started out as a weed, for instance, but kept being harvested with the crops, and eventually became an acquired taste. So ubiquitous were weeds that the Romans had no specific word to encapsulate the concept. 'Crops' covered all.

For the modern farmer, the presence of weeds is a problem because anything that leaves a farm is representing a loss of the resources of that farm. Any crop that is leaving the farm gate is taking with it the stock of fertility from the land, and that of course is environmental credit driving right out of the farm gate. This is true whether the fertility is naturally or chemically created. The crop is also taking away the application of water, the effort required to grow the crop, and so forth. Of course, that loss of resources and effort is why farmers charge a price for their food. This is pretty basic economics. If weeds are being produced on the farm, however, there is a problem. The fertility of the land, the efforts of the farmer, the water resources and so forth are going into the production of something that has no economic value. This is something no economist can tolerate.

So, how big a problem are weeds? Peasant farmers are estimated to lose fully a quarter of their crop to the impact of weeds. Two poppy plants will replace a wheat plant in the field, which does not sound too bad a problem. However, one poppy plant will produce 17,000 seeds on average. Assuming that the poppy plant is not seen as a cash crop to be cultivated for economic profit, the presence of a poppy in the field is a terrible threat to the economic return that the farmer can achieve.

So, what can be done? Again, technology can help. Planting seed in rows using a seed drill rather than broadcasting seed around at random means at the very least that the gaps between the rows of seed can be kept weed free by hoeing. Pre mechanisation, hoeing was the single most labour-intensive aspect of farming, and it remains so in many less-developed countries today. With mechanisation, ploughs and harrows can be constructed so as to go up and down the field, removing weeds from in between the crops. But of course, to really become efficient in an economic sense, the farmer embraces the chemical hoe of weedkiller.

The economically low-cost inputs into farming are fertiliser and sprays. Assuming one has access to a crop sprayer of some description, economic efficiency is going to dictate that weedkiller is applied. Glyphosate weedkillers are of sufficiently low toxicity that they can be sprayed before a harvest, ensuring that what leaves the farm is what the farmer wishes to leave the farm – a cash crop, not nutrients and water bound up in weeds that are of no economic value.

There are some environmental benefits to weedkiller, along with the economic. Applying weedkiller means that the soil does not need to be ploughed so often, if at all. That can allow the soil to retain more of its natural fertility, and indeed help to prevent soil erosion and water loss. Untilled soil retains 25 per cent more carbon than tilled soil – so the application of weedkiller could be construed as something that helps to reduce a farm's carbon footprint. Ploughing and harrowing are also more energy intensive than spraying (this is fairly logical – a tractor pulling a spray boom meets far less resistance than a tractor dragging a series of blades through the soil). Indeed, soil tillage is the most energy-intensive aspect of the crop cycle.[6] The use of weedkiller in the United States is estimated to save 300 billion gallons of fuel every year by avoiding the necessity of ploughing.[7] There is also the potential benefit gained from leaving soil-based carbon sinks in place by not ploughing. Environmental and economic trade-offs are extremely complex in the field of agriculture.

The economic efficiency in the near term of applying weedkiller is summarised in the price premium that is paid for organic produce. Organic crops, free from the application of chemicals, are priced at a premium for two reasons. First, their yield tends to be lower (most estimates put it at about 15–25 per cent lower). Less supply means higher price. Second, the supply that does make it to the market comes with higher production costs, in terms of either human or mechanical labour.

The arguments of the environmentalist on the topic of weedkiller centres on the issue of externalities – for instance, the potential impact on bees and other pollinators. It is not the impact of the weedkiller on the weeds, necessarily, but the risks of larger-scale environmental damage that arise from the regular application of weedkillers. This is not reflected in the economic price of the crops, because (for the most part) it is not something that is immediate or geographic specific. The adverse external costs of applying weedkiller may take years to reveal themselves, and they may not show up on the farm that was applying the weedkiller: they could arise as an issue of health or of water contamination for instance. Economics is not very good at capturing costs like that.

Bugs

Closely related to the economics of weed control is the economics of 'pest control'. This is basically about dealing with insects rather plant diseases (the issues are often related when insects act as a means of spreading disease). The desire to maximise agricultural yield and economic return suggests the use of pest control sprays. Indeed, the consequences of not controlling pests can be horrific, as the failure of the Irish potato crop in the late 1840s demonstrates (it had also failed several times in the past). A quote from the academic Benjamin Jowett highlights the potential for economic devastation: 'I have always felt a certain horror of political economists since I heard one of them say that he feared the famine of 1848 in Ireland would not kill more than a million people, and that would scarcely be enough to do much good'.[8] In defence of that noble profession, the economist (Nassau Senior) was pointing out, perhaps somewhat callously, the economic realities. Population had outstripped food supply when the constraint of a diseased crop was added to the equation. Ireland was suffering an extreme environmental credit crunch in the collapse of food supply on existing terms.

Box 3.3 Fungal infections

There is evidence that fungal infection is causing an unprecedented level of mortality amongst plant species, and this could in fact threaten food security.[9] It is likely that a two-pronged response to this problem will be needed. Prevention is always better than cure, and cure is not yet fully on the table. Thus, investment in research and development is needed to find a cure. It is unlikely that approaches to agriculture will change rapidly enough for either to be delivered with any speed, for both require capital investment at a time when capital is constrained.

If money were no object and food risk a non-issue, disease prevention (or at least reduction) could be achieved with fewer chemicals, by moving away from single-crop agriculture. Somewhere out there is the optimum proportion of land assigned to single crops receiving the optimum application of fungicide, combined with an optimum proportion of land managed on a multi-crop rotational basis (to avoid infections). This would not solve all environmental problems, but might minimise them. The point we look to emphasise here is that in the context of large population numbers balance is needed: huge prairies planted with a single crop are potentially risky for food security because of plant diseases; and it is not known whether a fully organic system would be potentially risky for food security, or not, from the perspective of productivity per acre.

An answer to this conundrum may lie in technology: it may not be beyond the wit of man and woman to find a sustainable treatment for fungal infections in food crops. The European Crop Protection Association turns over more than eight billion euros annually and 32 per cent of this consists of fungicides.[10] This gives an inkling of the considerable global scope. The global crop protection market turns over at least twenty billion dollars annually[11] and 40 per cent of this consists of fungicides. The size of the global fungicide market reflects the scale of both problem and opportunity. Research appears to be underway to find sustainable or 'green' fungicides.[12] In 2009, the media was suggesting that such a solution – a plant defence that blocks potentially malign fungi from gaining access to weak spots in the first place – might be two years away.[13] A patent was applied for by the University of Saskatchewan in December 2010.[14] Since then, the news wires have been silent.[15]

The medium-term challenge

We need to improve yield to arrive at the Hudson–Donovan 'optimal' scenario, but we need to do so without damaging the environmental sustainability that is necessary for future generations. If, year by year, environmental costs are ignored, we just add environmental liabilities to the future environmental credit card bill. Developing this analogy further, the resilience of any of the three major food grains could be at risk as a consequence of a long-run accumulation of environmental deficits – the amount by which, each year, environmental borrowings exceed environmental savings. As we know from the financial credit crunch, repeatedly incurring deficits leads to a large amount of debt, and some of the debt built up over years can be toxic, eventually exploding to trigger a credit crunch. An environmental grain credit crunch is something we really want to avoid, and we could avoid doing this at all costs by investing in the survival of the environment. A dystopian future would not be terribly pleasant.

There is no shortage of evidence to suggest that human beings are capable of extremes of myopic behaviour – the John Steinbeck novel *The Grapes of Wrath*, which describes hunger arising from soil degradation, is just one example. In large commodity markets potentially constrained by concerns of affordability, the trade-off will *tend* towards the 'profit at any cost' scenario, to the detriment of the environment. (It should be noted this is an extreme example, we are not suggesting it is a description of reality today.)

As the opening chapter of this book suggested, creating a system that can survive is best approached from as many angles of attack as possible at the same time. Investing in good soil stewardship will be a futile exercise if sustainable water supplies are not available, and investing in either or both of these may be futile from the perspective of food provision if there are no pollinators. Sustainable approaches to agriculture therefore need to be designed to avoid or minimise all of the following: soil degradation, water stress, biodiversity losses and adverse social impacts. Beyond this, some systems effects can be quite far-flung.

Box 3.4 **From mud-bath to Bath**

The residents of Bath, in the west of England, are enduring a plague of seagulls. These creatures, fully understanding the power their numbers confer upon them, swoop threateningly on individual residents, dropping glistening green gobbets of glutinous guano with an unerring aim. Pointing out that this is good for the garden is unlikely to amuse anyone regularly beset by the so-called rats of the sky. The root cause of the seagulls' success is currently not fully understood but the curious scientific sleuth seeking answers might do worse than consider an explosion in the population of snow geese in the Arctic in the 1980s.

The eating habits of snow geese leave much to be desired from an ecological perspective. They tear up vegetation by the roots, leaving nothing for the next goose, rather than just nibbling at the green shoots on the surface. Thanks to such eating habits huge swathes of vegetation were turned into a mud-bath. This was an animal version of the tragedy of the commons in which overgrazing wiped out plant life and led to the collapse of the coastal salt marsh systems in the Arctic with significant repercussions for the ecosystem.

The rapid rise in snow goose numbers was a puzzle but of course had to have something to do with food. Ornithologist Bob Jefferies[16] discovered the root cause of the problem to lie in changes in agricultural practices that left spare food in abundance for the geese, in combination with over-enthusiastic hunting in the snow geese's usual wintering grounds, to which the geese responded by moving on. So, the snow geese, responding to several man-made food-related environmental changes, moved to the Arctic. The cause of the Arctic environmental degradation lay far from the Arctic. The answer to this particular whodunit was, well, human beings done it. So, when the puzzle of the UK seagull population explosion is resolved, we might just discover that this a case of anthropogenic guano-slinging in which the seagulls have simply moved on in response to an over-availability of human food waste.

Avoiding soil degradation

The second chapter of this book mentions soil degradation as a potential consequence of some farming practices, ranging from underinvestment to overinvestment in chemical fertilisers. Sustainable farming seeks to avoid either extreme. Farming practices that tend to follow from producing large volumes of grain as cheaply as possible are known to degrade the fertility of the soil. An alternative approach to intensive tillage is, simply, not to till. An approach known as 'continuous no-till' is said to be the most effective and practical approach to restoring soil quality while still maintaining productivity.[17] As 'Turnip Townshend' and others have described[18] it is possible to have a number of operations in which legumes are applied directly to the soil to replenish nitrogen stocks. Such operations suggest what is possible. Of course, the success or otherwise of organic farming operations may depend on technical developments. The surprisingly narrow gap between the yields of chemically fertilised and non-fertilised crops observed in some oat and triticale varieties, but not for wheat, perhaps suggests that some crop seeds could be bred for productivity in an organic context (whereas modern wheat varieties may be less well-adapted to compete in an organic context).

Avoiding water stress

Whether the cultivation of grains and other soft commodities results in water stress depends on what is done where and how. Thus, wheat grown on land where there is sufficient rainfall and capture (whether through natural or artificial means) is unlikely to be a problem for either agricultural productivity or the ecosystem. On the other hand, wheat grown in dryer territory requiring the draw-down of water stored in aquifers that do not readily fill up again is unlikely to be sustainable. A particularly ominous example is the Ogallala Aquifer which irrigates roughly 27 per cent of America's farmland.[19] The water stored within has been there for so long that it is best described as 'fossil water' but it may not be there for much longer. It is being gradually pumped out to provide water for America's 'breadbasket', so called because this area produces a significant percentage of American wheat crops.

Water stress can be traded cross-border; stating the obvious, the idea would be for crops grown in water-abundant land to be exported to regions less well-endowed with water. In practice, this is unlikely to happen because the water embedded in crops traded internationally is not priced. However, virtual water trading may be possible in the long run with the right institutions and information in place.

Avoiding biodiversity losses

The most obvious direct impact of modern agriculture upon biodiversity is the tendency towards fields (or prairies) of single crops as far as the eye can see. Crop protection also impacts insect life, because generally speaking that is what it is supposed to do. A third problem for biodiversity is our old friend, market structure. The drive towards efficiency and lower costs has led to a focus on a small number of species in fruit and vegetable markets; even in these relatively fragmented markets there is the drive towards the homogeneity of the product on the supermarket shelf. Such practices have visible, direct effects, but also, potentially, indirect effects which arise from the point that our food-provisioning systems depend upon the broader, interconnected ecosystem.

Inefficient agricultural practices, including over-use of fertilisers and high-density livestock farming, are implicated in the widespread pollution of water with phosphorous and nitrogen. This pollution comes from widely dispersed, therefore hard-to-regulate, sources, suggesting that the solution must be very broad. The importance of the issue is emphasised by the range of problems to water-based plant and animal life, as well as damaging biodiversity.[20] This includes the loss of species that are part of the human food-chain. Out of the water, there are concerns that such practices may be killing pollinators, which creates a very direct feedback to agriculture.

Avoiding the loss of pollinators

A couple of years ago, the BBC's *Doctor Who* programme had a running reference to the decline of the world bee population. Theories abound as to the cause – *Doctor Who* ruled out extra-terrestrial interference. Changes in countryside (bees' 'habitat') and the spraying of crops are possible causes. There are reasons to be concerned about the potential loss of bees. At first sight, since grains are wind pollinated and therefore will be unaffected by the disappearance of insect pollinators – honeybees, bumblebees, moths, butterflies, beetles and flies – this issue may seem to be irrelevant to grain production. Human beings would be able to rely on wind-pollinated crops, but variety goes. Apples, pears, oranges, lemons, almonds, cherries, strawberries, passion-fruit, raspberries, gooseberries, blue-berries, blackberries, melons, plums, squash, alfalfa and tomatoes depend on non-wind pollination. Some of these crops have to be pollinated, for the best possible results, by 'buzz pollination', something only the bumblebee (not the honeybee) is capable of.

As this list of fruits is intended to suggest, the loss of insect pollinators kills off things we love to eat – the 'season of mists and mellow fruitfulness' would be much impoverished. The key question is not could we survive without pollinators. Of course we could. If they have no apples, pears, oranges, lemons, almonds, cherries, strawberries, passion-fruit, raspberries, gooseberries, blue-berries, blackberries, melons, plums, squash, alfalfa and tomatoes, then let them eat cereals. The real question is *should* we risk surviving without pollinators?[21]

The reason for the reduction in the number of pollinators is as yet not fully understood, but some suspect that the presence of non-toxic doses of chemicals used in crop protection may be implicated. Others suspect that the long swathes of mono-crops may contribute by making the landscape impossible for insects to cope with. Whatever the cause or (more probably) the causes turn out to be, the costs will be potentially considerable. The value of hive-bred honeybees as pollinators, supplementing the work of native pollinators, has been put at 1.6 billion dollars. Without native pollinators, the Ecological Society of America puts the value of the humble hive-bred bee in the United States rises to 8.3 billion dollars *per year*.

Biodiversity (and the system of pollination that works within it) is a particularly challenging problem. Cause and effect are not easily identified. Human beings tend to respond to such threats by thinking about survival in the aftermath of extreme change. This is the wrong approach. The right approach is to consider whether we should pursue high-risk ways of growing food (the answer clearly being no, whether viewed from an economic or ecosystem perspective). Let us be quite clear about this. By 'high risk' we are growing food in a way that might potentially put the environment at risk of irreversible change, forcing a shift to fall-back foods.

One-shot solutions to the biodiversity threat are considered unlikely – multiple solutions drawing on international expertise and global governance will probably be needed. One-shot ideas within the system of ideas might need to be collaborative. As an example, crop rotation is well recognised as an approach to grain production that can keep pests down as well as maintaining soil fertility. New ideas derived from old ones include crop rotation across the landscape, in which effective weed control through crop rotation 'requires coordination between farmers with regard to cropping sequences, crop allocation across the landscape, and/or the fraction of each crop across the landscape'.[22]

The economics of pest control, as with the economics of weed control, basically come down to the externalities of the situation. As Ireland demonstrates, there are ways of adjusting to deal with diseases which do not involve spraying. Had Ireland had more crop variety the economic and environmental consequences of the potato blight would not have been so severe (and indeed the spread of the disease may have been checked by having other crops planted between the potato fields). Changing the varieties of the crops grown can help. Yet even with this, chemical pest control sprays are estimated to increase crop yields by 10 per cent to 15 per cent.

From an economic rather than environmental perspective, the decision is whether the economic benefit of spraying crops outweighs the economic costs of spraying. The costs are generally environmental externalities, but these do have economic consequences. The use of DDT spray in the post-war era was very popular (it had been used during the war to control lice and through that to check the spread of typhoid). However, DDT is not a selective insecticide and kills beneficial as well as harmful insects. Pollination, which is economically beneficial, and natural pest control (also economically beneficial) are undermined by the use of DDT.

The banning of persistent organochlorine pesticides in the UK came about because of the economic-environmental externalities they produced. The chemicals in the pesticides led to a large number of foxes dying in the UK in the 1960s (the poisons in the insecticides were stored in the fat of the foxes). This provoked outrage from fox hunts, which were concerned about the economic damage (no hunts) of this environmental consequence (no foxes). The House of Lords was naturally enough motivated to investigate, and the pesticides were phased out. Economics, as well as the environment, was at work here.

The economics of good breeding

With weed and pest control, there is one final economic input to consider – breeding. This is more than genetic modification of crops, although that is a part of it. In a broad sense, humanity has been genetically modifying plants for centuries if not for millennia, through selective cross-breeding of different strains of plants. In modern times this moved from the random to the more scientific with the Agricultural Revolution of the eighteenth century. Agricultural societies sought to breed plants, with characteristics that were thought to be desirable.

What is desirable in terms of crops? Nowadays, putting less effort into growing a stalk and more effort into growing the usable part of the crop is to be desired. A tall wheat plant will put a little less than a third of its biomass into the grain bit that the human farmer is interested in farming. A short wheat plant can put half its biomass into the grain. Those plants that are shorter by nature (or perhaps shorter by genetics would be a better way of expressing it) are likely to be more receptive to the application of fertiliser – however the fertiliser is applied. Those plants that put most of their energy into producing a stalk will fall over if fertiliser encourages more growth, as 70 per cent of the biomass goes into height. Shorter varieties will stand resiliently upright as fertiliser increases their incentive to produce biomass, because half their biomass is going to the grain, not the stalk. Similarly, shorter plants are likely to be easier to protect against disease and insect damage. Shorter plants require less pesticide, for example. (The whole of a plant has to be protected from attack, as a rule. Shorter plants mean less plant to protect and therefore less spray.)

The efficiency of the plant does not have to focus on the grain. All too often the stalk is forgotten entirely as an economic product. However, the stalk of a grain plant is still something that has consumed economic resources (the environmental credit of the field has enriched the stalk at least as much as the grain, if not more). If grain also produces a stalk that could provide a highly nutritious animal fodder, then the waste of an arable farm could provide an input into animal husbandry.

Perhaps the key point to drop out of the range of ideas mentioned in the above paragraphs is how much is still known unknown. Blogger Steven Savage describes two experimental scenarios – a low-intensity, low-risk approach (minimal seeding rate, one dose of fertiliser and no crop protection chemicals) and a high-intensity approach (using certified seed, applying an elite seed treatment, a selected herbicide instead of tillage and applying crop protection). Productivity was twice as high for the intensive approach, which also had a lower carbon dioxide and energy footprint per bushel, as well as requiring less land.[23] Efforts such as this could potentially be complemented by new technologies. The UK Foresight Report envisages breakthroughs in crop genetic improvement technologies and targeted gene mutations, making it possible to produce seed without pollination or fertilisation.[24] Wohlmeyer and Quendler consider the possibility of vanilla or cocoa production through fermentation techniques that would side-step the need to grow the plants from which these specialist products are extracted.[25] Economically, such technology would be disastrous for countries specialising in these goods, such as Madagascar and Ghana.

In search of the Hudson–Donovan 'optimal' scenario

The preceding pages have hinted that agriculture might need to combine the old and the new to move forward sustainably; hence, approaches such as no-till farming, discussed above, or organic farming. Old ideas such as crop rotation might be used in new ways to good effect. As an example, one study discovered that introducing dry peas into the cropping system improved the yield of spring wheat.[26] Whether the perspective is economic or environmental, ideas such as this, which use nature's own (non-fossil-fuel driven) fertilisers to enhance agricultural productivity, can only be a good thing.

The impossibility of a single magic solution is demonstrated by the problem of herbicide-resistant weeds. These now flourish happily alongside crops genetically engineered to be resistant to glyphosate weedkiller.[27] Perhaps problems like this could be addressed by moving away from blanket applications of chemicals typical of modern practice to precision agriculture: a precise matching of crop requirements with soil requirements within individual fields, made possible by adding computer power and satellite navigation to agricultural equipment.[28]

Vegetable economics are at once simple and complex. The simplicity is all about yield increase. The complexity is the extraordinarily broad range of inputs that are required to achieve that outcome. What is not in question, however, is that technology plays a critical role in increasing both the economic and the environmental efficiency of crop growing. Technology undoubtedly does represent a second Agricultural Revolution, and it is unlikely that the developed world will become concerned by the lack of horse horsepower in agriculture.

The challenge is how quickly the most up-to-date technology can be disseminated through the agricultural community – both in developed and eventually in emerging markets. The financial credit crunch limits agriculture in this regard, and the shortage of capital globally may well lead to some difficult choices in how humanity feeds itself in the years ahead.

Notes

1 Food and Agriculture Organization of the United Nations (2011a).
2 Population Reference Bureau (n.d.).
3 The Ecological Society of America (n.d.).
4 Bacon *et al.* (2008).
5 Rickert (2005).
6 Food and Agriculture Organization of the United Nations (2012b).

7 Cited in McWilliams (2009), p. 100.
8 Cited in Woodham-Smith (1962), p. 375.
9 Fisher *et al.* (2012).
10 European Crop Protection Association (ECPA), at www.ecpa.eu/information-page/industry-statistics-ecpa-total (accessed on 15 February 2012).
11 Markets and Markets, at www.marketsandmarkets.com/marketreports/crop-protection-380.html
12 Farm Chemicals International, at www.farmchemicalsinternational.com/news/cropprotection/?storyid=1503; alternatively, Environmental Health News, at www.environmentalhealthnews.org/ehs/newscience/towards-more-sustainable-fungicides/
13 The name of this type of chemical defence is the phytoalexin detoxification inhibitor, or paldoxin for short.
14 MacPherson (2009).
15 Lest we be misunderstood, we interpret silence (and delay) as an illustration of the uncertainty inherent in science at the cutting edge.
16 British Ecological Society, at www.britishecologicalsociety.org/journals_publications/journalofecology/virtualissue_jefferies.php
17 Tischner *et al.* (2010).
18 Fairlie (2010).
19 Zielinski (2012).
20 Carpenter *et al.* (1998).
21 The reader who thinks this may be echoing the work of Kahn on nuclear war is correct.
22 Gonzalez-Diaz *et al.* (2012).
23 Savage (2011).
24 Foresight Programme of the UK Government (2011a).
25 Wohlmeyer and Quendler (2002), p. 21.
26 Tanaka *et al.* (2010).
27 Thompson (2012), citing Professor Charles Benbrook, of Washington State University's Centre for Sustaining Agriculture and Natural Resources, Puyallup.
28 Tischner and Kjaernes (2010).

4   Raw material inputs
Animal

> In an old batboard smokehouse they found a ham gambreled up in a high corner. It looked like something fetched from a tomb, so dried and drawn. He cut into it with his knife. Deep red and salty meat inside. Rich and good. They fried it that night over their fire, thick slices of it, and put the slices to simmer with a tin of beans.
> (Cormac McCarthy, *The Road*, p. 17)[1]

For the man and his son in Cormac McCarthy's *The Road*, eking out an existence on the basis of dwindling stocks of tinned beans and sausages, the find of the forgotten ham was worth its nutritional weight in gold. The ham itself, hanging up in a smokehouse, seems to have been the product of the 'slow food' industry rather than the factory farm. Thus, in the context of McCarthy's novel, it becomes deeply ironical as an artefact of a green culture killed off by McCarthy's fictional disaster, and food for thought on the subject of the animal as a store of nutritional and other value.

The fat of the land

The animal part of the agricultural production process is about more than meat. Animal farming tends to bring steaks and chops to the mental eye, but from an economic and environmental perspective it goes further than this. Meat is a part of what animals represent, but so are fish, eggs and milk. Animal products do not have to involve the slaughterhouse.

Traditionally, meat was not even the most economically valuable part of an animal. In an era before vegetable-based cooking oils and electric light, it was dripping and tallow candles that gave the economic value to a carcass. Fat was the valuable part of a cow, pig or sheep, and meat was in many ways a by-product. Animal husbandry bred according to that demand. The paintings of prize farmyard animals that were such a peculiar form of eighteenth century art tend to show animals that are generously proportioned – pigs that look like captive barrage balloons and cows that are basically rectangular in shape. By the late nineteenth century, prize pigs had splints strapped to their legs, as their limbs were liable to break under the weight of the body they had to support. Really prized specimens were given wooden pillows to support their heads – not to pamper them, but because without the support the animals would suffocate in the rolls of fat that formed their surfeit of second chins. These animals were prized because they were fat, and that fat meant economic value.

As consumer tastes have shifted, and as tallow candles do not play a large role in modern living, so the economic value of animal husbandry has changed. The economics of animals in food is certainly unrecognisable when set against the economics of animal husbandry from the eighteenth century, or even from the 1930s. Remarkably, the comprehension of what meat actually is has also changed from the eighteenth century, and from the 1930s.

In Cormac McCarthy's novel, all food, including meat, has lost its connection to the land because the land is dead. In real life, in the twenty-first century, the connection between meat and the land is reportedly forgotten by younger urban generations in many developed nations – youngsters who can grow up without ever having seen a farm animal in reality (Peppa Pig does not count). The resulting nature-blindness inevitably translates to a reduced cultural awareness of environmental or other constraints (such as animal welfare) about what eating meat means.

Whether this cultural shift matters from an environmental perspective depends on what happens in the future; should meat become an entirely factory-based synthetic product, today's environmental constraints would become irrelevant, although of course there would almost certainly be new environmental constraints that have not yet been thought of. As long as meat still originates on the land we would argue that being aware of the connection between meat (and associated products such as dairy) and its origins is vital from the perspective of the environment, and the sustainability of food supplies in the long term.

The deracination of meat from the land in the minds of meat-eaters is a relatively recent change. Films like *A Private Function*, set in the late 1940s, in which a stolen pig is memorably pursued around a small house by an ineffectual carving knife-wielding posse, remind us that the backyard pig was until very recently both food-waste recycling machine and warehouse for future meals. It was also then (as now, if in a different way) an important cultural symbol. In this film, those who had access to meat and could wastefully afford to feed the pig food that was good enough for human consumption thought of themselves as the 'in' crowd. The aspiration to eat meat seems to arise from a complex mix of physiology (the urge to take in calories and nutrients efficiently), cultural conditioning (what tastes good or looks good) and fashion (because we're worth it). A similar mix also appears to drive the consumption of fish.

Box 4.1 The silver darlings

An appreciation of economic value and the enjoyment of food are both reflected in the Scottish nickname for herring: the 'silver darlings'. In the novel *The Silver Darlings* and in the later play of the same name,[2] families were forced off the land by the so-called Agricultural Revolution in which people were required by corporate and government interests to make room for sheep. Some of those displaced from their homeland went to sea in pursuit of wealth, and thus joined the herring boom of the early twentieth century.[3] In *The Silver Darlings*, one of the economic shocks suffered by the protagonists is the removal of government subsidies, an event that forced the fishermen to work ever harder to bring back bigger fish hauls. The novel is not specifically about conservation, but does refer to the 'luck' required to bring in the definitive haul alongside the sparse catch found by most other boats.

In more recent times the influence of government regulation upon the herring industry has moved in a different direction: in 2008, the Scottish pelagic fleet netted the first Marine Stewardship Council eco-label for herring in the world.[4] When there is a lack of balance between the needs of human beings and the ecosystem, all food stocks are affected. The message is perhaps at its most stark in the context of fish, for the potential disappearance of entire species once taken for granted – such as cod – has the power to shock. A report from the United Nations describes the proportion of marine fish stocks that are 'overexploited, depleted or recovering' as having risen from 10 per cent in 1974 to 32 per cent in 2008.[5] Moreover, just over half of the global extinctions of marine species that have been recorded over the past two centuries were caused by overexploitation. As single species disappear, sometimes the prey species population explodes. Lobster-lovers may live to regret the fall-off in shark numbers that leave more octopi behind to ravage the lobster, and this is not the worst thing that could happen – the disappearance of predators such as tuna, sharks and swordfish could cause a population explosion in other species lower down the food-chain. Anyone for jellyfish?

We should not denigrate the jellyfish, which can be both an aesthetic and culinary delight in its rightful place. The serious point is that fish is an important source of protein calories and micronutrients as well as being a favourite dish, and the disappearance of fish stocks can be absolutely devastating in economic, environmental and nutritional terms for the local community directly affected, particularly if they are economically less well off. When it comes to fish in the diet, and indeed meat in the diet, environmental concerns suggest that the emphasis should be on moderation and balance.

Wallowing in gravy – the economics of the luxury of meat

Meat is expensive, because meat takes quite a lot to produce. A calorie of fossil fuel burned will produce somewhere between one-and-a-half and two-and-a-half calories' worth of grain (largely because the energy of the sun makes up the difference). However, it takes three calories of fossil fuel to produce a calorie of free-range beef. It takes thirty-three calories of input to produce a single feedlot-reared calorie of beef. The difference between free-range and feedlot is because the free-range cow eats grass which has been pulling energy in from solar power as well as fossil fuels. On average, the grain fed to a cow will produce meat in the ratio of sixteen to one (sixteen pounds or kilos of grain will produce one pound or kilo of beef). Over a third of the world's grain harvest goes straight into meat production in the form of animal feed. Moreover, it takes on average four litres of water to produce a single calorie of feedlot-reared meat, eight times the amount of water to produce a calorie of grain. For a calorie of free-range meat, seventeen litres of water is required on average. For an eight-ounce steak, produced free-range, forty-five bathtubs of water are required.[6]

Raising animals is also land-intensive. If going for free-range grazing, then a hundred acres of land will feed around fifteen people in a year. That same amount of land, when ploughed and cultivated for crops, can feed one-hundred-and-fifty people in a year. There are fewer calories per acre if using free-range grazing. However, this does not mean that grazing should be disregarded as environmentally unsound. As we saw in Chapter 3 on vegetables, putting land to grass or clover restores its fertility. Putting animals out to graze on that grass or clover also helps restore fertility, by naturally spreading manure. The challenge is to get the right balance, of course.

Why is meat so input-intensive? Well, only 10 per cent of vegetation energy (grass energy) finds its way into the cow, and only around 5 per cent of *everything* put into a cow actually comes out in the form of meat that can be consumed. A total of 95 per cent of the environmental resources pumped into a cow find some other purpose. Fully a third of everything put into a cow is returned in the form of dung. As returns on an investment go, getting a third back in the form of manure appears to be somewhat unappealing (unless you are planning to found an educational establishment on the proceeds). A little over an eighth of all input is output as urine. These products have to be collected and applied to the land as fertiliser or used in other parts of the economy if they are to have any further economic benefit. After accounting for these outputs from the cow there is then the bone, fat and muscle that are not consumed, which have to be considered waste products. The five per cent that is left after all this waste product is accounted for is meat that can be sold to consumers.

The point is that economically all of that input must find expression in the price of meat. When we purchase a steak we are not purchasing three hundred calories of meat. We are purchasing up to 10,000 calories of input (for feedlot-reared beef) that is required to get that steak to us, plus the water costs, plus the rent of the land required, and the labour that is required to bring this all to the farm gate. Clearly, the price of meat is going to be high.

Traditionally, this has put meat into the category of a luxury good. Charles Dickens' Mr. Bumble was horrified that Oliver Twist was fed meat, for as a pauper from the workhouse he would have been unaccustomed to it. Meat was not for paupers. Those in a workhouse in the nineteenth century may occasionally have had a 'meat day', when the Poor Law custodians would add a cheap cut of meat to the diet, but the idea of a daily meat intake was clearly ludicrous.

The problem with having something that is a luxury good is that people will aspire to consume it. There is nothing like luxury for making something desirable to the mass consumer – the aura of luxury status is one of the great advertising techniques of this or any age. Thus, as people saw their standards of living rise relative to those of their parents, successive generations began to demand more and more of what once was considered beyond their means. Meat became an economic benchmark for the standard of living one could aspire to. The hunger for meat that increased wealth brings about is not a new trend: an eighteenth-century visitor to England, César de Saussure, observed 'that the very wealthy ate no vegetables at all unless they were served with meat'.[7]

Take meat away, or make it unaffordable, and all of a sudden an ugly political mood is created. Britain ran out of beef at one point in early 1941, and food minister Lord Woolton would ordinarily have had to resign over so outrageous a situation. He was saved by a victory in Bardia in North Africa, and was able to declare, with a certain amount of hyperbole, that the British had chosen Bardia instead of beef – casting the loss of meat as a very unfortunate price that had to be paid for the war effort. There was huge sensitivity to the availability and price of meat in Europe during the 1940s. This was a critical barometer of whether life was getting better or not. The comic novelist P.G. Wodehouse was told by his publishers to alter a passage in *Joy in the Morning*, published in 1946, because it referred to characters eating steak.[8] The reading public would not tolerate such casual references to the lost glories of the past; 'Ichabod' had been carved over the door to the dining room and the contrast between the glories of the past and the fallen standards of post-war austerity would be too much for the reading public to bear. The references to steak were converted into ham and eggs.

Fashionable economics – health and meat

Before we drown ourselves in a rich gravy of meat gluttony, it is worth reflecting that luxury can be swayed by the dictates of fashion. Concerns about health in the context of meat in the diet tend to be relatively prominent in the present day. Consider the soothing headline in the UK's *Independent* newspaper in 2010: 'Excessive meat-eating "kills 45,000 each year"'.[9] The recommendation of the research cited in the article was that people should eat meat no more than three times a week. Similarly, it was the human desire for healthier food rather than suffocation in double chins that killed off the eighteenth-century fat pigs and rectangular cows. Developed economies seem to have maintained a relatively steady proportion of fat in the diet in the post-war era.[10] Wealth has risen, meat consumption has risen, fossil fuel consumption has risen, but fat consumption has risen to a 'negligible' extent. There may be any number of reasons for this but surely the rise in the consumption of fats has been capped by health campaigns, as well as the arrival of low-fat food products such as spreads. What we see here is the fashion for health driving the demand for meat, which then changes the economics of meat consumption.

We should remember that eating meat is not bad for health: from the perspective of human physiology, meat and fish are an efficient store of key nutrients and amino acids. Looking back through history and pre-history, meat-eating is likely to have been a key force in allowing human beings to evolve. We would arguably not be where we are in evolutionary terms today had we not had meat in our diets, along with the ability to cook it to make the nutrients more readily accessible. Barbecuing is good for you.

Meat was described by primate diet expert Katharine Milton as a 'catalyst for human evolution' because the energy and nutrients it provided allowed the brain to develop.[11] Meat-eating should therefore not be seen in isolation, but as part of a shift towards a more varied diet (generally a good thing from the perspective of human welfare) as wealth increases. The modern perspective, which must take into account a myriad of technology developments and knowledge in the fields of agriculture, food and nutrition as well as cultural shifts concerning the ethics of killing animals to eat, must be taken into account in order to look forwards.

Luxuriating in meat

So meat is expensive to produce, requiring a large number of inputs, but it is something that consumers aspire to consume and increasingly (in developed economies) believe that they should be able to consume. The politics of this means that developed economies will have to provide meat for their consumers at an affordable price to keep their consumers satisfied. For emerging markets, governments will need to provide their consumers with an increasing proportion of meat in the diet (cultural exceptions like India aside), in order to demonstrate the relentless march of economic development. The economic challenge that this presents suggests that ways must be found for producing more meat for less money. Realistically, that can only happen if either there are fewer environmental inputs, or those environmental inputs are cheaper in economic terms.

Here we find an important distinction. If we can reduce the environmental inputs into meat, then both the economist and the environmentalist can be satisfied. We get meat at less economic cost, but also with less environmental damage. However, if the environmental inputs are made economically cheaper, there may be a conflict. If the environmental inputs into meat are cheapened because their environmental costs are not recognised in the economic price, then fights between economists and environmentalists are likely to break out. The concept of environmental credit is often a central part of this debate. If our generation has its beef steak and eats it, because we are consuming environmental resources at an unsustainable pace, the economic cost of environmental inputs (such as feed, water, energy and land) may well be low now. However, the action of over-consuming resources will hasten the environmental credit crunch, and create economic and environmental problems in the future.

The environmental beef with meat

The environmental credit crunch that runs through this book is exacerbated by the fact that more and more people want to eat meat, compounded by the arrival of more and more people on the planet. Thus, expanding population numbers combined with economic development must, it seems, inevitably lead to an acceleration of the rise in meat demand (and supply to satisfy that demand). If we want to reverse the environmental credit crunch and start living within our environmental means, then it seems that consumption habits must change. This is not all about eschewing meat and embracing the nut cutlet – waste and other factors can play a role as we shall see.[12]

Meat consumption directly contributes to the ecological footprint expressed in hectares of land, as described in Table 2.2, in several ways: through the biocapacity required to sequester carbon dioxide emissions from fossil fuel consumption, through cropland required to grow feed, and through grazing land. According to the analysis behind Table 2.2, 8 per cent of the world's ecological footprint per capita is explained by pasture, and 22 per cent by cropland.[13] What this means in the context of this chapter will depend on whether the output of cropland is consumed as a form of 'vegetable' not far removed from its original form, or is converted to animal protein. The breakdown in usage varies greatly from one country to the next. For instance, according to the National (United States) Corn Growers Association, some 80 per cent of all corn grown in the United States is fed to livestock, poultry and fish production worldwide. For wheat, the equivalent number is 22 per cent. Common sense would suggest that ruminant animals are likely to be at their most biologically and environmentally efficient when grazing on grassland.

Animal supply and implications for the environment

In the world of traditional farming, food production is supply-driven – the seasons, and the availability and cost of resources such as animal fodder and water determine what is available. Both of the authors of this book are old enough to remember when the strawberry was a summer fruit and when there was only one lambing season rather than the two we now know (January and April); mutton was on the menu at other times. For the benefit of younger readers, mutton is basically elderly lamb. (The preceding sentence may not apply by the time this book goes to print, since, under the pressure of the financial credit crunch, mutton is making a comeback.) As the previous section on economics has made clear, the agriculture of meat has become more demand-driven than supply-driven. Agriculture is also increasingly shaped to meet the food demands of the urban dweller. The urban dweller seems to prefer predictability, and this is reflected not only in the ubiquity of the hamburger restaurant.

The predictability of the urban diet is not new. That bastion of British culture, the fish-and-chip shop, might have cod, haddock and halibut but little else. This is a retail outlet where the pickled gherkin is regarded as an exotic and unnecessary variant in the diet. The need to service the urban dweller with predictable foodstuffs in scale may be one reason why the monoculture now tends to prevail in developed-market agriculture. The need to service the urban dweller with affordable (low-cost) food is highly likely to be implicated in the industrialisation of food production that increasingly prevails inside the farm gate as well as outside it. Whatever the cause, in this world, in the context of competition for land from other activities, the only way to reduce the impact of production on the environment is through an approach known as intensification. The question is whether there are limits to intensification, from the perspective of the environment.

Battery beef and other intensification

If the idea of agricultural intensification is mentioned to the man or woman in the street, it is likely they will think about eggs and milk, because they are both associated with controversies relating to high-volume production. Barns full of battery cages can be seen as an extreme example of intensification – each bird having 550 square centimetres to scratch around in such systems. In January 2012, European legislation made battery cages illegal. Welfare improvements for chickens have taken some forty years to arrive, testimony to the amount of time it can take for culture to win out over economics. The large-scale dairy herd may be the next 'battery' animal for people to worry about – this issue has even reached Ambridge, a fictional but prominent UK town known to listeners of the BBC radio soap drama *The Archers*.

The proponents of the mega-dairy herd idea talk about improved animal health due to careful monitoring and a high quality of feed. Opponents will point out that all of the impacts on animal welfare of this change not visible in milk yield will not be considered. (Are cows bred and fed to engineer daily production of gallons of milk per day actually being milked to death?) Moreover, the consumer demand ultimately driving these practices moves forwards without full knowledge of what is happening behind the scenes, whether in economic, environmental and/or animal welfare or indeed human welfare terms, for dairy farmers.

In recent decades, the change in the structure of the dairy industry appears to have resulted in a shift in allocation of value through the production chain, reflected in very low profitability for the dairy farmer.[14] Dairy farmers can follow one of two strategies to survive – move along the food food-chain to capture the value in high value-added products such as ice-cream or cheese, or become increasingly large. The second of these two strategies can be expected to put pressure on the environment in two ways. First, thin profit margins mean little left over to be invested in environmental stewardship. Second, the environmental impact of large (often indoor) herds is likely to be potentially high, the question being, what happens to the large volumes of waste? This system separates animal manure from the ecosystem in much the same way that human sewerage systems made it impossible for key nutrients to be ploughed back (as we identified in Chapter 2).

Animal farm

Private sector companies like to sweat their assets, getting as much return out of them as physically possible. The volatility of global livestock prices is likely to motivate meat farmers to keep their costs as low as possible. Some animals may be more readily subjected to a regime of intensification than others. This point – a combination of biology and economics – is actually already reflected in the structure of the global meat market, for animal farming for meat production breaks down into three segments – pigs, bovines (beef) and ovines (sheep and goats). Pig meat accounts for 56 per cent of total output, bovines for 36 per cent and ovines for 7 per cent.[15] As would be expected, economists (they get everywhere) play a part in shaping this production mix. One reason for these production percentages is the greater productivity of pigs. It takes less than three kilograms of food for a pig to put on one kilogram in weight, whereas cattle would need five kilograms of feed to get to the same place.

In some situations, feed-cost considerations will be irrelevant. The Japanese farmer will not begrudge the cost of cosseting his *wagyu* animals, massaging them with beer, because the beef from such cattle is a specialist, high value-added product.[16] For anyone else, the economics are what count. As the feed conversion numbers cited above suggest, animal physiology, at least initially, shapes economics: domestic cows and sheep are ruminants and do best on forage, whilst pigs can digest more or less anything and thus can be more intensively reared.

As production operations expand to meet consumer demand, the extent to which the environment is affected by meat production will depend upon this mix of animal physiology and economics. Intensification may at first sight seem to be the obvious way to go from the perspective of both the environment and economics. For this to be successful, however, there must be attention paid to animal health (intense meat rearing has the potential to create intense health issues). Animals finding themselves in uncomfortable surroundings suffer stress. This is bad for animal welfare and also bad for the quality of the meat: stressed bovines produce tough meat and the meat from stressed pigs can be 'pale, soft and exudative . . . with a loss in muscle structure'.[17] Trucking live animals long distances is considered bad for animal welfare and potentially also bad for the product; thus, the welfare constraint has economic consequences that could help reduce food miles, thereby constraining one of the environmental impacts of meat production.

Flatulent cows and greenhouse-gas emissions

The idea of intensification is unlikely to have been possible before the Industrial Revolution. The high agricultural yields that furnish fodder for productive animals are only possible because of an energy subsidy that has been facilitated for a relatively short time in the scheme of things, fossil-fuel-driven energy. The higher up the biological food-chain, the higher the subsidy. This is reflected, in turn, in the environmental footprint of meat products. Figure 4.1 shows the greenhouse-gas footprint of a selection of common proteins estimated by CleanMetrics.[18] Lamb and beef stand out as the most greenhouse-gas-intensive (hence the well-known fact that methane from livestock is the cause of almost half of New Zealand's greenhouse-gas emissions).

72 Raw material inputs: animal

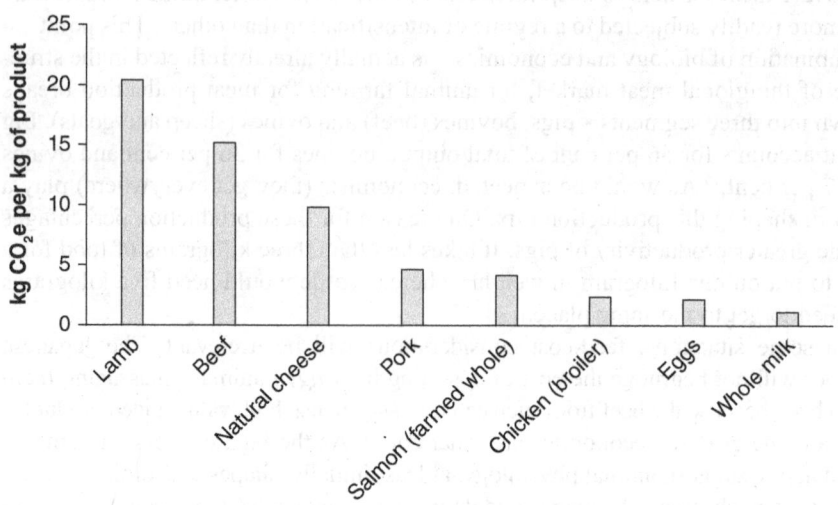

Figure 4.1 Life-cycle greenhouse gas emissions, selected food items (Hamerschlag and Venkat 2011).

Leaving aside the environmental footprint arising from animal fodder, animal husbandry also has a number of direct environmental impacts. From an environmental perspective, ruminants are a major source of greenhouse-gas emissions (methane and nitrous oxide). Animal slaughter is heavily water-intensive, and as we have already observed, up to 95 per cent of the animal is waste (blood and bone, and other less desirable by-products). Some of this waste can be recycled as biofuel, animal feed (where this is legal), pet food or as inputs to human food such as sausages.

Waste is more than waste at the slaughterhouse. At first sight, the waste problem could potentially be resolved if human food waste could be fed to animals, as still happens in developing countries, and as used to happen in developed countries too. This does, however, raise the risk of disease transmission. During the Second World War and after, pigs were fed 'Tottenham Pudding' – a mix of shop and bakers' waste. The unsterilised nature of 'Tottenham Pudding' led to recurring diseases in pigs, much as China's pig population experiences today for exactly the same reason.

Until 1991, UK slaughterhouse waste, rich in nutrients and known as 'rendered meat and bonemeal', was fed to pigs, constituting about 4 per cent of their overall diet. The same material was also fed to poultry and cows. The 'mad cow' crisis put paid to this practice. This failure was not rooted in the recycling practice itself but arguably in the way it was done. A failure to control risk here seems to have triggered other regulation such as the EU-wide ban on using kitchen waste to make pigswill.[19]

Deciding whether to use food waste to generate energy, or to feed to animals and grow dedicated energy crops is a good example of the trade-offs involved in the context of land use. Whether from the perspective of animal health or converting animal food into meat, animals need to be fed what best suits their digestive systems (this can also help with the greenhouse-gas problem). Thus, ruminants are best suited to pasture land, and pigs to a diet of more concentrated forms of protein. Common sense suggests that from an environmental perspective, having cows grazing on grassy fields is likely to be more efficient than feeding them with cattle food. However, when environmental externalities are not reflected in economics, a strategy in which animals are competing with other users may lead to a lower economic cost outcome. The efficiency gains from this come at the price of significant environmental degradation. This is economic efficiency but environmental inefficiency, and this seems to be the heart of the problem with meat. We need efficiency in both aspects. Economists and environmentalists need to find common ground (no pun intended) – perhaps using the waste from arable crop production as a source of animal feed.[20]

Getting the right cut of meat costs

Economically or environmentally, we need to get more meat with fewer inputs – or at the very least the *same* amount of meat with fewer inputs. We have been here before. The eighteenth-century Agricultural Revolution was not just about improving crops and the fertility of the land. It was also about coming up with ways of getting more animal products to the table. One of the earlier changes was the concept of better feeding – which was intimately associated with the aspects of the Agricultural Revolution pertaining to crops and soil. Traditionally, farmers would slaughter most of their livestock before winter, keeping a few animals for breeding purposes the following year. The reason, of course, was the lack of food for animals in the winter months. Historically, the main source of fresh meat in Europe during the winter was dove or pigeon, as they were animals that could forage and did not require too much grain to keep going. This is why older country estates normally come complete with dovecotes. Their original purpose was practical, not decorative.

With the growing of turnips as a food crop, and eventually with the development of silage as a source of food for animals, the practice of slaughtering and salting livestock became redundant. Animals could be fed year round, and the quality of the food they received gradually improved. Between 1710 and 1795, the average weight of sheep and cattle sold at London's Smithfield market doubled.

From the late eighteenth century onwards, there has been a gradual focus on breeding animals that offer a better economic return. This started with the agricultural societies, who encouraged better breeding through the use of shows – with prizes for livestock that displayed the most desirable attributes. As we have seen, originally the most prized attribute was fat. The idea of selective breeding is, in fact, relatively new compared with the history of animal husbandry. Robert Bakewell began cross-breeding in Leicestershire in the mid to late 1700s. In 1796, James Anderson advanced the idea of selectively breeding to maximise the most desirable attributes of an animal. The idea was revolutionary at the time, however obvious it may seem today. Prior to this, breeding animals was basically throwing together whatever males and females of the same species happened to be available in the locale, and hoping for the best.

With the widespread use of artificial insemination in the latter half of the last century, the ability to breed for selective attributes has advanced still further. Away from meat production, but still in the field of animal products, artificial insemination was used in the 1940s to breed cows that yielded the highest possible amount of milk. Cows that were genetically prone to yield significant quantities of milk were clearly worth propagating. This method of getting more for your money (more milk for the inputs) was shifted to meat specifically in the 1950s. The reason was Argentina. Since the introduction of refrigerated shipping, Argentina had become a major source of beef for the United Kingdom. While not quite a monopoly supplier, Argentina was providing 400,000 tons of beef a year to the UK before the Second World War (which works out at around the equivalent of thirty-nine steaks per person per year). In the 1940s, however, the government of President Peron repeatedly raised the price of beef exports (often at the last minute). In 1952, after eleven months of negotiation, there was a 29 per cent increase in beef prices.[21] This motivated the British government to start selectively breeding for beef. Along with Australian beef imports, this changed the pattern of trade away from dependence on the pampas of Argentina.

Box 4.2 Milk and efficiency

Milk is one area where economic policy has forced environmental efficiency, albeit accidentally. What used to be known as the 'Common Market' and which has now morphed into the European Union sets quotas for milk production. The idea is to control the total amount of milk produced in the European Union. This means that a dairy farmer's earnings from milk are doubly constrained – first by the market price for milk (which bears little resemblance to the supermarket price for milk, as we saw in the opening chapter), and second by the volume that can be produced under the quota.

Profits in dairy cannot be engineered by selling more milk, therefore. Efficiency of supply in terms of increasing the supply will not work. If farmers cannot control either the amount of milk they sell, or the price at which they sell, then the only way to change profit margins is to do something to control the costs of producing milk. There are two ways of doing that. The first is to have a smaller number of cows that each produce more milk – which is where the selective breeding of artificial insemination comes in. The second is to reduce the costs of keeping cows alive, through moving away from using cattle cake as a form of food (which is expensive) and towards pasture. Pasture is not costless, either in economic or environmental terms, but it is a lot less costly than manufactured feed in both cost senses.

Thus, the policy of limiting milk supply has forced greater environmental and economic efficiency onto the dairy industry. It comes at a price, quite literally, in that the price of raw milk is higher than it would otherwise be. For consumers, this is not necessarily that relevant (as generally less than half of what they pay for milk will go to the farmer who produced it), but manipulating the supply and thus the cost of milk does have implications along the supply chain.

The breeding for beef example is an important illustration of the dominance of economics. The Argentineans wanted to raise the price of beef for their own economic gain, of course. The impact of that on domestic pricing in the UK (which was slowly coming off rationing and controlled pricing) was to make beef increasingly unaffordable for the British consumer – hence, the concerns of P.G. Wodehouse's publishers over casual references to steak. Economics and pricing led to deliberate attempts to increase the yield of domestically reared beef through artificial insemination. This is basically a more technologically advanced process of the selective breeding practised by Robert Bakewell and James Anderson a century-and-a-half earlier. The economic objective was met (the UK became less import-dependent in the area of meat, and it was cheaper than relying on Argentinean imports). At a global level, more food is generated for any given quantity of environmental resources.

Pig husbandry is a similar story. As we saw above, pigs used to be reared to be fat, because that was where the economic value was. With alternative vegetable cooking oils and perhaps more importantly the knowledge of (if not the pursuit of) healthy eating, fat in meat became less desirable because it was less profitable. As a result, pigs became leaner, through a process of selective breeding. This took a while to develop – the tradition of having pigs that were fat was long established – but in the 1960s the wonderfully named 'Pig Improvement Company' began a process of breeding to ensure that more of the inputs into pigs (feed) went into what was economically demanded (meat) and not into what was now economically wasteful (fat). Today's pigs have much more in common with their wild medieval ancestors than they do to the balloon-like animals that were immortalised in eighteenth- and nineteenth-century paintings. With pigs, it went further than just breeding for the right attributes. Pigs were also bred to be disease resistant, reducing the drugs that were required and reducing the risk of loss from premature demise.

> ### Box 4.3 The economics of disease control
>
> In 1963, a quarter of a million pigs were slaughtered in the United Kingdom under a government scheme aimed at eradicating swine fever. The government paid compensation for the pigs destroyed (because whole herds were destroyed, healthy as well as sick pigs would have been slaughtered). The total cost was comfortably over two million pounds, which was thought to be a 'very large figure indeed' at the time.[22]
>
> Economically, a cost was incurred, but it also brought an economic return. The herds became disease free, and so the loss from diseased pigs dwindled. That loss had been both economic and environmental. Diseased pigs could not be consumed and therefore did not profit the farmer, and the environmental resources that had gone into rearing them were wasted. In reducing the losses, environmental resources were used more efficiently. As for the economics, it was calculated that the increased tax revenue coming from pig farmers (who were no longer losing pigs and the healthy profit associated with healthy pigs) more than offset the 'very large figure indeed' that had been paid in compensation.
>
> Today, the economic cost of poor pig hygiene is seen in China. A regular cycle of disease means sick pigs across the country, which in turn leads to pork shortages. This raises food price inflation, and through that overall inflation, in turn provoking policy reactions that have wider economic implications. Of course, any sick pig that cannot be consumed is also a complete waste of environmental resources.

Improving the output from animals is not all about breeding. Technology also helps to improve the efficiency of animal rearing. As we saw in Chapter 3, remarkable advances have been developed in recent years that allow a more specific agriculture to develop. Just as we have combine harvesters that 'know' what part of the field they are in, so we have milking machines that 'know' what cow they are dealing with. Personalising (or more properly, bovinising) the milking process to the specific cow means that the right amount of milk is drawn for the animal's health and position in the reproductive cycle. By careful timing of the milking process, lactation (and thus milk yield) can be increased. By making sure that the cow is not over-milked, the farmer can ensure that the cow is not damaged, and the risk of disease is reduced. The result is more output per input – which means more profit. Robotic milking machines were identified as the second most important agricultural advance by *Country Life* magazine in 2012 (after affordable global positioning satellite technology).[23]

Similar benefits from technology can occur when rearing animals for meat. Collars on pigs, for instance, mean that feeding can be customised for pigs that are not entirely free-range. Why should this matter? Because pigs (as everyone knows from reading George Orwell's 1945 allegory *Animal Farm*) are bullies. In normal circumstances, certain pigs will push others out of the way when it comes down to the business of getting snouts into the trough. While the amount of food for the herd will be appropriate, the distribution within the herd becomes highly unequal (there is an entire branch of economics dedicated to the manifestation of just this sort of behaviour in humans). Technology which identifies specific pigs, when coupled with feeding pens, can allow a sort of porcine socialism (where each is served food according to their need), without any of the unpleasantness of *Animal Farm*. This means a more efficient use of food, and better animal welfare.

The animal welfare benefit should not be overlooked. The taste for lean meat means that pigs bred today exhibit certain psychological characteristics. Lean pigs are pigs that are of a nervous disposition – the hormonal triggers that burn fat also mean that these breeds tend to like regular meals, a closed circle of acquaintances, and no loud noises (economists are much the same, even to the point of metaphorically being 'eaten for breakfast'). Somewhat counter-intuitively, today's lean pigs are at greater risk of heart attack and stress-related problems than their fatter ancestors. (We hope the same is not true of today's economists.) A pig that dies at an inopportune moment is an economic waste as well as an environmental waste.

So far, managing animal husbandry produced both economic and environmental benefits. Improving the food that can be derived from animals (meat, milk or eggs) through selective breeding or minimising instances of disease will be economically beneficial. It will also be environmentally beneficial, as environmental resources are being used more efficiently for any animal product that is consumed. But economics and the environment do not always coexist in perfect harmony, and the conflict tends to come in with the issue of what is popularly known as 'factory farming'.

Technology and innovation – solution or problem?

Technology developments have driven agriculture from time immemorial. The nature of innovations in the present day has changed because of developments in the life sciences industry and advances in knowledge about nutrition, breeding and health. Thus, in combination, selective breeding, together with tailored nutrition programmes and disease control (made necessary because of the much larger sizes of flocks and herds), have delivered an animal designed to make the job of the food processor easier. As ever, such practices can bring with them unintended consequences. As one example, the widespread usage of antibiotics on modern farms can be blamed for the increasing resistance of bugs to antibiotics in some situations, compounding a problem developing for other reasons such as the overuse or misuse of antibiotics to treat human diseases. Other human health issues include animal diseases that take advantage of large flock and herd sizes to proliferate, and could be potentially disastrous if they became transmissible to humans (e.g. H1N1, popularly known as 'bird 'flu').

Of course, technology is not universally bad. For food production, technology may still deliver solutions that could kill several birds with one stone. Professor

Mark Post of Maastricht University is reportedly looking to turn the laboratory into a substitute farmyard, except that no chicken would strut, and no lamb gambol its way to the slaughterhouse: meat would be artificially grown from muscle stem cells.[24] Progress is somewhat slow (the granting of the first patent was in 1999). What is changing is a dawning sense that moving meat from farmyard to factory could bring multiple benefits in its wake, freeing up cropland used for animal feed for other foods and reducing the environmental footprint of food into the bargain. If economics dictate that meat must be farmed on a factory basis for farms to survive and people are willing to eat the result, then once factory-made meat can be done on an economic basis, eating factory-made meat must surely be a no-brainer. It is best if the reader does not focus on the phrase 'lab rats' in considering this as a solution.

Meat substitutes such as Quorn have existed for some time and have taken very little share of the meat market. (The UK market for 'meat-free' meat products was recently estimated to be worth 787 million pounds.)[25] It seems unlikely that a step-change to meat from the factory from meat from the factory farm will happen overnight. However, the discussion in the previous two chapters of constraints against access to technology for the less wealthy may also apply here. It really depends what happens to laboratory meat (known less clinically as 'in vitro meat'). If laboratory meat retains its designation as an environmentally friendly substitute, conventional markets could exist alongside it. Should it turn out to be a true substitute then meat produced in the laboratory could potentially affect the price of meat in mainstream markets. In this case, technology barriers would likely deliver up the social problems typically encountered in industrial revolutions – job destruction in the first stage followed by job creation in the new world.

And now for the disagreement

The area where economists and environmentalists come to blows is over intensification. Animal husbandry in the early part of the twentieth century was not that much different from farming in the eighteenth century. Pasture for grazing, hens in coops and pigs in sties were part of the way of raising animals. During and after the war, however, there was an intensity introduced to farming that gave rise to the idea of farming as an industrial process. This allowed for food to be produced more cheaply, but not necessarily in an environmentally friendly manner.

One of the reasons organic food costs more is that it is less efficient as a whole. Partly this is about land. A country estate occupies more land than a high-rise development (and the accommodation will cost a great deal more per person as a consequence). Much the same thing can be said of free-range versus battery-farmed chicken. However, the economic efficiency of factory farming goes beyond this. Free-range animals are more likely to get diseases, which will require drugs. Drugs cost money, and that has to be reflected in the price. Even with the increased drug intake, free-range animals have a higher mortality. Battery hens have a 3 per cent early mortality rate, perchery hens 5 per cent, and free-range hens 10 per cent (in the early twentieth century, before drugs were introduced, the mortality for hens, which were by definition free-range, ran at 20 per cent).[26] In that statistic there is an immediate reason for free-range eggs to be more expensive than battery farm eggs – more chickens are required in free-range farming to replace the chickens that are lost.

There is also a seasonal element to consider. Hens are more inclined to lay eggs in the summer months than in the winter months. The result, pre factory farming (with artificial light), was a glut of eggs in the summer and a shortage in the winter (encouraging the pickling of eggs as a means of storing them). The seasonal nature of supply had a price impact that is not present anymore. No one thinks of eggs as a seasonal product in terms of price.

When we consider feedlot-produced beef, we know that it takes more energy to produce a calorie of beef in this fashion than it does to produce a calorie of free-range beef. That energy is environmental credit for the most part – fossil fuels that generate the energy required for the production of the food that the animals are eating. However, the free-range beef requires more land – which has a price and a series of competing uses to which it could be put. It also requires more labour per head of cattle to rear free-range beef when compared with feedlot beef. The economic costs of feedlot beef do reflect the environmental costs that go into the feed (at least in part; they reflect the current market value that is ascribed to the cost of consuming a finite environmental resource). But those costs are likely to be outweighed by the economic savings that arise from spending less on labour and land, and on losing fewer animals to disease.

This is where the economist and the environmentalist start throwing punches. The economist is concerned with producing food for the world's population as cheaply as possible (benefiting human welfare). The environmentalist is likely to raise concerns about consumption of finite resources. There are also considerations over animal welfare (although this is not strictly speaking an environmental issue). Economically speaking, there has to be factory farming in some form, unless humans are prepared to accept a substantial decline in the standard of living. The question is whether optimal economic farming can be combined with optimal environmental animal husbandry.

Environmental nirvana?

In light of the importance of resilience in our food systems, this chapter would be incomplete without a discussion of systems-based meat production, in other words, meat produced as an inherent part of an overall structure in which the animal wastes discussed above could once more be ploughed back into the land. This concept is a mix of old ideas and new ideas, and it would make for a more integrated approach to managing the environment (in the broadest sense of the word) – including animal husbandry, and forestry, and growing crops. This would make the animal more central than it currently is to the decision-making process (which sounds a bit like animals making the decisions, taking us back to *Animal Farm*, but means perhaps that we swing back towards a supply-based rather than a demand-based approach to meat). The role of the animal in traditional small farms

80 *Raw material inputs: animal*

was (and still is in small community farms) to act as some combination of waste disposal unit, living muck spreader and, if necessary, source of transport.[27]

The advantage of such livestock is that they are not dominating the agricultural landscape. Intensive farming has animals that monopolise land – anyone passing Stonehenge in Wiltshire is hit in the face (specifically, the nose) with the dominance of pigs in the landscape. The pigs are free-range, but *en masse* and clearly a long way removed from the cottage pig in its sty. Even if it is free-range, this sort of farming is not 'natural'. Neither monocultures nor the associated mass waste exist in nature. In nature, the norm tends to be a system of interconnected pieces that balance. Naturally, waste in one area becomes food for another area, without any real need for intervention. This is all tied to the idea of resilience that we met back in the opening chapter. If we can move away from environmental intensity, we can create a more environmentally resilient supply of meat. If we can do that in an economically viable fashion, then the problem is solved.

Animals and two credit crunches

We have to face facts. In environmental terms meat is an inefficient way of getting calories to the global population. At the same time, meat is something people generally wish to eat, and indeed aspire to eat as a signal of having achieved economic status. Economics cannot prevent this. The standard economic response, to ration demand (raising prices), could conceivably increase the luxury status and thus the desirability of meat consumption – while also creating political problems for those forced to cut their consumption (and their perceived standard of living) by economic circumstances. With current levels of meat production efficiency, if the emerging economies were to eat meat in the same quantities per capita as developed economies, the world would need to have two-thirds more agricultural land than actually exists.[28]

Clearly, we cannot consume finite environmental resources at the current pace. The environmental credit crunch is at hand – evolving more slowly than the abrupt nature of the financial credit crunch, but here nonetheless. So how do we satisfy the aspiration for animal products? At the level of animal husbandry, a mix of methods would seem to be required. Selective breeding to meet the demands of the global consumer as efficiently as possible can help. Reducing the instance of disease through better hygiene, the use of drugs (which will incur an economic cost), and the breeding of disease-resistant herds will reduce the economic and environmental waste of deceased, diseased animals. And then there is technology. Optimising the food that is input into an animal will get the best calorie-in to calorie-out ratio, at the end of the day. Whether this is efficient milking, providing the living conditions that maximise the egg production of hens, or allow the optimal feeding of animals bred for meat, the environmental credit crunch can be delayed or at least better managed.

The financial credit crunch is not likely to impact selective breeding, and need not impact issues like hygiene and disease control. The cost of global capital has some impact, in as much as research and development into disease control and breeding can be thought of as requiring capital – but much can be done to increase environmental efficiency by making best practice universal today. The hygiene problems of the Chinese pig population have similar causes to those that affected the British pig population seventy years ago, and which were conquered by British farmers fifty years ago. For developed-economy farmers seeking to improve the yield from their animals still further, the financial credit crunch is a challenge. As with arable farmers, technology can offer much to farmers of animals searching for the holy grail of better yields. But technology costs cash, and it is a form of capital investment that often requires borrowing for the farmer that wishes to take full advantage. We live in more capital-constrained times, and the financial credit crunch thus has a bearing on our ability to consume meat and other animal products cheaply.

The very fact that we decided to approach this section of the book by dividing the world into mineral, vegetable and animal says something about the culture that surrounds us. The modern-day tendency to chop-up industrial processes into pieces that can each be farmed out and performed in the most efficient way possible is present even in this book. As this chapter illustrates perhaps the most clearly, our food cannot be separated from the ecosystem that provides it. The ecosystem is a complex interconnected system and the way in which we procure our food needs to reflect the nature of the system that provides it if we are to arrive at resilient food supplies. Decisions about how much of our diet should consist of meat and fish and how that should be procured need to take the whole system into account. Our food security depends on it.

Notes

1 McCarthy (2007), p. 17.
2 This was Peter Arnott's adaptation for the stage of Neil M. Gunn's 1941 novel *The Silver Darlings* (reviewed by Fisher, *Guardian*, 2009).
3 See the website of the Scottish Fisheries Museum for further information at www.scottishmuseum.org/album/herringboom.html
4 Kelbie (2008).
5 United Nations Environment Programme (2012).
6 Water data from Mauser (2008) and authors' own calculations.
7 Colquhoun (2007), p. 197.
8 Letter from P.G. Wodehouse to William Townend, 24 December 1946, cited in Ratcliffe (2011), p. 399.
9 Hickman (2010).
10 Fairlie (2010) citing Dutch data between 1950 and 1990 in Gerbens-Leenes and Nonhebel (2005).
11 McBroom (1999).
12 The 2012 WWF *Living Planet Report* comments:

> Future scenarios for achieving Zero Net Deforestation and Degradation and 100 percent renewable energy are dependent on changed food consumption patterns. In particular, red meat and dairy consumption, and overall food loss and waste, must decrease in developed countries.
>
> (World Wildlife Fund for Nature 2012, p. 114)

13 World Wildlife Fund for Nature (2012), Table 2, Ecological Footprint Tables. According to the analysis presented in this table, the total ecological footprint per person is 2.7 hectares. The world grazing-land footprint per person amounts to 0.21 of a hectare (8 per cent of the total), and cropland to 0.59 of a hectare (22 per cent).
14 Tischner et al. (2010). See www.score-network.org (Sustainable Consumption Research Exchange).
15 Food and Agriculture Organization of the United Nations (2009).
16 Japan is not the only place where meat can command a high premium. Closer to the authors' homes, in February 2012, in Carlisle market, a Limousin bull glorifying in the unlikely name of Dolcorsllywn Fabio was sold for a record £126,000 by Alan Jenkinson of Penrith, Cumbria. The buyer would, said experts, quickly cover the cost from breeding revenues (*Times*, 2012).
17 Food and Agriculture Organization of the United Nations (2009), p. 8.
18 Hamerschlag and Venkat (2011).
19 Fairlie (2010) pleads for the return of the 'Environmentally Friendly' backyard pig (p. 53). After all, he argues,

> the more pork (or meat) that is consumed, the more land per kilo is needed to produce it, because a small quantity of meat can be reared on more or less worthless by-products, while larger quantities require high-value oilseed meal, or dedicated grain crops.
> (p. 60)

20 Nonhebel (2007).
21 *Glasgow Herald* (1952).
22 *Hansard* (1963).
23 *Country Life* (2012), p. 55.
24 Cohen (2011).
25 Taylor (2012).
26 Seddon (1989), p. 197
27 Fairlie (2010).
28 Vaclav Smil, cited in McWilliams (2009), p. 125.

5 Food processing

> They ate most of the day, picking fruit where they could reach it and not particular about ripeness and quality. They were used now to stomach-aches ...
> (William Golding, *Lord of the Flies*)[1]

In William Golding's *Lord of the Flies* the boys survive in a 'savage' state by picking fruit directly from the tree and devouring it unprocessed (making them ill). The hapless pig is slaughtered, dismembered, cooked on the fire and eaten without ceremony and with the minimum of preparation. Food processing – washing, extracting, peeling, gutting, chopping, preserving (heating, smoking, desiccating) and packaging in preparation for transport or storage – is one of the many trappings of civilisation and urbanisation. The absence of food processing was the first signal of the spiral into savagery in Golding's world. Complex societies tend to have relatively complex food-processing systems. Traditionally, these have been driven by a mix of necessity (year-round food security and safety), culture, ingenuity and taste – the desire for a variety of tastes and textures.

Bread-making happens to be a wonderful example of technology that began as a basic means of rendering wheat edible. Bread developed from simple flatbreads, to sourdough and eventually to leavened bread. Such innovation was the consequence of trial and error, achieved without an understanding of the chemical processes driving the fermentation that causes bread to rise. Elsewhere, someone discovered that by squeezing the poisonous juice out of cassava root it could be turned into an edible staple. A key step in the processing of the Korean delicacy *kimchi* is to bury cabbage and chillies under the ground in jars (so that they ferment). Cheese is a convenient medium of long-term storage for milk, and in some societies cheese is also a rich culinary experience with many regional variations. The making of bread, cheese and *kimchi* leverages natural processes that can evoke disgust (maggot infestation anyone?). However, these processes produce sustainable food provisioning and good nutrition, and of course good economics.

For, it is as we leave the farm gate and start on the processing part of the food food-chain that the economist becomes really excited (and an excited economist is a sight to behold). Processing is where the money is. Today, processing is where the economic value lies in our food food-chain. The farmer is a minor player in the economics of food. The biggest slices of the economic pie go to the processor and the retailer. In 1972, not far off half the money spent on food in a developed country went to the farmer. Although the sum varies from country to country, in the developed world today consumers give around a fifth of the money that they spend on food to the farmer. The remainder of the household shopping basket is given up to the processor of food, and to the distribution and retail networks.

The industrialisation of food processing means that both food content and preparation methodology are often taken out of the hands of the ultimate consumer. This has two important consequences. The first relates to *nutritional content* – the food that is the product of a large-scale industrial process may or may not have the same nutritional content as the same food prepared in a small-scale operation such as the farm kitchen or the home. The second is that the ultimate consumer can no longer *control* what goes into the food on the plate and instead must rely on the manufacturer to inform him or her what is in it. The 2013 scandal of horsemeat masquerading as different meat forms in processed food makes this point with great clarity. For the consumer this combination of conditions can result in a lifestyle that was never intended. Processed foods are often energy-dense, thus the unwitting consumption of calories can entail potential health costs in the form of obesity and tooth decay. Moreover, food processing itself can be resource-intensive, requiring energy, water and packaging materials, and often generating significant amounts of leftover packaging and food waste for the consumer to deal with.

The rest of this chapter therefore follows processing through a simple structure. How processing food came to be so economically dominant needs to be understood, because in order to address the environmental issues of food processing, a reshaping of the social forces that have rendered food so ultra-processed will be needed. We also need to consider other consequences of food processing, which basically boil down to nutritional consequences and questions of content control. We can then contemplate the environmental outcomes from the processing process.

How did food become so processed?

All food is in some way processed, even if the only processing required is a quick wash and a modicum of peeling and chopping – as might be required for vegetables taken directly from the kitchen garden. However, in modern parlance, 'processed food' tends to denote food handled in large volume in the factory. The economic idea that processed food is not food does not mean to imply that all processed food is unworthy of the name. What this means is that food, once processed, is a complex bundle of economic benefits and costs. In purely economic terms the value of processed food, as a product, is mostly about the labour and other inputs that went into preparing and packaging the goods for consumption. So how did the factory become so dominant in processing what we eat?

The rise of processed food reflects economic structures in society. The fictional Dowager Countess of Trentham of the film *Gosford Park* (set in the inter-war era), when eyeing the marmalade served with her breakfast, opines with supreme disdain 'shop bought. I call that very feeble'. What, after all, was the point of having a house full of servants dedicated to catering for one's lightest food catering whim if one could not get home-made marmalade? Processed marmalade from a factory was not to be borne.

Lest this be thought an issue that afflicted only the decaying aristocracy, it should be observed that the British government was confronted by near rebellion in the slums of east London in the autumn of 1939 over the lack of sugar. Sugar is a vital ingredient in jam, there was a bumper fruit crop that year, and the housewives of east London could not bear the waste of fruit which could not be preserved in the absence of sugar. This was an era in which the seasonality of food cultivation dominated food processing and the seat of food processing lay in the domestic kitchen. And yet, today, no one considers eating shop-bought jam to be 'feeble', and sugar shortages would not be associated with fruit preservation anymore.

Prosperity and processing

In modern times, where and how food is processed is intimately associated with economic prosperity. If we look at what a family in an emerging market consumes in terms of food, there is not likely to be a processed item in the weekly shopping basket. Raw vegetables, rice in a hessian sack, perhaps a cut of meat, unpasteurised milk. The processing involved (before the consumer purchases the food) is minimal. The packaging is also fairly minimal, and generally reusable. In all developing economies only 30 per cent of domestic food consumption is processed *at all*, once the food has left the farm gate.

Moving to a newly industrialised country (like the economies of Asia) the raw food content will still be fairly high. However, some processed elements are likely to creep in – generally in the form of soft drinks (packaged, of course, in bottles), and maybe some specific foodstuffs.

To look at the extreme end of the spectrum, a typical family in a developed country is likely to have a shopping basket laden with processed, packaged food. There may perhaps be an apple lurking somewhere in the basket, but one gets the sense that it has crept in purely by accident.

It is family income that is behind this desire to consume processed food. As incomes rise, the family can afford to pay for someone to process their food for them. Per Lady Trentham, members of the aristocracy in the 1930s were not going to roll up their sleeves and start cooking for themselves, because they could afford staff to look after them; it was just the natural order of things. Recall Jane Austen's Captain Wentworth in *Persuasion* gently ridiculing those who thought sailors on board lived 'without anything to eat, or any cook to dress [prepare] it if there were, or any servant to wait . . .'. This, however, is processing in the home (in the case of Captain Wentworth, on board ship). As the lower social classes aspired to the lifestyles of their social superiors, they wanted benefits of such food without the trouble and expense of hiring a servant. Processed food replaced the servant with a distant factory, but the result was the same – or thought to be nearly the same.

Moreover, as domestic labour became harder to obtain, the middle classes would increasingly seek to replace the in-house servant with the processed food of the factory – a form of outsourcing in effect. In 1911, 35 per cent of all women in the United Kingdom were employed in domestic service (which would have focused on cooking as well as cleaning). With alternative employments available in the aftermath of the First World War, the middle classes were forced to find ways of making their remaining servants more efficient, or in some cases replacing their servants with what amounts to external catering. Indeed, some inter-war apartment blocks came with a central restaurant that would send all catering to the apartment.

The changing role of affluence and processing

In the twenty-first century, the relationship between processed foods and affluence has become increasingly complex. Until the mid-twentieth century, processed food was a status symbol, and it was thus an aspirational purchase. To some extent that aspiration still applies in emerging and newly industrialised societies. There is no obvious nutritional reason why an emerging market consumer would wish to drink a cola drink in preference to a traditional beverage (indeed, there may be nutritional arguments against). However, the processed cola is presented as sophisticated, and associated through advertising with a certain lifestyle – and so it is preferred if it can be afforded.

In developed economies, 'processed' food is often regarded in a negative light, partly because it is perceived as bringing a raft of environmental and nutritional problems in its wake, partly because some see it as symbolic of corporate profiteering and power, and partly because when something does go wrong the scale and size of the market tends to give the issue a high profile. It is hard for the modern generation to realise that using 'processed' as a pejorative term is relatively new: the aged Miss Birdie character in the film *The Rainmaker* refers to a sandwich as being made with 'that good processed turkey' as a characteristic that would clearly increase the sandwich's desirability. For the consumer today, however, 'home cooked' has sufficient virtue as to be an advertising slogan in its own right.

In developed economies the relationship between processed foods and economic affluence has become complicated by changing working patterns. Purchasing processed food has assumed a more direct relationship with economic affluence and the value of time. This is particularly the case in the wake of the financial credit crunch. We tend to purchase goods (and in particular food) not as individuals, but as a household. Of course, there are exceptions – but a family of four is not likely to divide its food budget amongst its members, and allow each child to go and forage for food in the aisles of the supermarkets.

If the structure of the household changes, therefore, the pattern of food consumption may also change. The past two generations have seen a decided shift in working patterns in Anglo-Saxon countries, which is now being echoed in continental Europe and Japan. Female participation in the paid workforce has increased significantly, and this process is being encouraged by the financial credit crunch. If household income is less secure, or household access to financial credit is in some way impeded, one of the ways of maintaining a steady standard of living is to increase the number of people in a household who are working.

What this means, of course is that the household has more people working, potentially a higher income (depending on circumstances), but less time available for food preparation. The result is a greater inclination to purchase processed food. The financial credit crunch can make households time-poor, and it is that temporal poverty that encourages the purchase of increasingly processed foods. Who has time to bake their own biscuits, if all the adults in a household are working and pre-prepared biscuits are so readily available? Who has time to peel their own carrots, if all the adults in a household are working and pre-washed, peeled and cut carrot batons can readily be purchased by the bag?

Box 5.1 **Chips with everything**

Historically, chips (which for the benefit of American readers means 'French fries') were not eaten a great deal in the home. Chips are something of a pain to cook from scratch. The potatoes need to be peeled, and then cut, then dried, then immersed in a pot of boiling oil. It is all rather a lot of time and effort to undertake just to get some carbohydrate into the diet. Far easier to bake or boil.

Historically, therefore, chips were not a very regular part of a diet – or if they were, they were to be purchased from a professional who did all the preparation (a fish-and-chip shop is effectively selling processed food, after all). Chips were a holiday treat, purchased from a retail outlet, because of the effort required to prepare them.

Today, chips are the most common form of potato consumption in the United States. A quarter of all British potatoes used for domestic consumption wind up as chips. The reason is simple. Oven chips and now microwave oven chips have become ubiquitous. The preparation is done entirely in a factory, and the preparation time is effectively nil. With microwave chips, the time from desiring a French fry to actually eating one can be reduced to less than three minutes. (It would take around 25 minutes' walking to burn off the calories ingested from a serving – possibly giving rise to a new adage: 'A moment in the making, a minute in the mouth, an hour in the stomach, a lifetime on the hips'.)

Whereas chip preparation in the past involved potato peeler, knife and so on, the world of the oven chip is entirely mechanical. Skins are blasted off by steam, fired at high pressure through a grid of blades, small chips are rejected, blemished chips are deblemished, and then they are cooked, frozen, put into a bag or a box and shipped off. Human interaction with the potato is basically confined to its consumption.

In the United States the time spent on preparing food in the household halved between 1965 and 1995. It is safe to say that this is not because the amount of food consumed by the typical American household has halved. It is, of course, because the food consumed is processed and requires no or limited additional preparation.[2] In the twenty-first century around 80 per cent of American food is not food from the farm, but food from the factory. Of course, the food from the farm (those carrot batons again) may also be processed to some degree. In fact, 98 per cent of developed-economy food undergoes some form of processing after it leaves the farm.[3]

A British writer in 1955 could lament with horror that country women were acquiring urban habits and even that 'some have lost the desire to bake bread or make pasties or jam, or to keep up a generally high domestic standard'.[4] One gets a sense in the writing that civilisation is shaken to its very foundations by these trends, but of course all that was happening was that people were discovering that 'shop-bought' marmalade was not perhaps as terrible as it might be, and bread bought from someone else left time for other pursuits.

Thus, within two generations, we have gone from preparing food in the home as being the norm (with processed food the occasional aspirational exception) to prepared food in the home being the exception ('I made it all myself' being a dinner-party boast), and processed food the staple of developed-economy diets.

It is not coincidental that the outsourcing of food is so closely aligned to the industrialisation process. As more people work, and as they work longer, the value of 'non-work' time increases. If the cost of processed food is less than the value of someone's free time, then there is an economic incentive to purchase processed food. As more processed food becomes available, its consumption becomes more acceptable, and so it establishes a cultural role in society that can crowd out unprocessed food. Food retailers bias their shelves to what people demand, and the effort involved in obtaining unprocessed food increases, and so the relative advantage (in terms of time) of purchasing processed food rises, and so processed food becomes ubiquitous.

Of course, the consumer makes sacrifices in terms of surrendering the food production process from the home to the factory. There is then a virtual tug-of-war between the consumer and the producer of processed food. The consumer wants processed food because it is cheaper in terms of time, but they want reassurance that the food is produced to the requisite standards. The food producer, in order to create that reassurance, must package, advertise and standardise. All of these things entail an economic cost and generally an environmental cost as well. The equilibrium is found when consumers have enough confidence in the standard of the food they are purchasing to buy almost on auto-pilot, and the processor of food can keep the costs sufficiently low that there is no incentive for consumers to attempt anything as rash as cooking for themselves.

The economic complexity involved in this is why the processing of food is the largest part of the economic food food-chain. The complexity of the food product that emerges is why the processing of food is the largest part of the environmental food food-chain. This is why, in the developed world, farmers and their agricultural output are so little involved in the food that we actually consume. But the need for consumers to be reassured that what they are eating is as good as if they had prepared it themselves explains why so much of the presentation of processed food relies on images from agriculture. It is a fantasy, but who would not want to live in a fantasy realm?

You are what you eat – processing and nutrition

A common theme of this book so far has been that as people become wealthier, their diet becomes more varied. That rule applies to the inclusion of processed foods as much as anything else. However, processing does something to food. It processes it (self-evidently) but it also biases the content. *What* we eat is dictated by food processing and specifically by the choices made by the remote processor of the food that we eat. Processed food is more likely to be animal based and have more sugar than unprocessed food. It is also likely to have less fibre, vitamins and minerals.[5]

Industrialised food production very efficiently makes available foodstuffs that people had not customarily consumed in high volume. Processing moves humanity from 'a little bit of what you fancy does you good' to 'enormous quantities of what you fancy are now available (and won't do you any good)'. Processing efficiency, once again, makes it easier to access and thus over-use key resources. As an example, per capita consumption of refined sucrose was just 6.8 kilograms in England in 1815, and by 1970 had reached 54.5 kilograms. This trend has been further exacerbated by a key change in processing technology that arrived in the 1970s and delivered high-fructose corn syrup on a population-wide scale. Fructose consumption on such a scale would not be possible without industrial processing.[6]

Not only has the consumption of refined sugars, refined vegetable oils and salt risen steadily in modern diets, but modern farming may be compounding the problem by overriding the seasonality of what we eat. The seasonal fluctuation in the fat content of wild meat made it impossible for Neolithic man to consume meat heavy in saturated fat throughout the year, even if he had consumed meat on a daily basis. That fluctuation is not present in the consistently produced and processed meats of the modern diet – so say hello to saturated fat as a problem.

And now the science bit

At this juncture the reader may find it useful to have two key concepts to hand: the Glycaemic Index, and micronutrients.

The Glycaemic Index (GI) refers to the impact of dietary carbohydrates on blood glucose levels after eating. Basically, it stands for energy staying-power. Foods having a low GI will cause only a small upward shift in our blood sugar followed by a moderate downward adjustment. High-GI foods cause a 'sugar high' followed by a sugar crash. Like all addictive highs and crashes, this has the effect of making us reach for more.[7] A diet with lots of high-GI foods appears to lead to an increased risk of Type 2 diabetes, cardiovascular disease and some cancers. Unsurprisingly, health experts recommend a low-GI diet.

The industrialisation of processed food has made high-GI foods more available to consumers. Compounding the problem, food processing tends to convert some raw materials from potentially low-GI to high-GI food. White bread, as an example, is a more processed form of bread than is wholemeal bread. It is also a higher-GI foodstuff.

The term 'micronutrients' refers to vitamins, minerals, amino acids and other nutrients that are key to human health. It is possible to eat full meals every day but nevertheless to be malnourished. A shortage of vitamin D (which can also be caused by a lack of exposure to sunlight) is known to cause rickets; a lack of vitamin B1 causes beriberi; and those who have read old seafaring tales know that a vitamin C shortage causes the debilitating and eventually fatal symptoms of scurvy.

Micronutrients can be accidentally removed (or deliberately added) during food processing, but if they are not there in the raw ingredients in the first place and this is not realised, the food-processing industry may find it difficult to improve food quality. As they say in the land of computer programming, GIGO (Garbage In, Garbage Out).

The problem of spotting micronutrients

Micronutrients can be removed from the food by the way the raw ingredients are grown. What happens to food once it is outside the farm gate can also affect its nutritional content, compounding the risk of nutritional deficits that potentially arise from some agricultural techniques. Cereals are domesticated grasses, and left to themselves they are rich in vitamins, minerals, carbohydrates, fats, oils and protein. However, when they have been processed according to modern methods, what is left is mostly carbohydrate. For this reason, B-complex vitamins are often added to white flour, and niacin, riboflavin and thiamine are added to breakfast cereals.

To anyone who has read Mrs Beeton's famous *Book of Household Management* (first published as a bound edition in 1861), the idea that modern processing techniques are not the best thing since sliced bread from a nutritional perspective is nothing new. She describes the process of 'bolting' in which brown flour is made into white flour by being passed through a series of sieves which progressively remove the bran. She then recounts an experiment in which one dog was fed on brown bread, while another was fed white bread. The latter died. Mrs Beeton concludes 'in fact, we may lay it down as a general rule that the whiter the bread the less nourishment'.[8] The statistical significance of this single study may be rather suspect, not to mention the methodology (the Royal Society for the Prevention of Cruelty to Animals had existed for almost forty years in 1861, but appears not to have investigated). What it demonstrates, however, is an early concern for the damage that processing could do.

The tale of three loaves

Bread-making, however undertaken, requires four basic steps – mixing the ingredients; proving (so that the bread rises); baking; and cooling. In the food-processing industry there are two approaches to making bread – the bulk fermentation process (BFP) and the Chorleywood Bread Process (CBP). The first of these methods requires a period of fermentation for several hours – it is, thus, a version of the traditional approach to bread-making. The CBP makes use of high-speed mixing machinery to develop the gluten structure in the dough, helped along by so-called dough improvers – ascorbic acid and an emulsifier (or fat).[9]

Table 5.1 suggests that the industrial maker of bread saves time by short-cutting the proving stage and applying energy at the cooling stage. Supporters of the process note that the CBP can make use of lower quality types of flour that contain less protein, thus it is an efficient way of using wheat breeds typically grown in the UK. Those who would prefer to consume a less highly processed bread point to nutrients released during the proving process, and to the additives used to 'improve' the flour, not all of which may be as benign from a health perspective as ascorbic acid (vitamin C).

Table 5.1 The tale of three loaves in detail

Factory-made bread[a]	*Mrs Beeton's bread*[b]	*Traditional bread*[c]
Steel-rollers mill the flour (20 tonnes per hour), also separate it into its constituent parts – bran, germ, carbohydrate	Keep freshly ground flour dry for a few weeks until it becomes less glutinous. If damp, dry it by the fire for an hour or two	Stone-grind the grain (250 kilos per hour)
Ingredients: flour, water, vinegar, salt, yeast and 'flour improver'	Ingredients: wheat flour, milk, yeast from home-brewed beer, washed to remove bitterness, is preferred	Ingredients: flour, water, yeast, water, salt
Mix (time taken – depends on machinery – a few minutes). Rest (90 seconds)	Mix the yeast mixture with the flour, set to rise for an hour. Knead. Knead further. Set to rise for about 45 minutes	Combine ingredients. Set in a warm place to rise. Knock down, repeat (overall time required: approx. 2 hours)
Divide into loaves	Turn into pans	Divide into loaves
Bake (21 minutes) (p. 13)	Bake (1 hour to 85 minutes)	Bake (50 minutes)
Cool (110 minutes; significant energy use, p. 113)	Bread should be at least a day old before it is eaten and properly kept will be good to eat after three or four days (p. 448)	Leave to cool
Slice	Slice	Slice

Sources: [a] Lawrence (2004); [b] Beeton (2012); [c] Scott (2012).

Content is more than nutrition

Processing clearly has a bearing on the nutritional content of what we eat. But there is more to the power of processing than that. The quantities we eat are similarly influenced by food processing, as are the structures of meals. A strong argument has been made that the rise of processed foods has influenced levels of obesity – not because of the content of the food, but because processing has made certain foods more readily available.

In the modern age, food processing has been taken to a scale that would have been unthinkable even fifty years ago. Felicity Lawrence, returning from a two-year trip to Peshawar, reacted in shock to the plethora of choice on British supermarket shelves – said ironically in reference to 'twenty ways to process and market near-identical ingredients'.[10] Although there appears to be more choice than ever before on the supermarket shelf, Lawrence's comment suggests that in practical terms consumers do not have a choice over the content in their diet in the post-industrial food-processing world, even though on the face of it they appear to have more choice than ever before.

This is unfortunate, for the change in the composition of people's diets towards a larger proportion of processed food in the shopping basket as wealth increases is widely recognised as resulting in epidemics of obesity, heart disease and diabetes. It should be stressed, of course, that processed food is not the only reason for this. The World Health Organization places the blame for the fact that in a 2008 study about 10 per cent of the world population was found to be obese (having a body mass index of thirty or greater) on two key trends: the increased intake of foods high in fat, sugar and salt and low in key micronutrients; and the decrease in physical activity because of the increasing numbers living in an urban environment.[11] Of course, urban living can be said to encourage the consumption of processed foods through the prevalence of retail outlets. The web of links seems to multiply indefinitely.

Biscuit power – the convenience of overconsumption

There is a final economic and environmental issue that arises from the availability of processed foods. The amount of food that an individual consumes, and specifically the amount of calories that an individual consumes, seems to be strongly linked to the availability of processed food in the economy.

Imagine a poor economist, slaving away over a hot laptop computer in the relentless pursuit of economic knowledge. The work is arduous (of course) and the economist is moderately hungry. A biscuit would seem to be a ready solution to stave off the pangs of hunger.

So far, so good. Now, consider what that entails in a world without processed food being readily available. If the economist wants a biscuit, they will have to heat the oven, mix the ingredients (which they will have had to have had the foresight to purchase), bake the biscuits, clear up, allow the biscuits to cool, and can then consume the product. Even with a relatively simple oatmeal cookie recipe to hand, this is three-quarters of an hour or more, and quite a lot of effort relative to the outcome.

In a world with processed food the economist goes to a vending machine, inserts a coin and purchases the biscuits in a packet. The process takes perhaps thirty seconds (economists being decisive individuals, and not given to irrational dithering over available choices).

The availability of processed foods therefore gives the consumer two incentives to overconsume in terms of calories. First, the time cost of preparing food drops dramatically. What economist would give up an hour of research for so trivial a pursuit as food? But thirty seconds of research might be sacrificed without too much concern. Second, the instant gratification means that those with less self-restraint can more readily access surplus calories.

There is economic evidence for the relationship between overconsumption and processed food availability. Comparison of food processing over time, and between countries, with trends in obesity certainly indicates a correlation. Survey evidence supports the idea that a key cause of obesity is 'snack' foods between meals, rather than meals, or portion sizes. This is, of course, where processed food is most prevalent. Indeed, one economic study goes so far as to suggest that reducing the time spent preparing food by twenty minutes per day will add ten pounds to a person's weight if about three-quarters of the time saved is not assigned to exercise.[12]

Thus, developed-economy overconsumption of food can be attributed to the ease with which food can be obtained, which can be in turn attributed to the availability of processed food. Overconsumption of food is (by definition) wasteful in both economic and environmental terms. If developed economies made it harder to obtain foods – metaphorically putting the biscuit jar on the top shelf of the larder – then overconsumption of food and of the economic and environmental resources that produce that food could be lessened.

Food additives

Anything added to food in the course of processing to make it taste better, be more nutritious, look better or last longer is a food additive. Food additives are required to be disclosed on the basis of a well-known global numeric system, usually described as 'E numbers' in Europe. Additives fall into a small number of broad categories: for instance colourings (E1), preservatives (E2), antioxidants (E3), emulsifiers (E4), anti-caking agents (E5), flavour enhancers (E6) and glazing agents (E9). Colourings have been added to food for centuries to make it look more appetising, or indeed, for fun. If the alternative to colouring food is that less appetising-looking food would be thrown away uneaten then the addition of colouring may even be a positive from an environmental (or, indeed, economic) perspective. The caveat, of course, is that food colouring can also be used to make food that is empty of nutritional content edible. Traditionally speaking, some food is preserved by being made into something else. Hence, milk is stored as cheese, fruit can last for years in the form of jams and pickles, and other food, especially meat and fish, can be salted.

Some of the substances used to prevent oils and fats going rancid have nutritional value – in the instance mentioned above, the bread additive ascorbic acid (E300) is vitamin C. Jam-makers are familiar with pectin (E440a). Others seem less appetising: anti-caking agents (E5) include talc, kaolin and China clay, whilst flavour enhancers (E6) include monosodium glutamate. In the world of food additives there is huge scope for confusion: d-alpha-tocopherol (found in avocado and other foods) and dl-alpha-tocopherol (found in the factory) are the same thing, yet not the same thing, the first being natural vitamin E and the second a synthetic version. Whether these two versions of vitamin E have the same nutritional properties is open to debate.

Food additives can be put to good use – hence, sugar prevents fruit from going off in jam, and pectin causes it to set, making it easier to store and handle. However, in a world of processed food, the risk is that adding additives morphs into adulteration.

If you are what you eat, what on earth are you eating?

Surrendering control of food preparation to some distant factory is about more than giving up the preparation time. In surrendering control of preparation, one is also surrendering control of what actually goes into the food. True, you can add to the processed food in some sense – putting salt on oven chips, or pepper in a purchased soup – but generally speaking the purchaser of processed food is impotent as to the choice of what the food contains. The narrator of the film *Fight Club* ordering 'clean food' in a restaurant is a rather unpalatable (and, hopefully, fictional) example of that impotence in action.

As soon as the consumer and the producer of food are separated by a chain, the risk of adulteration in food increases. This is not exactly a new problem. The ancient Greeks knew the problem of wine adulteration, and adding chalk to bread was known to the Romans. As urbanisation took hold in mid-nineteenth century Britain, processed food became more prevalent. Geographic separation from agriculture was accompanied by a longer food food-chain. By the mid-1850s the respected medical journal *The Lancet* could report that some foods were impossible to obtain free from adulteration (if processed), and that every one of forty-nine breads sampled had contained alum. In 1985, diethylene glycol (an anti-freeze ingredient) was discovered in Austrian wine; Austrian wine exports dropped 90 per cent and the industry was forced to shift away from the sweeter wines that had been affected.[13] In 2005, Worcestershire sauce was discovered to contain an orange dye known as Sudan 1 not designed for human consumption. In 2008, melamine (used to make melamine-formaldehyde resin) was discovered in Chinese baby milk. In 2013, tests by the Food Standards Agency (FSA) discovered that beefburgers on sale in the UK contained varying amounts of pork and horsemeat alongside the rusk more usually used to bulk-out burgers.

This all goes to illustrate the higher risk introduced by long complex supply chains. The point, of course, is that when we eat food that has been processed by another party, be it jam made in the kitchen or corned beef produced in the factory, it needs to be trusted. If that trust is absent, then processed food will not be consumed. In the Worcestershire sauce example, many products were withdrawn from supermarket shelves in the UK with a speed reflecting a well-organised, transparent supply chain. In some countries food is regulated by a government body – such as the FSA in the UK, which was established in 2000 by an Act of Parliament to 'protect the public's health and consumer interests in relation to food'.[14] How hard this is to achieve in practice was demonstrated by the above-mentioned horsemeat scandal, arguably produced by a collision of financial credit-crunch conditions and the drive to provide cheap food.

This risk of adulteration adds to the cost of food, and increases the economic importance of processing in the food food-chain. Consumers have surrendered control over what goes into the (processed) food that they consume, but they want some reassurance that certain standards will be maintained. This is achieved through packaging, and through advertising. Both of these are, of course, economic costs to be considered. Food adulteration in the nineteenth century helped to propel the growth of tinned and bottled branded goods.[15]

Packaging food is intimately bound up with food processing. Home-processed food may be stored in sealed jars – pickles or preserves, for instance – but rarely is it regularised. With the advent of mass processing in food, regular and sealed packaging becomes essential. Tea was one of the first items to be retailed in sealed packets, from 1826, because tea was at that time very susceptible to adulteration. (Quality tea could be mixed with the sweepings of the warehouse floor, with lower quality tea dyed for the purpose, and even with recycled tea leaves that had been dried after use.) Thus, processing and packaging go hand in hand. Packaging gives some expectation that the contents are what they purport to be, and reassures the consumer that they are getting what they are purchasing.

Of course, the relationship between packaging and processing is a two-way flow. Processing necessitates packaging to demonstrate the purity of the product, but packaging can also allow more food to be processed. Canning is the obvious example of this, which allowed a wider range of foods to be processed, and then to be distributed to a wider geographic audience. The development of plastics in the 1980s allowed for far more foods to be processed, as control of temperature and moisture in the packaged foods could be controlled. Pasta is a classic instance of this. In 1957, pasta was such a rarity in the United Kingdom that the BBC could conduct an April Fools' day hoax about the threat of frost to the spaghetti growers of Switzerland (who were shown tending their spaghetti bushes). By the 1970s, spaghetti in the United Kingdom was available in processed form – in hoops, served in brightly coloured tomato sauce (from a can), or dried from a packet. Now, almost half of the population of the UK consumes fresh pasta, from plastic packets that allow the product to be processed and distributed without drying out.

Food processing and its environmental impacts

Food processing has developed from the structure of our economy, and has implications as to the nutrition and substance of what we eat. But what does food processing mean for the environment? It is stating the obvious to suggest that when food is mostly not food, its environmental footprint must be bigger than it was when food was in its raw, pre-prepared state. However, for much of the food we consume, the lion's share of its environmental impact is found in the procurement of raw materials. As an example, Kingsmill publishes a breakdown of where the carbon emissions of its soft white loaf come from, and the breakdown is as follows:[16] raw materials, 40.4 per cent; processing, 18.8 per cent; packaging, 2 per cent; distribution, 4.6 per cent; store, 0.7 per cent; in home, 29.8 per cent; disposal, 3.7 per cent. Tesco reports that processing accounts for 9.2 per cent of the total carbon footprint for skimmed milk.[17]

Judging a recipe book by its cover – packaging food waste

Processed food tends to require packaging – in paper, boxes, tins, plastic or glass containers – although, as the examples above suggest, this is a small part of the overall environmental impact of processed food. Nevertheless, in industrialised countries, the food industry is the largest user of consumer packaging. In 2008 it was estimated that waste packaging makes up 26 per cent of UK household waste.[18] A number of techniques have been used to reduce the amount of packaging needed: closed-loop recycling (for instance, the collection at point of sale of containers designed to be recyclable or reusable); light-weighting (for instance, using thinner materials); using re-usable containers; and redesigning the product so that less packaging is needed (e.g. some products can be sold in concentrated form). Some manufacturers have found that these changes also reduce processing costs. Technological developments are still underway – for instance, in biodegradable plastics and bio-based food packaging. In the meantime, packaging some foods can vastly increase their economic value. For instance, washed salad in plastic bags retails for several times the price of a lettuce. The environmental costs are unlikely to be priced in and, even if they were, the value thus created is unlikely to be ploughed back into the environment because the economics are not there to trigger this.

Waste

Food processing has an impact on how much food is wasted in two ways: the process of processing will involve 'scrap' – food that is not used. It may also involve flushing away of some nutrients that might be recycled in a less factory-driven environment. (Sometimes the reverse happens – the alert reader will point out that mechanically recovered meat is a misapplication of the idea of frugality.) Second, the outcome of the process itself may determine how much of the content the consumer eats and how much is thrown away. (This point will be discussed at greater length in Chapter 10 on waste.)

For every kilogram of cheese produced, up to nine litres of whey can be generated. In a small farm context, absorbing this would present no problem; however, the millions of tons produced worldwide are a different matter. This waste product contains about half of the nutrients in the milk used to make the cheese. It has been suggested that it could be used to grow mushrooms.[19] Whey and lactose are used directly in small but growing specialist food product markets,[20] and biogas production is an obvious possibility. As this suggests, such food-processing waste (liquid, solid and gas) cannot be dealt with on the basis of a silver bullet. The economics of re-using elsewhere in the process for other products, repurposing by chemical means, or converting to fuel will ultimately drive what is done.

Box 5.2 **Waste case study: coffee**

Coffee processing involves wet milling in which the bean is separated from the pulp, dry milling in which the 'parchment' skin is removed from the bean, and finally roasting. In this process, water and energy are significant inputs. The average coffee berry is about 68 per cent pulp, 6 per cent parchment and 26 per cent bean, thus in traditional manufacturing approaches almost three-quarters of the berry has traditionally ended up as waste, often sent down the river to pollute the environment. In an ideal world the organic matter left over after the bean has been extracted would be recycled, and because of the low bean-to-berry ratio could potentially go a long way to avoid or neutralise some environmental impacts.

In 2011, Coope Dota, Costa Rica, produced the first carbon-neutral coffee in the world based on the full life cycle from agriculture (including fertilisers) through processing, transport, consumption and waste.[21] The means by which carbon neutrality was achieved included significant changes in the coffee production process: the substitution of no less than 95 per cent of the firewood formerly used in the drying process with the dried pulp and parchment that had been waste matter; the composting of pulp to be ploughed back as organic fertiliser, vastly reducing organic waste and presumably also reducing fertiliser needs back on the farm; energy efficiency in the plant through computerised controls of machinery; the installation of a small mill for small high-grade quantities; 100 per cent recycling of water used in the process; and last but not least, small-scale experimentation (e.g. waste water from the wet milling process was fermented to generate bioethanol that could be ploughed into the mill).

Waste as a standard

Because the consumer has surrendered control of food, they also surrender control of food waste in processing. However, the consumer is perversely insisting that if they surrender control of food waste there must be more waste. Essentially, if one is buying food from a food producer, one needs to know that nothing untoward has happened since it left the producer (no adulteration), that the food producer is reputable, and critically that the food product that you purchase today is as good as the food product you purchased yesterday. In other words, processing requires a standardisation.

Standardisation is about more than a standard innate quality to the food purchased, however: it concerns not just consistency in quality, but the *perception* of consistency in quality. This is absolutely critical. The chip that you eat today must not only taste identical to the chip that you ate yesterday, it must *appear* to be identical to the chip that you ate yesterday if you are to have faith that the chip you eat tomorrow will taste the same again. This then introduces the element of waste into the process of processing food. If a food product is the wrong shape, or the wrong colour, or the wrong size then the food processor must reject it, for fear that the consumer will perceive a difference in the quality of the product. This is not rational, of course, but sadly consumers are not economists – they do not behave in a rational manner all of the time.

Here, then, we see an economic and an environmental cost of increased food processing. The purchase of processed food must increase food waste (and that waste will have to be paid for by someone, the 'someone' being, of course, the consumer). At the same time, the food that is rejected by the manufacturer of processed food represents wasted energy, wasted water, and wasted nutrients. One can hope that the waste food is recycled in some fashion of course, but the fact that it has made it off the farm and into the factory still represents a considerable amount of environmental effort.

In choosing processed food, there must be packaging (as we have established). That packaging must be produced, with both economic and environmental costs involved. The packaging must also be transported with the finished product (in most cases), which will add to the costs of transport. Thus, even if the packaging is recyclable and is recycled (the two not being the same thing), there are still economic and environmental costs to be borne.

The act of processing food itself on an industrial scale involves energy costs. The processing of food is the single most *energy* intensive part of the food foodchain (far more than home preparation or transport, and more than agriculture). It is a process of mechanisation. The human energy expended in peeling a potato is replaced by the steam jets of the industrial potato-skinning process. This can also be seen as renewable energy (human) being replaced by potentially finite energy (depending on what power source is used to generate the steam that skins the potato in the first place). Creating processed food requires energy to be used up and down the food food-chain as well. The raw ingredients for chips prepared at home do not require particularly specific storage conditions. Frozen oven chips require freezers from factory, to wholesaler, to retailer, to home (and on most of the transport stages in between). Those freezers require energy, entailing economic and environmental costs.

Why bigger can be beautiful in food processing

Generalising, the above paragraphs suggest that, for food, environmental issues arise in the context of large-volume production. However, this may not be the case for all dimensions of environmental performance. Considering energy per unit of production, for instance, it is likely that there is an optimal production volume, below which energy use per unit of product will be higher. A comparison of three Norwegian dairies found that the smallest of three dairies was the most energy- and, therefore, resource-intensive, and the explanation for this lay in the greater frequency with which the equipment was cleaned.[22]

New technology is a double-edged sword. The shift to closed-loop processing, which can vastly reduce the problem of waste, is an example of a benign change. Some so-called functional foods might be good for human health. Companies such as Nestlé and Danone put millions of dollars into nutritional research and development with a view to developing such products. This is the benign side of the 'sword'.

Elsewhere, technology has also been used in not-so-benign ways. It is possible to inject beef protein into chicken. Whether it is desirable to inject beef protein into chicken is an entirely different question. From the producer's point of view there may be economic advantages. The consumer may be less enthused. However, the consumer would be unaware that this process is taking place because it was not described on the label of the chicken (nor is there a requirement that it should be so described). Moreover, even those equipped with technology designed to detect such content would have been powerless to find out what was there – processing had rendered the source of the added protein undetectable by breaking down the DNA.

Elsewhere, Modified Atmosphere Packaging is used to lengthen the shelf-life of foods. Research suggests that the impact on nutritional content depends very much on how this is done; if there is any reduction in the level of micronutrients in some foods, this may be an acceptable trade-off against the likely reduction in unwanted microbes. The environmental impacts are likely to be more significant – for this process requires energy, water and other resources.

Market structures

The struggle between economics and environmental considerations in food processing is evident in the market structure of the industry. The food-processing industry has become increasingly consolidated. The largest firms have revenues counted in billions of dollars. However, large firms absolutely require high volumes to survive; large markets tend to function on razor-thin margins, and large players (generalising) tend to compete on price. In practical terms this makes it difficult for smaller players to survive. This, in turn, raises questions about the ability of free-market competition to supply answers to the nutritional and environmental problems evoked by practices followed in the global food processing industry.

Some hope may (possibly) lie with the consumer. UK consumers, post financial credit crunch, are said to be showing a preference for locally produced food.

The aftermath of the horsemeat scandal has led to increased interest in knowing exactly what we are eating. Should this preference catch on, size might become less important for survival in the food-manufacturing industry. However, that would only happen if the food-distribution industry were to respond comprehensively to the challenge. That is a subject for another chapter.

Conclusions

Summing up, the meaning of food processing in the post-industrial age has expanded to include many activities that once happened in earlier or later parts of the food food-chain. As a consequence, what food contains and how it is delivered has been taken out of the hands of the farmer and the consumer, with negative consequences for nutrition and the environment. This is a particularly significant point in the context of this book. To reiterate, processing is where the economic value lies in our food food-chain, but many of the environmental impacts of modern food production lie elsewhere in the food food-chain. The question is how to hold on to some of the positives delivered by the expansion of the food-processing industry, such as greater efficiency in some aspects of resource usage.

Notes

1 Golding (1954), p. 58.
2 Data from Cutler et al. (2003).
3 Food and Agriculture Organization of the United Nations (2012), p. 29.
4 Cited in Martin (1955), p. 253.
5 Millstone and Lang (2008).
6 Cordain et al. (2005), p. 313.
7 Foster-Powell et al. (2002).
8 Beeton (2012), p. 447.
9 The Federation of Bakers, at www.bakersfederation.org.uk/the-bread-industry/how-bread-is-made/production-methods.html
10 Lawrence (2004), p. xi.
11 World Health Organization (2012).
12 Cutler et al. (2003), pp. 28–29.
13 *Stuttgarter Zeitung* (1985).
14 UK Food Standards Agency, at www.food.gov.uk/about-us/
15 Colquhoun (2007).
16 Kingsmill, at www.kingsmillbread.com/fresh-thinking/environment/carbon-footprint/
17 Park (2009).
18 Waste Watch (2008), p. 9.
19 Song and Hwang (2000).
20 US Dairy Export Council.
21 Source: Presence of one of the authors on an Earthwatch expedition, 2012. Huffington Post also commented on the presence of this coffee at the UN Climate Conference (Peterman 2012).
22 Høgaas Eide (2000), cited by Mattsson and Sonesson (2003), p. 13.

6 Transport

> The railways had brought distant parts of the country nearer ... food bought at shops, much of it from distant countries, was replacing the home-made and home grown.
>
> (Flora Thompson, *Lark Rise*)[1]

As we set out to travel the byways of transport in the context of food, honesty is probably the best policy. A full understanding of the environmental impacts of transporting food is not within our reach. This does not mean we do not know what we are talking about. After all, economists always know what they are talking about. Rather, it means that advances are needed in food transport-related information flows and the presentation thereof, for anyone trying to understand the environmental impacts of transport in food.

Understanding the environmental impacts of transporting food

When man was still in hunter–gatherer mode, food could be consumed on the spot. Generally speaking, food is no longer consumed in situ where it is found. Of course, as anyone who has frequented a 'pick your own' strawberry field knows, a certain amount of illicit consumption from the plant may take place. Modern society also tends not to be too surprised (and is often moderately relieved) when a screaming child is placated with food direct from the supermarket shelves prior to checkout – but while that experience is somewhat barbaric, it is hardly foraging in the wild. For the most part, food undergoes a journey before it is consumed. This is hardly new. Cicero's letters give us evidence that the bread of Rome was made with grain from Sicily, and one of the reasons the Romans acquired Egypt for their Empire was to provide food for Italy. *Panem et circenses* (bread and circuses) relied on rather a lot of transport to get the bread (and to get the circuses too, for that matter) to where they were needed.

The structure of this book is framed as a journey through the various staging posts that food passes through to arrive at our tables (or more frequently today, trays), but it is more than that. It is also describing a journey in terms of physical distance travelled. The economics of our food, and the environmental consequences of our food, are intimately bound up with transport.

When faced with a complicated problem, it is human nature to try and simplify. Thus, transport of food has been translated in the public consciousness into the idea of food miles. 'Food miles' is a mantra that is widely understood by the food-consuming public. The simplicity of the concept (which is basically 'how far has the food travelled to get to the shop?') has perhaps encouraged its popularity. A certain patriotic appeal can also be added in – the stirring slogan of the British magazine *Farmers' Weekly* was 'Local food is miles better'. This attitude implicitly looks down on the competing imported products and could be interpreted as implying a certain inferiority or lack of freshness in the foreign food. This is environmentalism as an advertising slogan – could there be a more perfect union of economics and the environment? The answer (inevitably) is that there certainly could.

The simplicity of the concept of food miles has perhaps led to an exaggerated emphasis on the physical distance from food processor to food consumer. This does not in fact tell us very much about the total use of transport in the food food-chain. Transport is also a visible part of the food food-chain – every time we pass a supermarket or food processor's lorry on the road, we are reminded about the role of food miles in what we eat. As such, we are hyper-aware of the role of transport in food. But transport and food is a complicated process. We need to get to grips with that complexity if we are to have any chance of understanding the role of transport in food, and fortunately there is a technique that can help.

Life-Cycle Analysis

Transport is relevant at all stages in the food food-chain, from land to waste. This is not just a matter of common sense – there is analysis in place to prove it. The analytical approach capable of telling us what proportion of the environmental footprint of food comes from transport is known as Life-Cycle Analysis. This is a process which essentially looks in detail at each link in the food food-chain, and assesses the costs at each stage. The good news is that the private sector is increasingly using such analysis. This means that the quality of information available to the general public about supply chains is slowly improving. These glimpses into the arcane world of the supply chain mean that those consumers that choose to make environmentally informed decisions in buying their food could in theory have the necessary information at their disposal.

The bad news is Life-Cycle Analysis is typically specific to a certain situation, and the results are not always published. In the normal course of business, publication is not necessary as Life-Cycle Analysis is typically used for control purposes within a production line and deployed in management accounting. However, much could be gained from consolidating the lessons learned from such analysis, and putting key principles and a few simplified models into the public domain. The carbon-footprint concept is a good parallel example of how this might work. Carbon-footprint analysis can help better inform interested consumers in the many small decisions they make on a daily basis. If something similar to carbon footprints could be done for food, it might lead to better-informed decisions along the food food-chain in relation to food and transport.

Here's something I prepared earlier – uncovering the unseen food miles

The economics of food transport starts on the farm. Remember that much of the US grain crop is turned into animal feed. Cows do not get their grain-derived feed direct from the field. The idea that farmers suddenly turn herds of cattle loose into fields of corn or wheat to consume their calorie intake fresh from the plants is ludicrous (and would be very inefficient in economic and environmental terms). Obviously the grain is harvested, it is moved to storage on the farm, then it is moved to be processed into animal feed, then the animal feed is moved to wherever the cattle happen to be. In the absence of self-contained mixed farms (making silage in one field to provide fodder for cows in another), transport is a big part of what happens *before* the food leaves the farm gate.

It is a similar process with vegetables. As we have observed, fertiliser rarely finds its way to the field automatically – only if one is going to graze livestock over pasture will fertiliser find its way to the fields under its own steam. If artificial fertilisers are to be applied, they must be acquired and transported to the farmer. Fertiliser is applied in significant quantities, as to weight. While more efficient application may reduce the overall weight of fertiliser that needs to be transported, inefficient application is still very much the order of the day in many developing parts of the world, and even in developed economies fertiliser still has to be transported from factory to farm. Once the farmer has the fertiliser, it must be applied to the field – which requires a further form of transport in most advanced economies.

The importance of transport to the farmer is reflected in the fact that the British government voluntarily gives up tax revenue. Governments do not lightly give up the chance to tax, but in the UK 'red diesel' is used in agricultural equipment (the fuel is named for the colour of the dye that is added to make it distinct from conventional diesel and to prevent its use in non-agricultural vehicles). The diesel carries a lower tax than conventional motor fuels, and means that the transport costs of the farmer are reduced. Of course, the transport costs of buying-in animal feed or fertiliser are embedded in the price of those products, and the farmer has no choice over paying those specific transport charges, tax and all. But the principle of minimising transport costs on the farm and through that providing cheaper food (as a politically desirable outcome) is well established. We have not, perhaps, moved so very far from the bread and circuses of Cicero's Rome.

What this means is that we need to be careful about the casual assessments of transport costs in food. Typically, the transport component of food in a developed economy is put at something like 10–15 per cent of the total energy consumption across the food food-chain.[2] This, however, tends to be focused on the transport process that takes place *beyond* the farm gate. The transport of inputs to the farm is generally overlooked, or rather amalgamated into the overall category of 'food production'. This disregard for transport before the farm gate perhaps understates the sensitivity of food prices to transport costs. The price of meat will be impacted by any increase in transport costs, even if 'local' meat is consumed – because the inputs into the meat will still be transported. Life-Cycle Analysis can help to uncover the transport costs of these earlier stages of production.

The cutting-edge of environmental Life-Cycle Analysis is an analytical model known as Publicly Available Specification (PAS) 2050.[3] Let us ignore the horrendous branding ('food miles' beats 'PAS 2050' in spin, but not in substance, every time). Instead, consider the results. The model was designed to help firms manage greenhouse-gas emissions, but it has the potential to do more. The model takes into account a wide range of the environmental inputs that are relevant to greenhouse-gas emissions. A well-thought-out Life-Cycle Analysis for carbon dioxide must offer insight into other environmental issues. This is because a detailed understanding of the business model and its operations all the way along the supply chain (including transport) is essential if the greenhouse-gas analysis is to be meaningful.

The production of orange juice is a very good example of how this model can help consider the environmental impacts of transport within the food food-chain. Figure 6.1

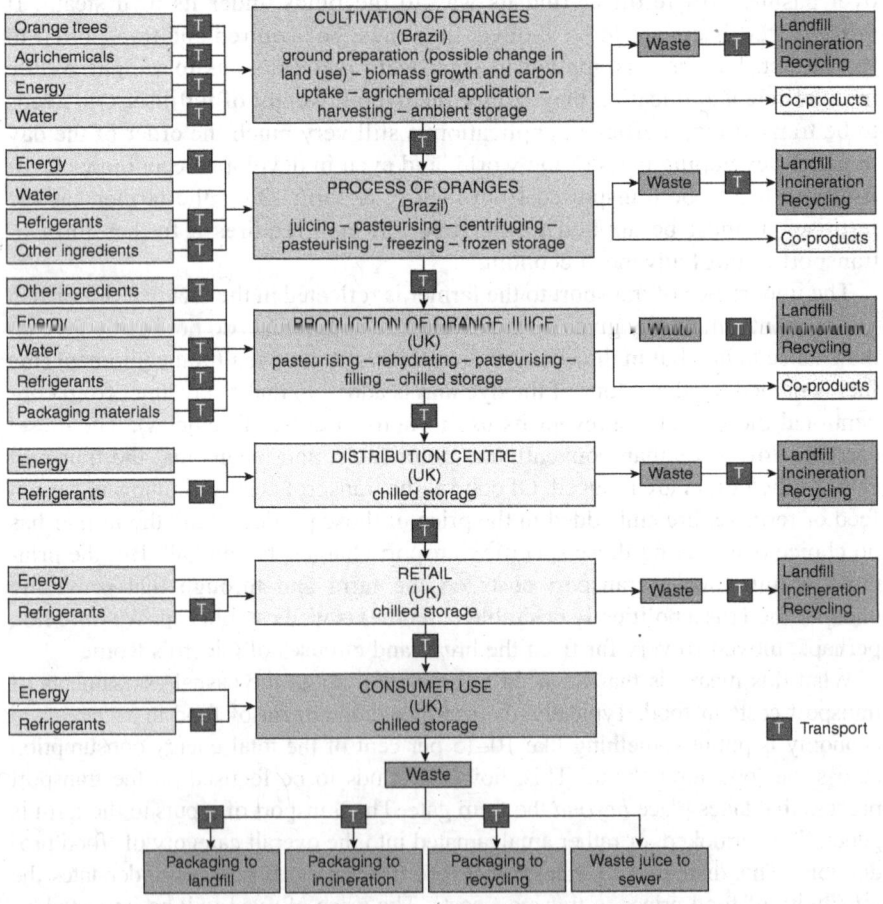

Figure 6.1 Where the orange juice flows (British Standards Institution 2011a, p. 8).

shows the metaphorical flow of orange juice, and each 'T' marks the point in the flow at which transport is required.[4]

It is obvious from this that transport is woven through every stage of food production, and thus has a direct economic and environmental importance to food. However, the more significant point about transport that drops out of this picture is that transport shapes the structure of the food sector as a whole. To take just one instance, supermarkets depend on existing transport networks to survive. Historically, transport systems have not been designed with the environment in mind. The impact of transport systems on the way the economy works, including food provisioning, may automatically mean that the way the economy works will encourage waste. (We note that this is by accident, not design!) It is no surprise to find that the environmental impacts of the food production system *as shaped and facilitated* by transport are potentially more significant than the direct impacts of transport. In other words, it is not transport itself that has the biggest impact. It is how the transport that we have impacts the topics covered in all the other chapters of this book that packs the powerful environmental punch.

Food transport from farm to factory

Having left the farm gate, the transport costs increase in visibility. This is the food mileage that excites advertisers and patriots alike, and which can appear in a readily quantifiable measure on the packaging. Essentially, there are three additional transport components once food crosses the threshold of the farm and heads out into the wider world: farm to processor; processor to retailer; retailer to consumer.

As we have just seen in the previous chapter, food processing is a big part of the modern diet, in the developed world at least. Economies of scale are an inherent part of the food processing process, and can indeed bring some environmental benefits. What this means, however, is that the food processor must have a large 'hinterland' to each factory. It is similar to the problem of feeding a large urban population. A city needs a large amount of agricultural land to supply it with food. Now, with outsourcing, a city that consumes processed food requires a food processor that has access to a large amount of agricultural land. Indeed, if food processors are supplying more than one city (and, of course, they can be supplying more than one country), they will need even more farmland to supply their factories.

The quantity of land needed to provide ingredients for a factory means, inevitably, more transport. The furthest-flung farmers still have to get their raw foodstuffs to the producer as quickly as possible.

The transport of food therefore requires speed and appropriate storage techniques in order to get to the far distant food processor in a suitable condition. The reason for urban cows in the UK was the lack of a swift transport system before the advent of the railways – to which, perhaps, may be added the risk that bumping along in a cart would rapidly churn the milk into butter before it got to even the suburbs of an urban conurbation. Flying food around the world reflects the importance of freshness – always a desirable commodity. The rail network meant that the Carlton Club of mid-nineteenth century London could serve, at seven in the evening, a salmon from the River Severn that had been caught that morning. Today, the consumer considers this entirely unremarkable. To a consumer used to stagecoaches as the fastest form of travel, this was nothing short of a miracle.

If speed is not practical, or economic, then alternatives must be found. The New Zealand meat industry is only possible because of freezing – which has been a feature of food imports into the UK since 1880 (when the SS Strathleven brought frozen meat from Melbourne). Temperature control helps banana boats bring in their fruit, and allowed Argentina to develop its beef industry. Developing the modern transport network allows the domestic processor to use raw materials from wherever it is cheapest to source them. By 1902, the UK was importing the equivalent of fifty-six pounds of meat per person per year, because, of course, it was cheap to import the meat (because of low transport costs). That level of meat import is the equivalent of over four hamburgers per person per week.

Economically, faster transport or temperature-controlled transport from farmer to processor is only viable if the price paid by the processor will exceed the costs of that transport. This was why milk rushed around by train in the nineteenth century – train transport was cheap. Milk took its first rail trip in 1844. Within a decade, the Eastern Counties Railway *alone* was transporting three million quarts a year.[5] The cheapness of the transport transformed the food industry. However, the costs of the transport will tend to focus on the pure economic costs. If the price of transport does not reflect the environmental costs then the economics of trade in food may create an environmentally negative outcome.

If transport costs rise, then there is an incentive to source locally, if that is possible. If local substitutes are not possible, there is a desire to maximise the efficiency of transport costs. The obvious example of this is the UK's experience during the Second World War, when shipping came with a human as well as an economic cost. The food convoys that supplied the UK often carried dehydrated foodstuffs as a means of maximising the highly costly space available.

Even in peacetime, economic transport costs are complex. We tend to imagine transport in terms of fuel, and that certainly is a part of the economic cost – but shipping freight rates can owe as much to the supply of ships as to the cost of running them. Shipping supply tends to be quite erratic – it takes a while to build a ship, and the orders for new ships can reflect economic conditions three years before the completed ships are ready to sail. Therefore, even if fuel costs are high (reflecting, at least partly, environmental costs), the economic costs of freight can be low if lots of ship owners are looking for business in order to pay for the ships that they have bought.

Transport of raw ingredients also raises the issue of food security. The issue of food security and transport between farm and producer is not so much about the risk of piracy on the high seas or highwaymen stopping lorries laden with frozen meat. The issue of food security and transport rests (as the horsemeat crisis of 2013 in the UK amply demonstrated) on the length of the supply chains and the disruption to international trade. This is where local political economics can triumph over global economics. Because food is such an important political issue, and because consumers tend to be very sensitive to food prices, international trade is periodically threatened by protectionism. This can come in the form of protecting domestic farmers, or it can come in the form of hoarding domestically produced foodstuffs.

As we saw in Chapter 4, it was the threat to the security of British beef supplies from the Peronist government in Argentina that led to the expansion of the UK beef herd. This was protectionism from Argentina (designed to raise prices) encouraging local production in the UK. In modern times, the vulnerability of food supplies is emphasised by bans on the export of food in times of shortage. The Ukraine banned the export of grain in 2010, and again in 2012, to make sure that local markets were supplied at a low price. The consequence, of course, was to push up international grain prices to the detriment of grain-importing regions (in 2010, the Middle East was impacted). Transporting agricultural commodities has implications that go beyond the mere cost of transport.

Globalisation and food

Here we take a slight detour on the food-transport journey. The global trade in food is something that happens both between farm and factory, and also between factory and retailer. However, global trade in food is more likely to occur earlier in the food food-chain, and is implicitly vilified in the food miles concept, so now seems the right moment to consider it.

Done in the right way, international trade can render economies more resilient by diversifying the resource base and sectors the economy is involved in. This is the counter-argument to concerns about food security. All other things being equal, this should be good for employment, as well as theoretically resulting in risk reduction, thereby lending the network of economies involved in this system greater resilience in the event of shocks. (This is a simplification. It assumes a reasonable distribution of power between trading partners and ignores the potential for the tragedy of the commons to get in the way of resilience.) One of the ideas running through this book is that resilience is a good thing in general terms, particularly in the context of environmental considerations, but also in the slightly more specialist field of environmental economics.

The same general points about the productivity and resilience-related benefits of international trade apply to food systems as fully as they do to economics. With the global population still growing, agriculture needs to be as productive as possible without doing long-term damage (known as sustainable intensification). This is only likely to be possible if different regions can make best use of what they have in environmental terms – for the environmental resources available will be vastly different from one region to the next. As an example, it makes little sense for wheat to be grown where there is a structural water shortage: it is rational for countries that are short of water to import wheat (and in effect import the water that is necessary to grow the wheat). China, as a country that is short of water, imports nearly all its soya (one of the most water-intensive crops to grow). From this perspective, transport is critical to supply food to people. Transport also facilitates the export of 'virtual' water (that used to grow the wheat or soya). If that is from 'water-rich' to 'water-poor' countries, all is well.

Where it is the other way around, environmentalists protest and economists mutter darkly about market failure.

Globally optimal food supply

The environmental costs of transporting food cannot be totted up as a simple fuel bill; it is more than that. International trade can allow economic and environmental efficiency – grow food where it is best grown (in economic and environmental terms), and ship it to where it is to be eaten. It is highly likely that the environmental gains arising from an environmentally optimal global food production model could vastly outweigh the direct environmental costs of food transport. The problem, of course, is that so environmentally optimal a system would place the food supply of one country under the control of another country – and given the political sensitivity of food, that could be problematic.

To an extent, economics will look after resource optimisation. Food systems are vulnerable to environmental shocks. With a surprising regularity, drought dramatically reduces the yield on crops in one region of the world or another (as the 2012 harvest demonstrated). Economics suggests that drought creating a supply shortage should then increase the price of the crop, and the price increase should then lead to increased production elsewhere. If the drought is permanent, then the price change should be permanent, and the forces of economics and the price mechanism will do their work and production will shift to other regions. The former grower of wheat will still be able to access wheat through import markets. Thus, sufficiency (although maybe not security) can be attained through global trade and economic forces. Of course, this positive effect is not the end of the story. It is easy to talk about structural changes to food provisioning. The difficulties actually undergone by people trying to put food on the table in the context of a limited budget, or, worse, forced to go hungry or malnourished, because of the turbulence caused by change, must not be brushed off.

As the above suggests, it must be recognised that international food trading can have other unwanted environmental and social consequences, for instance when environmental costs are not properly taken into account or 'externalised', or when imbalances in the food food-chain are produced by cross-border competition effects. These two points are considered below.

Globalisation and its impact on economic and environmental costs

Trade and transport allow those involved in the food food-chain to reduce food production costs by working on a larger scale, consolidating production and then transporting raw ingredients and finished products to where they are needed. This is also good for the consumer wallet, for in mass production the cost of each food item tends to be reduced. At the same time, manufacturing activity (including food processing) that is done on a large scale is likely to have a large environmental consequence. The question is whether transport, facilitating the reduction in financial production costs, does so at the expense of the environment.

Putting this in another way, would food-related cost savings arising from global trade still be in evidence if all direct environmental costs were fully factored in? This is a very hard question to answer because of the way transport networks develop and the economics driving usage. In general, once transport networks are there, experience finds that they fill up, and they tend to be used to capacity unless someone (a regulator, for example) steps in and puts the brakes on. Adding more supply is not the answer to congestion – it tends to fill up all over again. Someone once asked Edmund Hillary why he so badly wanted to climb Everest, and he replied 'Because it's there'. One reason why people and freight move around so much is because the transport networks are there: in economic terms the marginal cost of another user making use of the transport system is virtually zero after fuel costs.

Once infrastructure is in place, it is hard to change it, thus transport systems can be seen to have the effect of hardwiring habits and behaviours. If all environmental costs were fully factored in to economics, with the effect of putting up transport costs, it is quite possible that price effects would still be over-ridden to some extent by such network effects. As things stand, they are not, and so transport supply has burgeoned over the past few decades, permitting the expansion of food miles at the same time.

A hitchhiker's guide to the food industry

Over the past half-century, the volume of air freight, and of food air freight, has grown dramatically. This has happened because the rise in long-haul travel by *passengers* increased the available capacity for freight over the same time period, bringing about a collapse in freight rates.[6] Consider the humble green bean. Almost 90 per cent of green beans consumed in the UK come from sub-Saharan Africa (indeed from five countries in sub-Saharan Africa). The beans are transported by air. This will cause the food-mile fanatic to fulminate about the resources used in flying a vegetable almost half way around the world. However, most of these beans are flown in on passenger flights that would have been in the air anyway. Effectively, the bean is hitchhiking. Certainly, the fuel consumption of the plane will have increased as a result of the additional weight coming from the beans, but generally speaking this is a low-cost way of moving beans around the planet. In economic terms it thus became rational to move perishable goods such as food around in increasing volumes.

Box 6.1 How green are African green beans?

In a much-cited paper,[7] Professor Gareth Edwards-Jones of Bangor University, an expert on African agriculture, pointed out that the food miles travelled by hitchhiking Kenyan green beans are not the most important consideration for the consumer deciding between beans from Kenya or the local farmers' market. Kenyan farmers do not use diesel-snorting emissions-spreading tractors, and

(Continued)

> *(Continued)*
>
> rather than using fossil-fuel-intensive fertiliser they plough animal manure back into the land. Moreover, the irrigation model in Kenya is small-scale and relies on a range of technologies in which water is variously moved around by gravity, hand, foot, small motorised pump, rope-and-washer, small earthen dams and wind power.[8] The shared air miles used to transport Kenyan green beans to retailers in far-flung places need to be weighed against the better environmental profile of Kenyan produce even before other effects of economic development (such as local employment) are taken into account. When this is the case, the environmental advantage gained by moving to a seasonal pattern of consumption might not be the best answer. Gareth Thomas, in a 2007 speech made when he was the UK Minister for Trade and Development, observed that driving a few miles to buy food emits more carbon than flying a packet of green beans to the UK.

Is this hitchhiking a good thing or a bad thing, from an environmental perspective? It depends on whether this question is answered in relative or absolute terms. In relative terms, it is said to be better to air-freight green beans, tomatoes or strawberries to the UK than to grow them in hothouses even after the environmental impacts of the air journey, the connecting land journeys (usually by road in the UK) and the chilled storage on the way are taken into account. In absolute terms, however, it might be better for the environment if food consumption patterns were more often driven by the seasons than by the shape of our available transport infrastructure. Eating fresh tomatoes and other perishables when in season (and relying on preserves when they are not) might cut at least some transport usage out of the food food-chain. At the same time, it hardly seems fair to attribute all the environmental costs of flying green beans, tomatoes or strawberries to the food if the flights will take place anyway, for the benefit of air passengers. Why should shoppers for green beans pay the environmental price of holidaymakers going on safari?

The question we cannot answer here (it would take an entire book) is whether the environmental cost of whichever comestible took the place of the out-of-season tomato in the diet would wipe out the environmental gain from a reduction in food miles achieved via a shift to seasonal food consumption. The transport required for food in our complex culture is significant. It is worth pointing out that attributing the full consequences of transport to food is not necessarily fair.

From factory to retailer

Moving – temporarily – away from global trade issues, we proceed to the next link in the food food-chain; getting the food from factory to retailer (for the purposes of simplicity we can bypass the role of the wholesaler in all of this). Here the economics is all about volume, speed and appropriate storage.

When food can be easily transported, this tends to consolidate the supply chain. This means that rather than moving straight from the farm gate to the table, food is brought to central points in a transport network, and from such hubs is moved on to retail outlets. As long as the logistics are well designed (for instance minimising the number of empty trucks zooming around) such processes can bring efficiency gains with them, reducing the marginal economic and environmental costs of transporting many food items. This is something the consumer is likely to welcome – indeed, such cost savings are one reason why food-price inflation in the developed world has remained relatively low. The consumer may also benefit in other unseen ways from scale – for instance, highly developed food transport systems help maintain food quality between the farm gate and the food store. Well-designed food transport systems bring many benefits.

Food distribution systems of a significant size tend to be well capitalised. The storage and transport infrastructure should minimise the food waste that comes from natural degradation between the time it is produced (harvested and brought to the farm gate, or manufactured and packaged for the factory gate) and consumed. The example of developing countries shows what life can be like when food transport is not always available. If food producers are unable to get their produce to food retailers they cannot sell it and it goes to waste. If the logistics and infrastructure are creaky (for instance, food cannot be kept in good conditions through the journey), waste is once again the outcome. Waste is something covered in more detail in Chapter 10 – for now it is enough to point out the role transport has in helping to minimise waste at other stages of the food food-chain.

While it is clear that there are numerous benefits to be gained from investing in an infrastructure that makes it easy to move food around, there are also some downsides. One of these is that the consolidation in end markets that transport brings about can increase competitive pressure on the supply chain. This can happen in domestic markets and global markets. Consolidation in the name of efficiency gains is likely to cause few problems when buyers and suppliers are of a similar size – however, in modern food markets, many producer markets and some food processor markets tend to consist of many small players servicing large buyers. The balance of power inherent in such systems forces smaller, higher-cost suppliers out of the market, causing supplier markets to consolidate. From an environmental perspective, this could be good or bad. On the negative side, if consolidation is forced on suppliers, this may have the effect of bringing about a structural increase in the number of miles local produce needs to travel to get to the local supermarket.

Beyond this, there are shorter-run risks to consider. Far-flung transport infrastructures can be complex, and this reduces visibility, thus transportation systems (which can be described as a very effective vector for the transmission of risk) need to be accompanied by a good reporting system so that, in the presence of health-related food scares, food items can be tracked down and removed from the system. Shock absorbers are also required in case of unexpected interruptions to the transport chain. The 2000 UK fuel crisis was a good example of what happens when the transport infrastructure that delivers food fails: supermarket shelves emptied in the food-hoarding panic that followed.

The general concept of food transport as an environmental benefit may come across to some as an environmental travesty: moving food around generates greenhouse-gas emissions. The first point about this is that greenhouse-gas emissions are not the only thing that matter – there may be a trade-off between food security, population health, water security, employment levels and other social considerations that also need to be taken into account. Moreover, we would argue that adding transport and storage to a developing-country infrastructure would not automatically lead to an increase in the carbon footprint of said produce. Recalling the food food-chain, carbon emissions are more significant where food is *grown*, thus adding a decent transport infrastructure to the food distribution system is likely to shift some carbon emissions *along* the food food-chain by *reducing* the carbon emissions arising from avoidable food waste. Overall, it seems fair to suggest that excessive carbon emissions (such as those embedded in food grown and thrown away) avoided by minimising wasted agricultural production could be greater than those added by transport.

Minimising transport costs (economic and environmental)

This is not to say that economics and environmental considerations should accept the transport status quo. Even if environmental costs from transport are the lesser of two evils when weighed against the environmental costs of waste, transport costs should still be minimised. Let us turn once again to the staple example of bread. Initially bread (as the finished product) was not transported. It was baked in the home, because where else would one get bread? The houses of the wealthy had bakehouses (entire structures dedicated to baking), and villagers in their cottages would have a range (perhaps) or would rely on some form of pan bread. Transport of bread involved carrying the loaf to the table. Urbanisation put paid to a lot of bread production in the home. One reason (in poorer households) was the lack of fuel. Obtaining wood to fuel an oven is difficult in a city setting, and coal was expensive. Therefore, urbanisation led to outsourcing of baking to bakers – still local, as a general rule, but requiring some transport to get the bread to the home. Then the 1930s saw the introduction of sliced bread, and remote production distributed via the transport network to shops. The transport element increased to its maximum, and there it stayed – until recently. As transport costs have started to rise, as consumers have become more sensitive to food miles (perhaps hypersensitive to food miles), and as technology has changed, so the early indications of a shift in transport and food may be discerned.

One reason why even the smallest village shop can have an in-store bakery today is economics. Partly, of course, it is because the smell of fresh bread is an inducement to buy food. But equally, an in-store bakery facility will reduce the transport costs. Bread contains water and quite a lot of air. There is weight in the former, and volume in the latter. Transporting bread around the country therefore is weight- and space-intensive. However, transporting the raw ingredients around the country, to be mixed with water and baked in-store takes up less transport space, and weighs less. As the components of bread are less likely to go 'stale' than the bread itself, the problems of storage are minimised; bread can be made to order (near enough), minimising transport costs and waste costs.

The demise of the local baker in a town or village came about because of economics; the consumer wanted a one-stop shop, and did not wish to have to visit a baker regularly when a weekly supermarket shop (perhaps combined with the ability to freeze bread at home) would suffice. In a world of low transport costs, there was no problem with selling bread direct from a 'plant' baker. Indeed, this is still the dominant form of bread sales – around 80 per cent of UK bread comes from a 'plant' baker,[9] and around 75 per cent of all bread is sold sliced and wrapped.[10] In-store bakeries are often replacing the local craft baker, but the fact that technology allows even small shops to run bakeries may lead to a further shift towards more localised bread production.

One could even go further and say that the prevalence of bread-making machines for home use allows for a complete return to the tradition of bread-making in the home. This is probably a bit of a stretch, but the popularity of ready-mixed dried ingredients (to which one just adds water) is testament to some reversion to tradition.

The reduced transport cost (economically and environmentally) that comes from substituting plant bakeries with in-store bakeries is largely because a dehydrated set of ingredients can be hydrated and prepared simply at source (it should be noted some in-store bakeries use pre-prepared dough, not dry ingredient. In such cases only the volume of food that is transported will be reduced and not the weight). With the water transmission network in place in most developed economies, dehydrating more food products or concentrating food liquids before the retail stage of distribution would seem to make economic sense in lowering food transport costs. However, from a customer point of view, this is likely to be a step too far.

Shipping dry bread ingredients around is acceptable to consumers, because bread has to be rehydrated somewhere, and some pastoral idyll can perhaps be invoked if the rehydration takes place in the shop where one purchases that bread. (Quite why a pastoral idyll is conjured up by baking bread in a service station on the M3 motorway is a mystery only advertising agencies or psychologists can solve.) A more concentrated orange-squash concentrate is also something that consumers may accept – because of course the principle of a squash drink is that one adds water at home. However, consumers are likely to shy away from other dehydrated foods, because they are clearly processed and carry an aura of 'artificial' about them. The modern consumer is edging towards fresh rather than dried pasta, for instance. Perhaps the solution is to have fresh pasta prepared in-store through some simplified pasta machine, in the way that bread is prepared in-store today.

If dehydration is not acceptable, the retailer has some other options available. Better packaging (meaning lighter or less packaging) will help reduce transport costs by reducing volume and/or weight to be transported. Thus, using lighter-weight glass bottles can reduce the economic costs associated with packaging itself (less glass), and transport (lighter bottles are cheaper to move about). The

UK supermarket Tesco removed the trays from the bagged chickens it sold in-store, and as a result reduced the volume of packaging by 68 per cent (equating to a presumably theoretical 540 fewer lorries on the road).

As we shall discuss at more length in the next chapter, the pattern of food retailing may be undergoing another shift in the face of sensitivity to food waste. This is a return to higher-frequency food purchases, but generally also processed- food purchases. However, the food purchase here does not necessitate any additional journey on the part of the consumer. Rather, the food is purchased en route from the workplace to the home, as part of a journey that would hopefully be undertaken anyway. The food purchase is hitchhiking onto a pre-planned journey (there are parallels to the African green bean here) – and this is the final consideration that we need to ponder in examining the relationship of food and transport.

Food transport and the consumer

The consumer is under pressure to make food choices that minimise food miles. Estimates suggest that over a third of freight on the UK's roads is part of the food food-chain (either production or distribution).[11] It takes 88 calories of energy to fly one calorie of carrot from South Africa to the UK (albeit those calories are also probably flying humans at the same time).[12] Given the quantities of energy required to transport such food items, it is no wonder that food transport is seen as contributing significantly to greenhouse-gas emissions.[13] From about 2007 onwards, the idea of food miles entered the consumer consciousness as something that should be avoided.

In the intervening years, however, the idea of food miles has lost some of the credibility it once had, because understanding the environmental impact of food transport turns out to be more complicated than it appears at first sight. Focusing on a single numeric target or metric can have benefits, but the problem with single metrics is that they can leave a lot out. So it is with food miles.

As we suggested in a previous volume,[14] the tomato flown in from Spain may be greener (in an environmental sense) than the tomato grown in a British greenhouse. The source of this story is a UK government study that suggests that outside the harvesting season it can, from the perspective of energy efficiency, be more sustainable to import tomatoes from Spain than to grow them in climate-controlled (heated) greenhouses in the UK.[15] However, there are exceptions to this rule-of-thumb. Unlikely as it may seem to those who suffered from the trauma of the UK's miserable wet summer of 2012, there are times of year when the tomato can be grown in some regions of the UK under cover but without the help of climate control (but with irrigation). In season, it would thus make more sense to eat the locally grown British tomato rather than its overseas cousin from an environmental perspective, but whether this happens or not may still depend on the eventual price of said tomatoes, as well as consumer taste. Through the year, should the consumer insist on having fresh tomatoes all year round, the insuperable obstacle is that, owing to the vagaries of British weather, local tomatoes grown without climate controls can only be harvested for four months of the year, whereas in Spain the so-called 'long growing season' allows harvesting to run from October through June. It is easy to see why this source of comparative advantage in ecosystem services enjoyed by Spain relative to the UK could be economically exploited thanks to cheap freight, over-riding environmental concerns.

So it is with other food items. As Table 6.1 suggests, the short UK harvesting season for apples means that chilled storage for up to ten months of the year is required for the UK consumer to be able to eat them all year round. The amount of energy used to keep apples in storage for that time is highly likely (all things being equal) to overtake the carbon cost of 'hitchhiking' from, say, New Zealand, thus in the summer months shipping is likely to be a better environmental choice. Similarly, winter lettuce may be better imported from Spain, whereas in the summer, buying local is likely to be better.[16]

However, there is a missing ingredient in the above commentary. This is the question of seasonality in food production. The UK government report observed that a full Life-Cycle Analysis would be needed to make a proper assessment of the relative environmental virtues of the stay-at-home British tomato versus its well-travelled Spanish competitor. A full Life-Cycle Analysis would have to take seasonal effects into account. At one level of analysis it might be better, out of season, to import rather than grow stuff in heated greenhouses. The main question is all-year-round consumption of summer produce: why insist on out-of-season produce?

Although Life-Cycle Analysis is in its infancy as a decision-making tool in the public domain, when it is possible to find examples, it can be used to establish rules-of-thumb applicable to many other contexts. In a telling piece of research focusing on tomato and carrot consumption patterns in Sweden, the conclusion is that seasonal produce should be very much on the table as a means of reducing the environmental footprint of our food. This example – a Life-Cycle Analysis of the tomato- and carrot-eating habits of Swedish consumers, who eat an average of 10.4 kilograms of tomatoes and 9.2 kilograms of carrots per person per year – suggests that in the context of how we handle the seasonal availability of perishable

Table 6.1 UK sowing and harvesting seasons for beans, lettuce, tomatoes and apples

Produce	Jan	Feb	Mar	Apr	May	Jun	Jul	Aug	Sep	Oct	Nov	Dec
Runner Beans				I	IO			H	H	H		
Lettuce		I	I	SH	SH	SH	H	H				
Tomato	I	I	I	I				H	H	H	H	
Apples									H	H		

Source: Allotment.org.uk, at www.allotment.org.uk/grow-your-own/sowing-harvesting-vegetables-chart (accessed on 16 September 2012).

Note: I = sow indoors; O = sow outdoors; SH = sow outdoors/harvest; H = harvest. Apples: one of the authors has an apple tree in the back garden.

Table 6.2 The share of selected environmental impacts from transportation, heating and electricity for greenhouse tomato and carrot production (combined)

Impact	A		B		C		D	
	GWP	FFD	GWP	FFD	GWP	FFD	GWP	FFD
Transportation (%)	4	3	6	6	13	8	56	57
Heating and electricity (%)	56	68	3	12	57	72	5	7
Other (%)	40	29	91	82	30	20	39	36

Source: Karlsson (2011), extract from Table 24 (p. 23).

Note: GWP = global-warming potential; FFD = fossil-fuel depletion.

produce, the environmental impacts of transport may matter a great deal, outweighing all other environmental considerations. The writer Hanna Karlsson considered four different scenarios: Habit A – Swedish seasonal produce including tomatoes from climate-controlled greenhouses; Habit B – Swedish seasonal produce without climate-controlled greenhouse production; Habit C – European seasonal produce (longer transport distances) including tomatoes from climate-controlled greenhouses; and Habit D – European seasonal produce (longer transport distances) without climate-controlled greenhouses. Table 6.2 contains an extract of climate-change-related numbers from Karlsson's data.[17] As would be expected, the profligate 'Habit C' carrot and tomato eaters indulging in transport and heated greenhouses were also the most greenhouse-gas intensive (6.2 kg CO_2e – here half of the impact is explained by the heating of tomato greenhouses with natural gas). Not far behind in terms of carbon footprint came the 'Habit D' consumers, where cutting back on heated greenhouses made little difference (5.7 kg CO_2e because of the impact of bringing tomatoes from Spain). Transport is clearly shown as the problem in Karlsson's work. Habit A (little transport but using heated greenhouses) had significantly lower greenhouse-gas emissions (3.9 kg CO_2e) and Habit B (eating locally in season) boasted the lowest emissions (3.1 kg CO_2e).[18]

The above implies that we should only eat perishable produce when it is seasonably available. Does this apply at all times? Not necessarily. The answer may also depend on what happens where crops are grown. If the tomato were grown in the most sustainable way possible, the environmental benefits arising in the agricultural part of the food food-chain might be great enough to outweigh the environmental impacts of transport. Thus, food miles and refrigeration costs may not always be the dominant issue for perishable produce produced thousands of miles away from where it is consumed.

From shop to mouth

The concept of food miles does not generally take into account the distance travelled by the shopper. The relationship between consumers and food retailers is a story for the next chapter (and a thrilling tale it is too), but the role of transport and the consumer is intimately bound up in a whole series of changes in the way in which we consume food. Additives to processing, coupled with changes in packaging, mean that the consumer can purchase food and store it for longer. That means that they can shop less frequently, with higher volume. In the 1970s, the idea of shopping on a weekly basis was an anathema to almost all. This was when the farmer received almost half the value of the weekly food shopping basket, and by inference food was less processed, more likely to be fresh and therefore more likely to spoil quickly. It was not practical to shop on a weekly basis, and the structure of the economy facilitated daily shopping.

As economic structures changed, and processing became more significant in foodstuffs, the daily shop for fresh produce became both impractical and unnecessary. The age of the out-of-town superstore was born. The descriptor is rather telling there – out of town means a longer trip to acquire food. Moreover, because the food is being purchased in bulk, it is not practical to carry it home in bags or wheel it in a shopping basket. A car is required. All of a sudden, foraging for food has become something that requires fossil fuels and a lengthy journey.

This increase in the transport element (and in the environmental transport cost) of food acquisition is coming from shifts in economic circumstances. Like most things in this world, the driver of change can be boiled down to an economic motive. Increased participation in the workforce, in particular increased female participation, means that family units become time-poor. This, as we have seen, motivates an increase in the consumption of processed food. It has (until recently) encouraged fewer shopping trips, for more items – condensed shopping for processed product.

Transports of delight – the economics and environmental issues of moving food

Transporting food from producer to retailer is not that economically significant, nor is it terribly environmentally significant. It is, however, a very visible economic action. Moreover, the concept of food miles is simple to understand. This gives weight to food freight, and perhaps overweights the importance of transport in the mind of the modern food consumer. At the same time, transport is intimately bound up into the way in which we receive our food today, and so changing the way we transport food may be part of how we become less environmentally expensive as well as less economically expensive in our consumption habits. Certainly, localisation of the later stages of food processing has an impact on food transport costs – and can also have implications for food waste. The environmental benefits via changed transport patterns may be incidental to this – but the emphasis supermarkets place on control of transport costs in their environmental strategies tells us that the image of transport as an environmental link in the food food-chain still has considerable significance.

Transport has the potential to add both environmental and economic value by facilitating environmental as well as economic gains from trade. It could potentially be the means of facilitating the sustainable exploitation of the many different resource endowments enjoyed by different countries in an optimal fashion with the overall goal of furnishing global food needs sustainably. As currently deployed and used, however, it seems to be a two-edged sword, destroying value as well as creating it.

As Figure 6.2 suggests, the environmental and economic impacts of transport in the upstream pieces of the food food-chain can sometimes work well in harness, protecting the environment, as well as improving quality of life for human beings. However, it is clear that transport in the context of food has a number of adverse environmental consequences, several of which are rooted in behavioural and cultural shifts facilitated by transport.

At a global level, we have already noted that different countries have different environmental advantages when it comes to food production (some have ample water, some ample sunlight). How those environmental resources are managed will depend on the strength of local institutions against the forces of competition and the associated economic benefits. The Amazonian rainforest is a very good example. In some areas of Amazonia, deforestation has been actively leveraged in order to free-up land for crops such as palm oil, which has become ubiquitous in food products and other staples. Economic forces cannot protect such land because the ecosystem services embedded therein are not priced in conventional economic models. Protection has to depend almost entirely on the strength of local institutions. In the absence of such institutions, global trade and the transport infrastructure associated with it allows untrammelled economic forces to determine what happens to important global commons such as rainforest that happen to get in the way of global demand for key food items.

A number of things are needed for transport to become a benign influence within the food sector. The most important is the connection between the consumer and the environment in the form of food knowledge. As things stand, for instance, it is unlikely that the hungry hardworking economist looking for an energy boost will

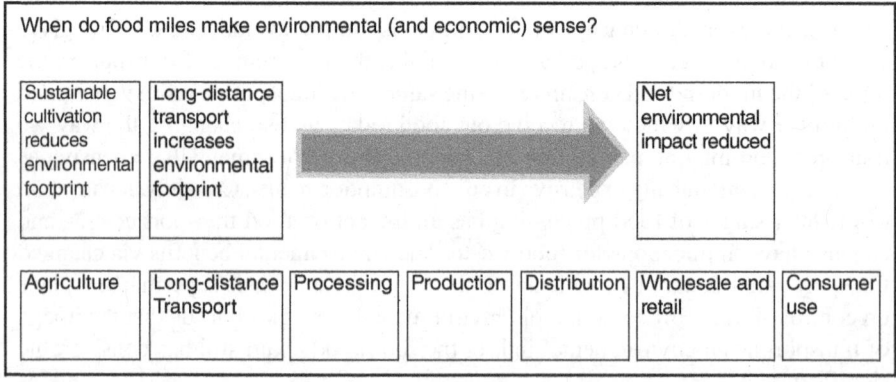

Figure 6.2 Using transport to reduce environmental footprints: environmental gains from trade.

associate the 'vegetable oil' on the chocolate-chip-cookie label with palm oil from far-flung environmentally challenged climes, no matter how rational. Without better labelling, it is hard for the consumer to make the environmental connection. Elsewhere, a cultural shift back towards seasonality in the diets of some developed countries could potentially give the consumer more power (through the acquisition of knowledge about what grows when) in making sustainable food choices. Other than allotment owners, how many are aware of the short harvesting season for many staples? This may be a cultural change too far, perhaps – particularly given the tendency to purchase processed foods that are further divorced from the raw ingredients and thus the harvesting cycle. Improved access to soundly based and simplified Life-Cycle Analysis food could change the decision-making culture around transport and the food food-chain. Finally, recognition of the need to protect aspects of the global environment like the rainforest may add a necessary cost to transport. Transport is a force for good in the context of food provisioning if consumed when needed rather than because it is there.

Notes

1 Thompson (1939).
2 McWilliams (2009), p. 24.
3 British Standards Institution (2011a, b). PAS 2050 provides the methodology for assessing life-cycle greenhouse-gas emissions of goods and services (see www.bsigroup.com/Standards-and-Publications/How-we-can-help-you/Professional-Standards-Service/Pas-2050/). PAS 2060 provides the methodology for demonstrating carbon neutrality (see http://shop.bsigroup.com/Navigate_by/PAS/).
4 Permission to reproduce extracts from PAS 2050 is granted by BSI. British Standards can be obtained in PDF or hard-copy formats from the BSI online shop (www.bsigroup.com/Shop) or by contacting BSI Customer Services for hard copies only (tel. +44 20 8996 9001 or email cservices@bsigroup.com).
5 Burnett (1966), p. 6.
6 Department for Transport (2009).
7 Edwards-Jones et al. (2009).
8 Purcell (1997).
9 *Farmers Guardian* (2008).
10 The Federation of Bakers, at www.bakersfederation.org.uk
11 Lawrence (2004), p. 83.
12 Jones (2001), cited by Lawrence (2004), p. 93.
13 Transport 2000, UK.
14 Donovan and Hudson (2011).
15 Smith et al. (2005).
16 McKie, R. (2008).
17 Karlsson (2011). Global-Warming Potential is discussed on p. 31. Karlsson's results will appear in a forthcoming article by Elin Roos and Hanna Kärlsson in *The Journal of Cleaner Production*.
18 Karlsson, p. 24.

7 Food wholesaling and retailing

> Customers are often induced by considerations of fashion or convenience to pay high prices; but they can hardly be said to be overcharged, since they chose to pay for such costly luxuries as spacious premises, handsome shop fronts, numerous shop assistants and long credit.
>
> (Mrs Beeton, *Family Cookery*)[1]

Mrs Beeton, one of the more famous cookery writers of the nineteenth century, would probably have resented her categorisation as a cook. Mrs Beeton wrote explicitly on the topic of household management, and could justly aspire to the role of economist. While Mrs Beeton is not usually thought of as an environmentalist, her awareness of the influence of the environment upon our food choices runs throughout her work – in part because the circumstances of the age meant that it must. Hence, a 'Calendar of Food in Season' is made available to the family cook in *Family Cookery* and for every single recipe in the New Edition she indicates when the main ingredients are in season, as well as their average cost, and the preparation time required. The user of this book in the days when Mrs Beeton's word was law could go shopping for food armed to make decisions that would take full account of nutrition, economics and the environment, without even thinking about it. However, the way consumers shop for food now is so changed that the book would need to be rewritten for this still to hold true. For an explanation of what has happened, we look to economics.

The death of high-frequency shopping

The economics of how food is sold to us has changed significantly in the course of little more than a generation. In the United Kingdom at least, in the 1970s food was still sold in smaller shops, and the supermarket was a supplement to that process. Food had to be sold locally because cars were less prevalent as a form of transport; an 'out-of-town' supermarket is wholly impractical for the pedestrian consumer. Food had to be purchased frequently (often daily) because of the problems of keeping food fresh for any length of time. Freezers were less common, and the preservation of food offered by modern packaging and processing technology was not available. Moreover, in a world with lower female participation in the workforce and generally shorter working hours, daily shopping for food was feasible.

The high-frequency purchase of food was the norm for the urban consumer, at least. Historically, the rural consumer would have had food to hand from their own gardens, supplemented by occasional visits to the market and perhaps a little light poaching. In an urban setting, where storing fresh food was a problem, purchases had to be frequent. A survey in the nineteenth century found that an urban family would make (on average) seventy-two purchases of tea over a seven-week period.[2] That, of course, suggests more than a daily purchase of food. It also reflects the economic practicalities of a time when the amount spent on food was a higher proportion of the family budget. Small purchases of tea were necessary because bulk buying would have been beyond the means of a working family income. The urban consumer also has far greater *opportunity* to buy sustenance on a frequent basis. A 1751 survey revealed that London and its environs was the proud home to 17,000 gin shops.[3] While gin may not conventionally be considered a form of sustenance, it is indicative of the urban proclivity for frequent purchases of food and drink (a city does not support 17,000 gin shops if its consumers are buying on a monthly basis). Why bother to stock-up with bulk purchases of gin, when a convenient shop is within stumbling distance?

We can also see that an alternative form of grain-based sustenance, bread, was increasingly an urban frequent *purchase* as long ago as the eighteenth century. Bread was not *made* in the urban home. By 1831 there was a baker for every 295 people in the local population of the British county of Berkshire (the more rural Cumberland had a baker for every 2,200 people). Again, a baker is going to require a high frequency of sales if he or she is to make a living with fewer than 300 customers. Urban consumers could buy bread readily, and it was easier to buy from a baker than to make at home (it was also possibly cheaper, given economies of scale associated with fuel costs). The demand was for fresh bread, meaning frequently purchased bread. This was a trend which worried the government enormously. Consumers were buying fresh bread while it was still warm; a wanton display of extravagance and luxury by the lower social orders that was simply intolerable. The trend led to the passage of the Stale Bread Act in 1801. The Act did not seek to prevent bakers from dishonestly selling stale bread to their customers; it banned them from selling fresh bread to their customers, and insisted that the loaves be allowed to cool and dry somewhat before being retailed. It was about as effective as one would suppose.

Consumers historically have been sensitive to the prices that they have to pay in the shops for the food that they purchase – something that continues to this day. There was a revolt by housewives over high food prices in England in 1795, with one Sarah Rogers of Fordingbridge being sentenced to three months' hard labour for the impudence of campaigning for cheaper butter.[4] A key point here is that the unfortunate Ms Rogers was buying the butter, not making it herself in her home. This was a food retail culture, and in the world before refrigeration it must have been a high-frequency food retail culture.

The concept of high-frequency purchases of foodstuffs by urban consumers therefore has a long history. By 1939, nearly a third of UK economic activity was generated from the retailing of foodstuffs to the domestic population. It was a pattern that lasted until the 1970s. It was during the 1970s that the economics of the historical consumer model changed profoundly, and with the change in economics we have witnessed a change in the structure of food shopping. (Economists lead and society follows once again.) Perhaps the defining shift was the increase of women in the workforce. Daily food shopping and the labour required for daily food preparation became too difficult if the household had two adults working. The recession of the early 1980s saw the numbers of women in the workforce start to increase in the Anglo-Saxon economies. This was the best way of preserving household living standards at a time of job insecurity for many, and the trend once it had begun has not reversed. This then created a demand for prepared food, and for fewer shopping trips. There was just not enough time for a visit to the butcher, the baker, the grocer and so on. One-stop shopping, to take place once a week rather than every day, was the demand of the food-buying public. In a capitalist economy, demand is generally met by enterprising supply, and so supermarkets became ubiquitous. The combination of demand and opportunity, the latter provided by better packaging and preservation techniques, led to lower-frequency shopping.

The importance of economics in shaping the structure of food retail can be glimpsed in an international comparison. The USA and the UK, as economies that experienced increased female participation in the workforce thirty years ago, have embraced supermarkets as the main form of food retail. In much of continental Europe, however, female labour-force participation rates have tended to be lower. While supermarkets are obviously significant (one thinks of the hypermarkets of France, for instance), they are not as dominant as in the Anglo-Saxon world. The economics of these countries has not forced the consolidation of the food retail experience.

Helping with this process, food has become a smaller and smaller part of the family budget over time. While spending on food in absolute cash terms has increased, the share of the household income dedicated to food cooked at home has declined. This has meant that there is increasingly room in the family budget to purchase, for instance, a month's worth of frozen food in a single trip.

Evidence from the USA suggests that by the middle of the last decade, comfortably over half the population conduct a major food shop only once or twice in a week, supplemented by smaller forays into food retail, and that a fifth of the population confine their food purchases to one or two large shopping trips alone with no side trips.[5] This is very, very far removed from the consumption patterns of the previous generation. This shift has significant economic and environmental implications. A weekly food shop almost forces the consumer into a car – carrying a week's worth of groceries for a family of four is no light task. Less frequent food purchases forces more packaging and more processing than in the traditional model, because food needs to last for a week. Distribution patterns from wholesaler to retailer shift as well. The growth of large supermarket chains gives them increased power as purchasers (tending towards what economists, ever adept with the English language, call monopsony power – which is monopoly power for the buyer rather than the seller). This has contributed to farmers receiving a smaller and smaller proportion of what we spend on food and is why we can claim that food is not food any more.

The increase in market share for supermarkets obviously threatened the smaller retailer. Essentially, the choice was to adapt or die. Relying on the custom of a non-car-owning minority continuing the shopping patterns of the past would bring about a slow commercial death for the small retailer. The alternative was to become a boutique retailer – offering some specialist experience that would entice shoppers away from the larger stores. Some combination of specialist products with the idea of 'shopping as a leisure experience' would allow some smaller stores to survive. This form of shopping tends to cater to higher-income groups, however.[6]

Food wholesaling and retailing – scope, scale and environmental impacts

About three-quarters of the environmental impacts of private consumption are accounted for by three areas of human activity: eating and drinking, getting around and where we live (including the equipment we rely on for food preparation and other domestic activity in our homes and the energy that powers it). Our aim in repeating these key points is not primarily to reinforce the point that consumption of food and beverages makes a significant contribution to the environmental impact of household activity.[7] The point is that what we eat, how we travel and where we live are interdependent, thus *in aggregate* they have a strong influence on how we shop for food, even if, in the normal course of events, this is not something the average shopper needs be aware of. It is clear that there is significant scope for food retailing to be relevant to a wide range of direct and indirect environmental impacts running through several aspects of private consumption, all relating to how we live and eat now. Global warming and carbon footprints may be the fashion of pop environmentalism, but they are also just the tip of the environmental iceberg. Issues such as the pollution of water, of the physical environment wild animals live in, and of the air and rainwater are no less important. Thus, according to a European Union study, the consumption of food and beverages in the EU-25 accounts for not only 31 per cent of global warming potential but also 60 per cent of eutrophication (for example, fertiliser run off into the water supply), 24 per cent of ecotoxicity (toxic pollution into the environment), and 31 per cent of acidification.[8] This is impressive for something that accounts for only 10–15 per cent of consumer spending. Some, but not all, of these impacts are brought about directly by the food retailing and wholesaling sector, but none are likely to head the consumer's shopping list as they head out to buy food. When it comes to shopping for food, economics trump the environment every time.

Food retailing and its direct and indirect environmental impacts

The direct environmental impacts of the food retailing and wholesaling industry include energy consumption, waste generation, and the environmental impacts of large-scale refrigeration. Direct social impacts include the influence of the food retailing and wholesaling sector upon nutrition, as well as positive impacts of good practice in food safety. The food retailing industry is not directly responsible for the environmental effects of other pieces of the food food-chain (such as nitrogen in the water supply, which is largely caused by agriculture) although its indirect effects are both significant and relevant. Retailers shape retail trends, and through that shape other economic trends up and down the food food-chain.

Moving back up the food food-chain first, the food retailing industry can have considerable influence over its suppliers. As we discuss below, experience has shown that if enough of the food retail industry demands produce grown or processed in environmentally friendly ways, this can potentially have a significant influence upon farming practices or the operations of food processors.

If we travel down the food food-chain towards the consumer, food retailers must be absolved of some responsibility. Retailers cannot be said to be entirely responsible for the decisions made by millions of consumers. Yet it is hard to deny that the food retailing and wholesaling sector can have an influence the consumer may not be fully aware of – what else is advertising for, after all?

On the evidence of initiatives already under way in the food retailing industry – such as investment in energy-saving programmes or clean-energy infrastructure – the industry is already aware of the need for change. However, economics very often drives decision-making in highly competitive sectors. Initiatives undertaken in the industry tend to be most readily adopted when there is no trade-off between the environment and profit. The most obvious example is the simultaneous financial cost savings and environmental cost savings that can come from energy efficiency. The British retailer Marks & Spencer has sought a more complex version of this with an initiative called 'Plan A' (introduced in 2007).[9] This is a combination of environmental initiatives, branding and advertising – involving the consumer in sustainability while promoting the commercial interests of the retailer.

If it were always possible to arrive at win–win ideas such as energy saving (which saves the environment and money) there would be no need for this book, as economics would solve all the environmental problems associated with food. However, not everything will fall in the 'win–win' category. Let us consider the options with regard to food waste and food retail. Win–win is not the most likely outcome here.

Figure 7.1 suggests that sustainability initiatives such as recycling (bottom right) are likely to be hard to implement for the food retailing and wholesaling industry as it is configured. Why is this, and does it mean the industry needs to be reconfigured?

Why the food retail sector cannot solve all environmental problems

While the food retail sector may be able to help the consumer avoid food waste, Figure 7.1 suggests that dealing directly with food waste itself is a different matter. The food retail sector should emphatically not try to deal directly with the problem of food waste. This is clear if we consider the most direct response to food waste, used in households since time immemorial – namely, recycling. Food waste

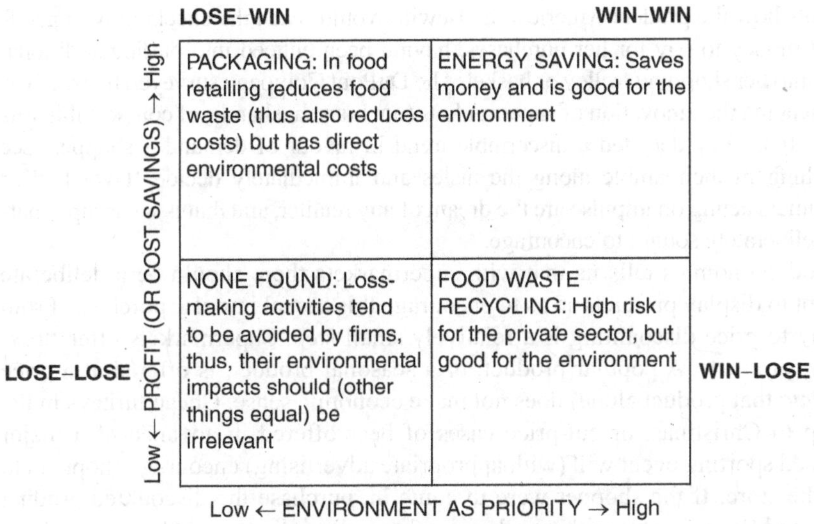

Food wholesaling and retailing   125

	LOSE–WIN	WIN–WIN	
High ↑ PROFIT (OR COST SAVINGS) ↓ Low	**PACKAGING:** In food retailing reduces food waste (thus also reduces costs) but has direct environmental costs	**ENERGY SAVING:** Saves money and is good for the environment	
LOSE–LOSE	**NONE FOUND:** Loss-making activities tend to be avoided by firms, thus, their environmental impacts should (other things equal) be irrelevant	**FOOD WASTE RECYCLING:** High risk for the private sector, but good for the environment	**WIN–LOSE**

Low ← ENVIRONMENT AS PRIORITY → High

Figure 7.1 Easy decisions versus trade-offs for food retail: or, why we need this book.

recycling is not a core skill for the retail sector: retailers' expertise lies in packaging, distribution and marketing. Retailers are well aware that to offer food waste management facilities would not play to their core strengths and thus it is avoided: the recycling facilities available in association with leading supermarket chains in the UK contain bins for paper, glass and even shoes and clothing, but generally they do not deal with food waste. There are sound operational reasons for this – food waste brings with it a range of potential health and safety problems that the average supermarket may not be equipped to deal with, and which would therefore be potentially bad for people, as well as bad for branding and bad for business. It is clear to see that the disposal of food waste is best left to the experienced municipal sector.

Although the food retail sector is not necessarily the best qualified sector to deal directly with food waste, however, retailing practices could potentially help change behaviour both ways along the supply chain – upstream and downstream – in such a way as to avoid food waste in the first place. Here, the core skills of the sector – merchandising, messaging, and innovating in areas such as logistics and packaging – could be a powerful force for change.

The economics of overconsumption

The aim of a supermarket is, of course, to sell as much food as possible, as profitably as possible. Daily food shopping is shopping with a purpose – one goes out to buy what one needs for the evening meal, and that is generally all. Shopping for food on a less frequent basis is different. If one is doing a weekly shop, and is confronted by food that will stay fresh for a week (or more), there is less certainty about what needs to be purchased. Impulse buying is possible.

A story of the introduction of supermarkets to the United States in the 1950s recounts how the prudent American housewife would reach the checkout with insufficient money to pay for her purchases, having been enticed into putting additional items into her shopping trolley or basket. The DuPont Company surveyed housewives experiencing the innovation of supermarkets (not househusbands, of course – this was the 1950s). They detected a discernible trend in favour of demand – shoppers see something in their amble along the aisles and immediately decide 'I want it!'.[10] Consumers acting on impulse are the dream of any retailer, and that is what supermarkets deliberately sought to encourage.

Good economics tells us that with supermarkets there should be a deliberate attempt to display products so as to encourage this casual impulse purchase. From display to price discounting is a relatively small step. Supermarkets offer 'loss-leader' products. A popular product, or a seasonal product, is offered at a price that (*qua* that product alone) does not make economic sense. Cheap turkeys in the run-up to Christmas, or cut-price cases of beer offered in advance of a major televised sporting event will (with appropriate advertising) encourage shoppers to visit the store. If the shopper were to come in, purchase the discounted product alone, and flee the store with no other purchase, the policy would be an economic disaster for the supermarkets. Indeed, when such products are offered below their cost, the supermarket would go out of business almost immediately.

Of course, this is not what happens. The supermarket offers these products knowing full well that shoppers will not wander around with blinkers on. As they wander the aisles in search of the discounted product (for rarely are such products placed near the entrance) the shopper will discover other products to purchase on impulse: snack food to accompany the beer, or stuffing to accompany the turkey. These products will not be offered at a discounted price, but as the shopper is in the supermarket they might as well buy them. The economics of the supermarket depends on the willingness of the consumer to impulse buy.

Related to this is the 'buy one, get one free' (BOGOF) principle, a strategy that is periodically used by supermarkets. There are variations on the theme, of course: buy two, get one free; buy one, get one half-price; buy two for a price that is less than twice the price of a single purchase. The economics of this form of selling is again to encourage increased consumption. There may be an element of enticing the shopper in, in the hope of encouraging more impulse buying. The economics of BOGOF are simple. As with the price-discounting model, there is the opportunity to sell other items alongside whatever is being retailed as a BOGOF offer. Alternatively, there is the expectation that getting an additional product free will not result in half the number of purchases of that product over time.

Imagine a consumer who consumes a packet of biscuits every week. Biscuits are offered 'buy one, get one free'. Will the consumer still buy fifty-two packets of biscuits in a year? Almost certainly not. If one has two packets of biscuits in the home, there must at least be a risk that the second packet is eaten more quickly (because it is there). Convenience food is consumed because it is convenient, and there is nothing more convenient than having food to hand, as our economist at the vending machine from Chapter 5 has already proved. Alternatively, the second packet of biscuits may have an expiry date on it that causes it to be thrown away without having been fully consumed. Either way, the BOGOF process will generate increased purchase of food.

In the past twenty years or so supermarkets have taken the economics of retail to what seemed to be the logical conclusion. If you are stepping out to your local supermarket to purchase a loaf of bread, why not purchase a flat-screen television, or a new shirt, or get a mortgage at the same time? If one can be persuaded to purchase food on impulse, then why not keep extending the principle?

Supermarket shopping changed the way that we consume food. Supermarkets took the shopper from daily focused shopping with a purpose into an environment of food shopping on impulse. DuPont, again researching the supermarket phenomenon over half a century ago, found that 70 per cent of food purchases in supermarkets were decided in-store, not in advance (the report from the 1950s, presumably written by a man, recounts with a certain fascinated horror that less than a fifth of women make a proper shopping list).[11] However, the changing economic climate in the aftermath of the financial credit crunch has led to a further change in supermarket sales, and to some extent is a return to past behaviour. Of course, we are not completely turning the clock back; that would be entirely unfeasible. But there is a definite shift in consumer patterns in the environment of the financial credit crunch.

The power to change behaviour

Food retailers can influence food consumption patterns. This thus raises three questions: Could food retailers reduce their direct environmental effects? Could food retailers shape the choices we make in allocating resources such as money and energy between food, travel and the home? Could food retailers shape the choices we make in terms of our food choices? The answer to the first question is likely to be 'yes', subject to competitive conditions in the industry, as well as economics. The answer to the second question is likely at first sight to be 'no', except perhaps for those food retailers also involved in retailing household products. (However, we return to this topic when we return to transport at the end of this chapter.) To the third question, the answer is an emphatic 'yes', for retailers influence consumer choices every day of the week – indeed it is their very bread and butter.

Consumer preferences or technology – drivers of change to food retail?

Global food retailing industry revenues amounted to over five trillion dollars in 2011. About 46 per cent of this was handled by hypermarkets, supermarkets and discounters.[12] Worldwide, the top thirty retailers look after about one-third of global grocery sales.[13] In developed countries the concentration of food provision in the hands of supermarkets is likely to be significantly higher. Studies suggest that 75–80 per cent of all food retail outlets in developed countries are supermarkets.[14] This number may be overstated because of the practical difficulties of properly categorising all stores properly, but it certainly tallies with the experience of the UK, where the top four retailers account for around 60 per cent of food sales.[15]

We have already noted the seismic change in food shopping behaviour that has taken place in developed economies over the course of a generation. For many food consumers in developed countries the weekly shop by car, facilitated by chilled storage in the home, has replaced daily food procurement in the local market or local shops. These changes were only possible because of technological progress. Food sold less frequently, and in volume, needs to be packaged and stored in a different way to food sold fresh for consumption the same day. Food processed on an industrial scale thus facilitates the new approach to shopping. Whether consumer preferences or new technology drove this significant structural change in food wholesaling and retailing is likely to be a 'chicken or egg' question. It is, in any case, a moot point – after all, the important point in this context is whether some combination of change in consumer preferences and technology could remedy some of the environmental and social ills that are perceived to be rooted in modern approaches to food retailing.

Different readers are likely to react differently to a juxtaposition of the environmental numbers cited in earlier paragraphs with the industry concentration numbers of the previous paragraph. If three-quarters of environmental impacts are caused by food and its linkages to transport and buildings, and thirty retailers account for a third of food retailing, then the food wholesaling and retail sector is enormously important from an environmental perspective. From the perspective of environmental degradation, scale and impact could come across as a profoundly negative story. However, the flipside of this is that a change in the prevailing culture surrounding the buying, selling, consumption and disposal of food could be transformational for society, human health and the environment.

Cultural change tends to have its roots in human knowledge. Thus, we briefly consider two topics that come up in later chapters – food preparation and diet.

Skill displacement from kitchen to factory

As described in Mrs Beeton's *Family Cookery*,[16] there are six reasons for the preparation and cooking of food: to make it easy to chew; to render it digestible; to change harmful substances into nutritional foods; to kill off harmful organisms (such as parasites in fish and meat, or bacteria and other organisms lurking on vegetables); to combine foods in proportions needed for nutrition; and to make it appetising to look at, and tasty. Put together these imply significant work together with a decent skill and experience base. Consider, as an example, horseradish sauce à la Mrs Beeton.

- *Method One:* This requires the cook to find the plant (requiring knowledge that it is seasonable from October to June); scrape the root; soak it in cold water for an hour; and wash and shred it with a sharp knife (being careful to begin at the right end of the plant). This done, the cook can decide between the cold recipe

(requiring 20–30 minutes) and the hot recipe (20 minutes assuming Béchamel sauce is ready to hand and a further 40–50 minutes if not).
- *Method Two:* Find the nearest supermarket and choose from the several varieties on the shelf.

Both of the authors of this book enjoy cooking. One of us makes a mean chocolate cake from scratch (no packets of cake mix are given houseroom in the pantry). The other has a stock of home-grown, home-made apple butter 'to die for' in the cupboard – delicious on crumpets, in yoghourt, or in the middle of a Victoria sponge.[17] Both of us might be willing to experiment with Mrs Beeton's horseradish sauce recipe for fun. However, we have to be practical – the modern man or woman is expected to hold down a full-time job, entertain guests and cook, preferably all at the same time. Mrs Beeton would have been the first to agree that multi-tasking has its limits in the kitchen. Method Two would undoubtedly always prevail.

Horseradish sauce is relatively complicated. What about far simpler tasks such as washing lettuce? We think it likely that there are many consumers whose culinary skills do not extend to washing lettuce. We give you the hard method and the easy one.

- *Method One:* Separate the leaves from the stalk, rinse them in salty water to kill off unwanted wildlife and then rinse in clean water. Should you wish for some mild exercise, put the wet lettuce in a clean tea towel and spin it around your head (preferably outside) to remove excess moisture. At the salty-water stage *never ever* leave the lettuce to soak even if your aim is to be absolutely sure that all caterpillars have been eradicated for the result will be severely wilted lettuce. (As one of the author's great-aunts could testify, getting this right can be a fine balance.)[18] Serve.
- *Method Two:* Thanks to technological advances in food packaging, a choice of lettuce and salad varieties washed and ready to eat can be found in many supermarkets.

Since practice makes perfect and we simply do not have the time to practice the delivery of home-made horseradish sauce or bug-free crisp lettuce to the table, or indeed many other complicated sauces from scratch, the supermarket will win for all but those most determined to be frugal. It is likely that many similar decisions are made in households across the planet. Although it could be argued that the supermarket has helped to displace activity from the kitchen to the factory by making it less-and-less necessary to know how to cook when putting a meal together, the fact is that economics also have a part to play. The disappearance of the skill-base that once resided in every kitchen in the land is a consequence of there being other careers to follow. Supermarkets can thus be said to have facilitated the social change, but it would be hard to argue that social change was entirely attributable to the food retailing and wholesaling sector. Once again we arrive at a 'chicken or egg' question. Is the food retailing sector responding to the cultural context, or shaping the cultural context? The answer is likely to be both.

The disappearance of the culinary skill-base once taken for granted in the family home may seem to be unimportant if those who cannot boil an egg or wash lettuce can in effect delegate those skills to the food industry. The question is whether such skill is too important to be so delegated. As Mrs Beeton makes clear, food preparation and cooking is designed to render food suitable to the human digestive system; safe to eat; nutritious; and appetising. All of these connect in some way to human health.

Food retailing and direct health impacts

Domestic science was regarded as a soft option when at least one of the authors was at school. Possibly this was reflecting contemporaries' low regard for skills in cookery and housekeeping, when women were generally expected to be found in close proximity to the kitchen sink. Yet, we are what we eat, and if we do not know how to eat well we will inadvertently damage our wellbeing. Some government bodies recognise the problem – hence the British government presents the 'eatwell plate', describing the balance between different food groups in an ideal diet[19] in an effort to make it easy (à la Mrs Beeton) for people to make rational decisions in the supermarket. Any economist will point out that the consumer is not rational, not even close, so we should not be surprised to find evidence of irrational behaviour in the context of nutrition as in economics.

The recommended proportions of the main food groups in a healthy diet are 33 per cent starchy foods such as bread, rice, potatoes, or pasta (wholegrain when possible); 33 per cent fruit and vegetables; 15 per cent milk and dairy; 12 per cent non-dairy protein such as fish, meat, eggs or beans; and 8 per cent of foods high in fat or sugar. The typical UK shopping basket reportedly contains the following: starchy foods 19 per cent; fruit and vegetables 23 per cent; milk and dairy 21 per cent; non-dairy protein 13 per cent, and food and drink high in fat or sugar 23 per cent.[20] These statistics suggest that the British government's 'eatwell' plate has not been as widely adopted as hoped (we are back to the Stale Bread Act of 1801).

It is clear to see from this that if 15 per cent of the typical UK food basket spent on foods high in fat and sugar were reallocated to fruit and vegetables and bread/rice/potatoes, the average diet would be far healthier. The question is whether the food retailing industry could or should do anything to bring about this single, simple change to the typical contents of the shopping basket. Whilst the change is so simple it may appear to be the equivalent of the 'silver bullet' (a single easily wrought solution that is close to the perfect answer), in practice it is unlikely to be easy to bring this conversion about. To understand why, think of the writers of this book sitting in their respective lonely garrets. Imagine a hypothetical packet of chocolate-chip cookies hidden in the cupboard.[21] On the one hand, the packaging informs its owner that a single cookie contains 120 calories and a significant amount of 'bad' fat. On the other, the sight, smell and sounds associated with said packet of biscuits is overpowering. Availability (and the power of the sensory experience) trumps information every time and the packet of chocolate-chip cookies is consumed well before its sell-by date.

In contrast to the brown paper bag in which the typical grocer would serve up portions of cheese, meat or fruit, the food packaging associated with food on the supermarket shelf often contains reams of information on flavour, texture, provenance and nutritional content. In contrast to the brown paper bag in which reasonable portions would be served up in full sight of the queue of acquaintances, the anonymous supermarket provides hundreds of chocolate-chip cookies, without the social constraints that might once have constrained volumes purchased.

Leaving aside the attractions of the chocolate-chip cookie, the relative affordability of food is the likely driver of food purchasing decisions for less well-off households. In the credit crunch, UK consumers saved money on the weekly food shop by trading down; however, the least well-off bought less food, cutting back on several food groups (carbohydrates, fruit and vegetables, and meat), thereby cutting back on calories by almost 9 per cent,[22] but also dropping protein and micronutrients in the process.

With the arrival of a significant proportion of 'own label' goods on the shelf, there is no doubt that the food retailing and wholesaling industry is engaging with the consumer through the medium of food packaging. The nutritional information adorning every packet is without question useful. It is, however, only part of the answer. Ultimately, affordability and availability are likely to dominate many food purchasing decisions, and it is likely that the same point will apply to environmental considerations.

Indeed, if environmentally friendly or healthy food options are more expensive than their less environmentally friendly versions, it is likely that many consumers will go for the cheaper option. Hence, a 2012 UK survey[23] found that price dominated all other decisions; promotions, quality and familiarity were the next most important, followed by taste or smell and the use-by date. Environmental or ethical inputs came tenth – named by only 16 per cent of consumers as one of the 'top five influences' in food purchasing decisions.[24] The 'ethical' food-and-drink market in the UK amounted to a mere 5.5 billion pounds in 2010 – just 6.5 per cent of all food sales.

Food retail in the brave new world

The financial credit crunch has generated many forms of irrational behaviour on the part of consumers. Bank depositors who rushed to withdraw their deposits from the British bank Northern Rock in 2008 were in many cases acting irrationally (the government guaranteed most of the depositors who queued to get their money out). Similarly, because food is a high-frequency purchase, consumers seem to feel that focusing their time and energy on economising on their food budget is a rational response to the financial credit crunch (and the savings that economising on food will allow that same consumer to justify spending huge amounts of money on the latest smartphone upgrade).

Economising on food spending is rational, up to a point. From an environmental perspective it is very helpful – or it can be. But because food is a high-frequency purchase, and because consumers are disproportionately aware of the price of food, in times of economic difficulty consumers are disproportionately inclined to economise on food spending.

This desire to economise on the cost of food has any number of implications for consumption patterns – and that means, of course, consequences for the food retail sector. There has been a decline in the tendency to eat at pubs and restaurants, as a high-profile form of higher than normal food consumption spending. That works in favour of the supermarkets, which have tended to see an increase in the sale of high-end processed 'ready meals' – a luxury dish that can be put in the oven while a bottle of wine is uncorked (or unscrewed, in this day and age) in the comfort of one's own home.

Less favourable to the supermarket's traditional model, consumers have acquired a concern over food waste. We shall examine the economic and environmental implications of waste at the end of this book, but for now it is enough to know that consumers generally do not like waste at a time of heightened sensitivity about income and concerns about the household's economic stability. The financial credit crunch has led to an examining of household budgets, and of course throwing away food uneaten, or only partially eaten, is a peculiarly visible form of economic waste. It is also an environmental waste, and that may eat at the conscience of some consumers, but (as with most things in this life) economic considerations tend to be more powerful than environmental considerations.

So why does this concern about food waste matter so much? It matters because there has been a discernible change in consumer behaviour as a result of this. Consumers want to minimise food waste. One way of doing that is to stop buying food in large quantities on impulse, and instead buy food that is needed.

In theory this could still be achieved with a trip to the out-of-town supermarket, accompanied by a shopping list which one follows with a fanatical zeal. However, we have to consider that every fibre of the supermarket's being is striving to overcome such discipline on the part of the consumer. As hard as the consumer is trying to be disciplined, the supermarket is trying harder to persuade them to give into impulse and temptation, and to part with cash in a two-for-one special offer. Shopping lists are but a flimsy defence against the commercial instincts of the food retail business.

In addition, temptation comes in many forms. Planning on a Monday to eat a healthy meal of fish and salad on a Thursday is all very well, but what happens if one does not want to eat fish when Thursday comes around? What happens if one has been kept late in the office, trying to turn the latest pronouncements of the Bank of England into some kind of sense (a Sisyphean task), and one no longer has the time, the energy or the inclination to prepare the meal? Nothing saps willpower and healthy eating intentions like the Bank of England *Quarterly Bulletin*. We all know that a pizza is just a telephone call away, and can be delivered to the door within minutes (those minutes being spent in opening a bottle of wine and trying to forget). In such circumstances economic and environmental efficiency are cast to the winds, the fish is jettisoned, the salad consigned to the compost, and the pizza meal-deal is ordered.

Controlling food waste by careful planning does not seem readily compatible with the supermarket-based consumption patterns we have fallen into in OECD countries, because of course that is not what supermarkets are designed to encourage. Instead, consumers have adapted to control their waste with some kind of parody of the food shopping habits of yesteryear. Consumers are starting to shop for food on a daily basis, once again.

The return of the daily shop, without too many of the shops

Shopping at smaller stores never entirely disappeared from the consumer's activities. As well as the boutique stores selling specialist products, smaller convenience stores made virtue of the fact that they were convenient (the hint was in the name). If the cornucopia of bargain biscuits on offer at the supermarket led one to forget to buy milk in some kind of sugar-induced haze of absent-mindedness, a convenient and local convenience store could remedy that omission until the next supermarket visit.

What has now happened, in the United Kingdom at least, is that consumers have shifted some of their shopping away from the big once-a-week marathon in the local supermarket, towards a series of condensed sprints to local stores. In recent years, UK convenience stores (stores with a surface area of less than 3,000 square feet, selling a range of products) have been outperforming their larger supermarket brethren in terms of sales growth. Indeed, convenience stores hold more than a fifth of the food retail market share in the UK, a share that has been steadily rising during the financial credit crunch and its aftermath. The UK shopper is attempting to reduce food waste by buying food on a daily basis. Buying food because of daily need, rather than buying food because of an induced impulse and some abstract possibility of future need, is likely to be less wasteful.

Generally speaking, this return to higher-frequency purchases of food is a more urban phenomenon, as it requires the food convenience store to be fairly nearby. Preferably, the convenience store is either located near to the commuter train station or to the office. One buys the day's food supplies near to one's place of work, and transports them home to suburbia. Think of the hunter-gatherer killing a deer on the open plains before retreating to a cave to consume it.

The financial credit crunch has also brought with it longer working hours for many. This also encourages the idea of buying food near the workplace on a high-frequency basis, rather than doing a weekly shop at a supermarket some way from one's home. If one is working longer hours, the economic value of leisure time will increase – leisure is in short supply, and anything in short supply tends to become more valuable. The prospect of ten minutes a day in a local convenience store en route home is more attractive than the two hours of supermarket shopping (including travel to and fro) once a week. The time saving may not actually be that great, as some supermarket shopping will probably still have to take place, albeit with less frequency, but the perception is of leisure time saved.

Lest we should be fearful for the economic health and viability of the supermarket chains, it is worth observing that the fastest-growing sector among convenience stores is the supermarkets' own convenience stores. Indeed, in the UK the independent convenience stores have continued to decline in number in recent years, in spite of the rapid growth of the sector overall.[25] Of course, the supermarket chains have the advantage of buyer power, which enables them to keep costs low. Remember that one of the key motives for more frequent food consumption is household economy. Anything that can visibly reduce waste and do so at a lower price will be favoured.

The limits to high-frequency shopping

We should recognise that the shift to high-frequency shopping requires certain conditions, and it seems unlikely to become the dominant form of consumer spending on food (though it may increase further in importance in the future). This pattern of shopping requires an urban workforce, and one that is relatively geographically concentrated in terms of working. As we have already noted, unless the rural household has at least one worker in an urban environment, or unless there is a village shop perhaps attached to a petrol station, high-frequency food purchases are more difficult. Economically, the food retailer needs to have a relatively concentrated source of customers to make the model profitable. Daily convenience-store shopping is relatively well suited to the British working pattern (urban concentration, with commuting by public transport). It is perhaps less well adapted to a more American urban landscape, which is still Sports Utility Vehicle dependent for the most part and with less concentrated office areas and more urban sprawl.

Even with the concentrated urban environment, high-frequency shopping will probably be supplemented by visits to the out-of-town supermarket. Food for the weekend is less readily purchased on the daily convenience-store model, although of course there is always the option of takeaway pizza. We need more than just food, and daily convenience shopping may not be so convenient when purchasing cleaning items or cases of beer. Such supermarket shopping expeditions will still expose the consumer to all the risks of impulse buying. However, the risks of exposure are reduced with less frequent supermarket-based shopping expeditions, and thus both economic and environmental waste is reduced.

The consequences of high-frequency shopping

Let us start with the good news. High-frequency shopping should reduce food waste in the household. The consumer is buying food on a daily basis, and are therefore likely to buy what they need rather than what they impulsively think that they might like in the future. If one is buying the ingredients for one's dinner ahead of a half-hour commute home, it is relatively unlikely that the consumer is going to change their mind about consuming the food over the course of that journey. That makes the higher-frequency purchase of food both economically and environmentally efficient. Further, the consumer will reduce the number of car journeys that they take. The daily shopping expedition is done as part of existing travel arrangements, and the consumer will therefore need to undertake fewer journeys specifically to purchase food. Again, we have economic and environmental efficiency from the consumer.

Against this there are additional costs. The modern consumer is buying in a rush – one motive of higher-frequency purchases of food is to try and spend less time shopping. This biases the consumer towards more processed foods. One does not select three carrots from a pile in the convenience store – one buys the bag of pre-washed and pre-prepared carrot batons. Convenience stores know this, and of course the store may not give their customers the option of selecting from a pile of carrots. The bias to processed food is particularly likely if the store is small and floor space is at a premium. Heaps of carrots take up quite a lot of space and are not generally a high-profit-margin business. Bags of batons are higher-margin business.

The problem, as we have already discussed, is that processed food outsources the food waste business. The consumer is throwing away fewer carrots at home, but those pre-washed and packaged carrot batons may have entailed more waste in the food processing factory than would have occurred in the home. This is waste that the consumer does not control – the consumer is forced to waste food in purchasing processed and packaged product.

Associated with the processing, there is the economic and environmental cost of packaging. Buying more frequently involves buying in smaller quantities, of course. The small quantities still need to be packaged. There is a lot more packaging per apple selling two apples on a cardboard tray with a film cover, when compared with selling a plastic bag of ten apples. It is true that daily food purchases may require less use of plastic on high-turnover items. Cardboard will do just as well if something is going to be consumed within a relatively short time.

This is a peculiarity. The move from the traditional model of high-frequency purchasing from several stores to supermarket-based shopping led to an increase in processing and packaging (because food had to last for a week in the home environment). However, we are suggesting that the move from supermarket shopping to a higher-frequency model of shopping will also increase the processing and packaging component. Why is this? There are two forces at work. First, the consumer has become used to less food preparation, and with leisure time at a premium they are unwilling to save time in shopping merely to spend those precious minutes peeling a carrot. Second, the convenience store today is not the butcher, baker and grocer of yesteryear. Today's high-frequency consumer is not returning to the romanticised idyll of a daily gentle amble along a village high street in some parody of Agatha Christie's Miss Marple (without the murder). There is still an attempt to do one-stop shopping. Consumers want one-stop shopping, because we are coming to this shift after a generation that has known little else. One-stop shopping is also faster. This means, if not quite a 'pile, 'em high and sell, 'em cheap' approach, an emphasis on maximising the profit per square foot or square metre of retail floor space. The profitable conclusion is packaged and processed product sold at a premium.

There is also an economic and an environmental cost associated with transport in a modern high-frequency shopping culture. While the consumer may be reducing the frequency of their journeys, smaller convenience stores are likely to require more frequent supplies from their wholesaler or central distribution centre. The smaller store is likely to have less storage space, as a central urban location means that the cost of a large warehouse would be uneconomic, even assuming that that location could accommodate such storage. We are trading the out-of-town supermarket for the out-of-town food warehouse. Little and often is likely to be the hallmark of the urban convenience store's delivery schedule. This is generally considered to be economically and environmentally suboptimal – the most efficient is fewer journeys using larger lorries (for preference conducted at night to minimise the economic and environmental costs of traffic jams).

Finally, a move to higher-frequency retailing may create economic and environmental inefficiencies in the home environment. If one is buying food on a daily basis from a convenience store, one is effectively paying the retailer to store the food for one – they run the fridges and freezers necessary. However, as consumers we have not yet abandoned the fridges and freezers associated with food storage for the longer term. The American concept of a fridge with two storeys, chilled drinks provider and a small annex for cheeses still seems to be dominant. The fact that such monsters contain a forlorn pack of butter and a screw-top bottle of Chardonnay and nothing else means that they are inefficiently used.

One possibility for the future is the greater role for technology to play a part in this piece of the food food-chain. Some of the components are present but, speaking in general terms, not connected: internet shopping and home delivery, intelligent home appliances and ubiquitous mobile communication technology. The sadly neglected state of the refrigerator described above (possibly nicknamed Marvin after the paranoid android invented by Douglas Adams) prompts the idea that such equipment might play a more intelligent role. Thus, Marvin could interrogate the shopping habits of its owner, correcting for weaknesses such as an inability to leave chocolate-chip cookies uneaten, and electronically arrange for a home delivery of healthy food. Consumer and food might thus become differently connected. We do not expect such a dystopian arrangement to happen any time soon; however, we note the possibility for internet shopping with home delivery to bring efficiency gains somewhere in the system on the assumption that 'because I deserve it' impulse buys do not wipe them out.

The economics of acting on impulse

Food retail is obviously where consumers and food interact most visibly. In most developed economies we still predominantly purchase food for home consumption. The advent of supermarket shopping in the past century has pushed consumers towards the impulse-based purchase of food rather than the demand-based purchase of food, which no doubt helps to account for the growth in the staggering levels of food waste (which we shall bravely wade into in Chapter 10). The trend for less frequent shopping for food encouraged bulk buying, and changes in packaging and processing to facilitate longer periods of home storage. It is a symbiotic relationship, of course. Consumer demand encourages new packaging techniques, which further influence consumer demand patterns, which influence demands for additional packaging innovations, and so on.

Following the financial credit crunch, consumers seem to be returning to a pattern that has a higher element of high-frequency food purchases. This is a perversion of the old model of high-frequency purchases, of course. We are not going back to clusters of stores serving customers on a daily basis. Rather, we have goods clustering into the aisles of convenience stores. As a trend it is remedying some of the environmental challenges of modern food consumption, while simultaneously increasing or creating other problems. The sensible economic and environmental response is to recognise this change in the trend of consumption and adapt policies accordingly.

Packaging, economics and the environment

Consumers who visit their local market to buy fruit and vegetables carry home the produce unwrapped in the shopping bag, while those who go to the supermarket can find themselves bringing home a substantial amount of packaging. One of the writers has monitored the shelf life of fruit from two sources (the local market where there is often no packaging at all (not even a paper bag) and the local supermarket where fruit finds itself cocooned in plastic). The finding is that packaged fruit tends to last longer, thus the packaging reduces the amount of food not eaten to the apple core, but leaves the shopper with the packaging. Paying more for packaged fruit than fruit unpacked could save money for the householder as well as reducing food waste, depending on specific circumstances such as the frequency of shopping trips and the throughput speed of the household consuming its regulation five a day. Which route is better, in the round, will depend on what happens to leftover food packaging – is it reused (and how often) or sent to be reprocessed into other packaging (with energy and other costs).

Summarising, and generalising, the benefits of food packaging are that it contains the food for the journey home, preserves food quality and reduces the use of additives, and provides information about nutritional and other content.[26] As this suggests, reducing the environmental impact of food packaging is less simple than appears at first sight, when trade-offs may need to be taken into account.

The accidental shopper

The structural change to the way we shop in the past forty or fifty years has significantly increased the usage of fossil-fuel-powered transport in our food shopping. This is a consequence of social change in several quarters. Working and living patterns have changed. The shape of the average household has altered. Car transport has become widely available. This may be a sweeping generalisation for some readers but, in developed countries we suspect that very few of us trundle the shopping trolley along the high street, moving from shop to shop – we get into the car and drive in order to trundle a trolley round the supermarket aisles. In the supermarket, food choices are made on many bases, but probably not having much to do with food miles. The flipside of this is that twenty leading food retailers examined in a recent survey did not appear to set a high priority on helping the consumer reduce car travel to the supermarket. The stores in this study building e-commerce businesses did not appear to consider e-commerce as a means of optimising food-shopping-related travel.[27]

In the aftermath of the financial credit crunch, this has changed, at the margin – for instance, people are keen to support their local farming community in tough times, supporting local shops and local produce wherever bought. If one consequence of this is a reduction in the environmental impacts of transport and packaging, it is a good illustration of the point that environmental issues may very often have to be approached on the oblique. As the Bard put it so well: 'By indirections find directions out'.

Notes

1. Beeton (n.d.), p. 31.
2. Burnett (1966), p. 146.
3. de Vries (2008), p. 166.
4. Martin (1955), p. 176.
5. Yoo *et al.* (2006).
6. British Brands Group (2007).
7. Tukker et al. (2006).
8. des Abbayes *et al.* (2009).
9. Marks & Spencer, at http://plana.marksandspencer.com/about
10. Packard (1961), p. 92.
11. Ibid.
12. MarketLine (2012).
13. Fox and Vorley (2004).
14. Reardon and Gulati (2008) cited in Moomaw *et al.* (2012), p. 21.
15. The share of the top four UK players was 62 per cent in 2010, the largest player (Tesco) accounting for 23 per cent. See Department for Environment, Food and Rural Affairs (DEFRA) (2012a), p. 19.
16. Beeton (n.d.).
17. We have not yet experimented with apple butter in the middle of chocolate cake but may do so once we are not spending all of our spare time on this book. We also leave you to guess whose recipe is which – answers on a postcard please.
18. The above-mentioned great-aunt invited her fiancé-to-be to lunch with her parents. Salad was served, complete with a small green caterpillar. He, responding chivalrously to the gauntlet thrown down by his mother-in-law-to-be, discreetly rolled a lettuce leaf round the persistent creature and ate it. Readers finding this story hard to believe should know that this took place at a time when plates had to be cleared, leaving no place for extraneous protein to hide.
19. DEFRA (2012a).
20. Eatwell Plate, UK Department of Health (cited in DEFRA 2012a, p. 58).
21. The observant reader will note that our obsession with chocolate-chip cookies is a good illustration of some of the behavioural issues at work in this book.
22. DEFRA (2012a), p. 23.
23. Survey undertaken by Institute of Grocery Distribution (IGD) ShopperVista.
24. Cited in DEFRA (2012a), p. 29.
25. Institute of Grocery Distribution (2012).
26. de Leo (2000), p. 130.
27. des Abbayes *et al.* (2009), p. 36 (footnote).

8 Eating food

> When icicles hang by the wall
> And Dick the shepherd blows his nail
> And Tom bears logs into the hall
> And milk comes frozen home in pail,
> When blood is nipp'd, and ways be foul,
> Then nightly sings the staring owl:
> 'Tu-whit! Tu-whoo!' – a merry note
> While greasy Joan doth keel the pot.
>
> (Shakespeare, *Love's Labour's Lost*, V.ii)

Finally, after seven long chapters, we come to eating. You would think a book about food might have arrived at this point somewhat sooner in the process – but the length of the journey to get to the table (or the tray, or the kebab van) is rather the point both economically and environmentally. A whole lot has to happen to food before it ever makes it to our mouths.

We are *what*, *where*, *when*, *why* and *how* we eat. This is beautifully illustrated by the above quotation, which is about food as much as it is about contemporary society and seasonal weather. In the days of greasy Joan, *what* was eaten was shaped by agriculture, the seasonal climate of the day, prevailing cookery know-how and culture; *where* by social status; *when* and how by social convention; and *why* (subsistence, enjoyment or self-indulgence) by social status and wealth. What is visible in the personal, micro-level scale of this quotation can be seen today on a global, macro scale. In this century, wealth and culture shape meat consumption from one country to the next. In some countries the range of recipe books, kitchen equipment and ingredients available is enormously varied when compared with what was available just a few decades ago, when spaghetti came to UK consumers in tins with tomato sauce, and curries mostly arrived in packet form. The extent to which people eat out or at home (and where they eat out) is shaped by what can be afforded, as well as what is in fashion. As wealth increases, food tends to become a less significant part of the budget, but if it were possible to measure the mind-share taken up by food, it would be far larger than the 11 per cent it typically takes up for the UK consumer on the weekly budget (calculated as food consumed at home).

We may not always realise the extent to which what we enjoy eating is likely to be shaped by our history. Most obviously the recent past shaped what we got used to and enjoyed as children, but the tastes we prefer may go even further back than that. What our mothers ate during pregnancy is said to shape what we like as children and adults, perhaps explaining why some of us find it so hard to 'eat up our greens'. A fusion of culture and genetics may also have a part to play, suggesting that our food choices may be more instinctively than consciously made because they are partly determined by genetics. Gary Paul Nabhan describes different ethnic cuisines as driven by the evolutionary response to the availability of different food materials or, as he puts it, 'we are what our ancestors ate and also what they had to regurgitate'[1] as they found out what was safe and what was not. If eating the wrong thing was once a matter of life or death and thus had a bearing on the survival of the fittest, it is entirely natural that food be associated with strong emotions and reactions.

Food – a game of two parts

Eating food is a game of two parts – home or away. The economics of eating food at home are very different from the economics of eating food at a restaurant or using some other external form of catering. Similarly, the environmental consequences of eating out are very different from the consequences of eating in. Unsurprisingly, the consequences of the choices we make about where we eat and how we eat are intimately bound up with all of the earlier chapters (in many ways this book is a recipe of ingredients, and omitting any of the earlier stages of the recipe would make a disastrous nonsense of the later stages). To keep it simple, let us examine the economics of eating at home and the economics of eating away as distinct sections along with some of the environmental and nutritional consequences of modern eating habits.

Food at home – the economics of hierarchy

If we look at eating patterns around the world, the spectrum of what constitutes 'food at home' has a considerable breadth. Food at home in a developed economy is far more highly processed. Food in an emerging economy is far more likely to be raw ingredients. The way in which we eat at home is also carefully intertwined with the development of society and most particularly with economic status in society. It is not so much 'you are what you eat' as 'who you are dictates what you eat' (not as catchy as the original perhaps, but apposite). Interestingly, one of the trends within a developed society, as we saw in Chapter 5 on processing, is that lower-income groups are more likely to eat processed food, while higher-income groups have a higher proportion of raw ingredients. Why this pattern of consumption has evolved is itself a function of economic evolution.

Back in the Middle Ages the idea of eating at home was in some ways a hybrid of eating at home and eating away. The household that ate together stayed together (in theory), and the great houses of the time had something approaching a communal mess hall. In the larger household units people did not cook for themselves, but were catered for by the household for which they worked. Of course, this was not quite the common eating of the staff canteen. There were clear gradations of rank, with the position above or below the salt being one of the key distinguishing features. The wealthy and the nobility were seated above where the salt was placed on the table, with the poorer people sitting in graded order below it according to their station in life – concluding of course with the economists occupying the seats nearest the door. The quality and variety of the food served would be differentiated according to rank as well. Economic and social status dictated what and where one ate in the home.

Such gradations still linger on today – the seating plans of weddings, for instance. The order of precedence in British society has a corresponding table of precedence, dictating (by social rank) where the guests should sit around the table relative to the host and hostess. One cannot sit down anywhere at a formal dinner – and indeed the host and hostess should sit as far apart as the physical constraints of the table will allow. The American television sitcom *That '70s Show* had an episode dedicated to the importance of whether one sat at the 'adults" table or the 'children's' table at Thanksgiving dinner, with the status of moving between the two of paramount concern.

To a generation used to dinners on trays in front of the latest reality television experience, the concept of formal seating seems archaic, and of course in many ways it is. However, the concept of seating underscores the relationship between social and economic position and how and where one eats in the home.

Income inequality and eating inequality in the home

One version of the soldiers' ditty 'She was poor, but she was honest' from the First World War ran: 'It's the same the whole world over; it's the poor wot gets the blame; it's the rich wot gets the gravy; ain't it all a bleedin' shame?'. The consumption of food at home represents that difference, of course. The rich metaphorically bathed in gravy, while the poor worried about making ends meet. We can talk about generalised trends in the economics of food consumed at home, but the difference between sitting above the salt and below the salt became more and more marked when the different social classes did not occupy the same physical space. Jane Austen's Mrs Bennett in *Pride and Prejudice* (who had married into the gentry) prided herself on being able to offer two courses for a family dinner in a story set at the opening of the nineteenth century. Yet by the end of that century, in 1895, an arbiter of fashionable etiquette, Lady Jeune, could opine that no dinner should consist of more than *eight* courses.[2] Well, quite; one would not wish to overindulge. And yet just five years before this salutary advice was being offered to the British upper class, the UK could still record a death from starvation. Indeed, eighty years *after* the idea that one should stop at course eight, malnutrition was still being recorded in the UK.

Economic trends infiltrate the kitchen

By the eighteenth century the upper classes were getting somewhat tired of having to muck-in with the masses at meal times. Even if the food served was different, one did not necessarily want the local peasantry in the same room at dinner, gently wafting the mingled scents of the farmyard and honest toil over the proceedings. Clearly, it was far better for the 'quality' to be physically separated from the people who actually reared the animals and harvested the crops that one was eating. The upper classes went one way, and the lower classes went another.

The great houses of the nineteenth and early twentieth centuries still kept a catered element. The domestic staff of the house ate in the servants' hall, and frequently mimicked the rigid formality of the table of precedence of the dining room upstairs (the hideous complexity of the hierarchy of a servants' table of precedence formed part of the P. G. Wodehouse novel *Something Fresh*, published in 1915). Outside of this sphere, however, industrialisation and urbanisation led to changes in eating behaviour. Industrialisation, an economic process, can be considered the inspiration for the traditional English breakfast. The 'full English' is basically a gastronomic riot of meats – bacon, sausage (which often has an element of meat in it, even today), black pudding – with eggs for more protein, fried bread for carbohydrates and coronaries (fried in animal fat it should be noted) and maybe a decorative tomato; there is a lot of energy in such a dish. The reason, of course, was that this energy was required in the industrial workplace, and breakfast became the critical meal of the day. Lunch was skipped or constrained by working circumstances, and breakfasting on a croissant and a dab of jam was never going to be sufficient for those toiling in the dark satanic mills of the Industrial Revolution.

For the upper classes the meat was just as profuse, for energy was required to lord it over the lower social orders. A hunting breakfast at The Duke of Rutland's place in the country in 1853 included kidneys, fowl, salmon, sheep's tongue, rump steak, rice and ham croquettes, chicken in Béchamel sauce, potted game, pressed tongue, ham, sirloin of beef, roast snipe, roast woodcock, roast thrush (admittedly there is not much meat on a thrush) – and stuffed tomatoes (one always aims for the balanced diet). Of course, toast, marmalade, prunes and similar fruits were available. Cognac was provided for those who felt the need. This preceded a day's fox hunting with The Belvoir, and presumably gave the fox a sporting advantage by weighing down its pursuers.[3]

Similarly, urbanisation changed the options for cooking for many families. Essentially, urbanisation reduced the choices available. The peasant of the Middle Ages had access to wood for a fire close at hand (even if the rights to gather that wood were owned by the local baron). In the slums and tenements of the industrial urban landscape, the lower-class worker found that their access to fuel was effectively cut off. In addition, cramped urban living conditions meant that space for cooking was restricted. This forced the decision between eating at home or eating away by denying or constraining the former option in many instances. As we have already seen, by 1831 the more-urban Berkshire had one baker for every 295 people. At the same time, the more-rural environment of Cumberland had a baker for every 2,200 people.[4] Why was this? Well, space was one issue – having an oven at home requires a home large enough to take a kitchen range of some form. More importantly, fuel costs were a constraint on the Berkshire poor. Why heat a range at home when economies of scale could be obtained by a baker cooking the bread for one instead?

The constraints of eating at home continued long after the nineteenth century. In the East End of London in the inter-war years of the twentieth century, it was very common for families to take their Sunday dinner to the local baker on the way to church or the chapel, to be placed in the baker's oven. The food could be collected on the way back home (and of course, the longer the sermon the greater the risk of a dry roast or burnt pie crust).

What we are seeing, throughout history, is the way in which the structure of the economy leads the structure of our food consumption at home. The great British public did not wake up one morning and decide to abandon their grain-based porridge at breakfast for a protein-based meat diet to start the day. The practical demands of industrialisation dictated that is what happened. Similarly, abandoning home-baked bread was not the result of a disinclination to knead dough in an era before electric bread-makers – the time constraints that industrialisation imposed on the workforce, coupled with the constraints of access to fuel and space for a range, created the shift. Economics leads food consumption patterns, which in turn creates new economic trends.

Economics leads, of course, but the problem with food is that politics interferes. Politicians are sensitive to food consumed at home, because their electorate is sensitive to it.

Panem et circenses *in the twenty-first century – food, politics and inflation inequality*

One area of food eaten at home that is peculiarly important to economics is the role that food plays in inflation inequality. Income inequality is generally well understood – 'it's the rich wot gets the gravy' and so forth. However, while the rich may get the gravy they also spend proportionately less of their income on gravy – or on any form of food at home – than do those of a lower income.

Why does this matter? It matters because inflation is a plutocratic rather than a democratic statistic, calculated on the basis of one pound/dollar/euro, one vote. One literally buys one's voting power in the election of goods and services to the Consumer Price Index (CPI). In the UK the rate of inflation is calculated using a weighting of 11 per cent for the food that is consumed at home. The bottom 20 per cent of the population by income distribution spend 17 per cent of their income on food, however. The top 20 per cent spend 8 per cent. The average weight ascribed to food consumed at home is clearly a lot closer to the top income group's weighting than it is to the weighting of the bottom income group. That is because 8 per cent of the top income group's disposable income is a great deal more in absolute terms than is 17 per cent of the bottom income group's disposable income. The top income group therefore has more votes when it comes to determining the shape of the average CPI basket.

In the past this inequality in the pattern of goods consumption has not mattered too much. The general tendency was for the inflation rate of things bought by lower-income groups to broadly equal the inflation rate of things bought by higher-income groups over time. However, the past couple of decades have seen a more noticeable shift. The prices of food consumed at home (along with energy and housing costs) have tended to rise more rapidly than have the prices of other goods and services – and have done so consistently over time. Because food (and energy and housing) are far more important to the low-income groups than to the high-income groups this means that lower-income groups experience a higher rate of inflation than higher-income groups. Average inflation typically does not represent the inflation of someone at the midpoint in the income level – but someone quite close to the top (around 70 per cent up from the bottom rung, as a rule). Anyone below that rung is likely to have a higher than 'average' inflation rate, and food plays no small part in that process. Put another way, it is more expensive to be poor.

Food consumed at home plays a very important part in the relative inflation inequality. Food is a high-frequency purchase, which means people are disproportionately sensitive to its price. It is more important to lower-income groups – and indeed more important than official statistics would suggest for a majority of the population. This is why the price of food consumed at home is so important politically – and why politicians have a strong incentive to provide economically cheap food almost without regard to the environmental costs. It is hardly a new trait – we are repeating the *panem et circenses* of Cicero once more. The circuses are replaced by reality television today, but the bread is still bread; consumed at home, its economic and political importance is disproportionately dominant.

Thus, the importance of food consumed at home for a democratic majority of the population has a bearing on politics, which has a bearing on policy, which has a bearing on economics, which has a bearing on the environment. This is the food-chain that matters most perhaps – but it is a food-chain where the political expediency of economic short-termism makes the environment the residual consideration – almost an incidental outcome of the process.

Food at home today – space, time and money

The post-industrial modern urban consumer has constraints on their home consumption of food that are not too dissimilar to those faced by their industrial forebears. Modern kitchens are often advertised as the 'heart of the home' in property programmes and magazine articles. The reality is that some modern developments have kitchens that barely go beyond the provision of a microwave and a fridge to chill the wine. Smaller living spaces reduce the cooking options available. The increase in single-person households encourages this trend. Heating an oven to cook a meal for one person, even if the food comes with all the incentive to consume exhibited by the oven chip we encountered in Chapter 5, is a very visible manifestation of waste. Better to go for a microwave.

What happens in the kitchen and at the table is driven by technological innovation as well as economics. Innovation in cooking equipment has arisen in part because the way energy is delivered to the household has changed, and in part because of innovations made in industry as in the kitchen. Such equipment facilitates the cooking of food to make it easier to eat; however, easy eating may come at the price of reduced nutritional value. When vegetables are cooked in boiling water or steamed, micronutrients leach into the cooking water and thus the nutritional value of the content is diminished. If the water is used elsewhere – for instance as vegetable stock as a base for gravy, soups or stews, or even given to children to drink as 'greens water' – some of the nutrients can be salvaged. Some micronutrients – such as vitamin B_{12} – are changed from active to passive forms when exposed to heat.[5] Some nutrients respond differently to being cooked in the microwave or on the stove. Unfortunately, there is no easy rule-of-thumb, other than to take the temperature no higher than necessary, to cook raw ingredients no longer than necessary, and to recycle the liquids in which food is cooked. The availability of pre-packaged stock cubes or gels may mean that cooking liquids tend to be sent down the drain, taking valuable micronutrients with them.

Use of new technologies like the microwave is also driven by other manifestations of economics. The modern consumer is increasingly time poor, hence the desire to outsource food preparation. Why not speed the process up further, and go for food in under five minutes? The time and effort, and energy required (human and heating) to produce from scratch a full-scale meal for one, or even for two, is measured in the scales against the preparation simplicity of a single-person ready meal, put into the microwave and providing almost instant gratification. It is like the chocolate biscuit in the vending machine all over again. We will return to this topic of time poverty with the gripping 'Tale of Three Fisherman's Pies' a little later in the chapter, but for now we just need to acknowledge that the economic climate has increased the time poverty of many – as families see more people working, and working for longer. It is no surprise to learn that sales of ready meals, which are often though not exclusively destined for the microwave, have grown faster than overall food sales during the aftermath of the economic downturn. The UK saw ready meal sales outstripping overall food store sales in 2010 and 2011 – once the slow recovery from economic downturn had made longer working hours a more frequent feature of the household.

The economics of modern food consumption (smaller households, time poor, in smaller living spaces) then pushes back up the food food-chain. The use of the microwave encourages the production and sale of processed food, and packaged food. Eventually, the household infrastructure starts to close off options for food preparation. Just as today few people would consider roasting potatoes in the embers of a kitchen fire (the lack of a kitchen fire being something of a handicap in this regard), so in the future the design of kitchens may push consumers into the embrace of microwave ready meals – anything else being impractical in the absence of alternative means of cooking. It is the tale of the nineteenth-century urban worker denied access to wood, updated to the modern age.

Economics can also dictate what a modern family chooses to eat. In the 1930s, mortality rose amongst those who moved out of the slums of Stockton-on-Tees in the north of England.[6] The reason was that the new housing, though superior in quality, was more expensive to rent and further from places of work. The family budget for food, after paying for rent and travel, was smaller than it was for slum dwellers and so the quality and quantity of food eaten declined. In the twenty-first century we encounter similar problems. A chocolate biscuit can be cheaper than an apple in a school lunch. Moreover, a pack of five chocolate biscuits can be readily divided to provide a daily 'treat' over a week. Half an apple (sold at an equivalent cost) is less appealing when it is the second half of the apple and when it is being consumed on the second day.

So the economics that style modern food consumption are not that different from the economics that styled food consumption in the past.

Even an environmentalist has to admit economics shape what, when, how and where we eat

Consider the tired economist wending his weary way home after a hard week in pursuit of economic enlightenment by plane, train and automobile. This is a person with no time to shop for decent food. Tearing the film from a microwaved double portion of Fisherman's Pie, after less than five minutes of preparation time, does not have the romantic resonance of taking a hearty home-made Fisherman's Pie piping hot from the oven. However, a home-made pie is a great deal more time-intensive in preparation and to indulge in 'home-cooked' food would mean eating around midnight. Even if it is possible to get home at a decent time, time is money and the cost of two hours' preparation and cooking time required to deliver the home-made version can seem prohibitive when set against the two minutes of effort it takes to heat up the ready meal version. Time-is-money economics drives the way in which a great many modern meals are prepared and eaten.

Delia Smith, writing in 2008, describes a younger generation not taught how to cook, and suggests that changing lifestyles requires a rethink of the way cooking is done. In *How to Cheat at Cooking* she does not present processed food and food made from scratch as polar opposites – rather, her solution is to cook imaginatively by using a combination of pre-prepared and fresh food in such a way as to save time.[7] The Fisherman's Pie recipe in the book is compared with two others, in Table 8.1.

Table 8.1 The tale of three Fisherman's Pies

Input	Cooking from scratch[a]	Cooking with help – or how to cheat at cooking[b]	Choosing not to cook – the ready meal[c]
Ingredients:	Filling: 30% of total uncooked weight, of which 18% white fish; 12% prawns; salt and pepper; a little beaten egg Sauce: 22% of total weight, of which 2% butter; 2% flour; 17% milk; 1% chopped parsley; salt and pepper Topping: 49% of total weight, of which 45% potatoes; 1% butter or margarine; 3% hot milk	Filling: 53% of total uncooked weight, of which 22% prepared firm white fish; 11% frozen peeled raw tiger or king prawns; 10% frozen scallops; 7% dry vermouth; 0.7% fresh chopped dill; 1.5% cornichons Sauce: 15% ready-prepared fresh cheese sauce Topping: 32% Aunt Bessie's home-style frozen mashed potato; Cayenne pepper; parmesan cheese	Ingredients list on packaging (flaked cod and haddock in a creamy sauce): 12% haddock; 9% cod; 30% cheese sauce; 43% mashed potato; 5% cheese crumb
Cooking time and temperature: (Fuel energy used in preparation = 30 minutes on stove top)	Preheat the oven (10 minutes) Potatoes: cook in boiling water	Preheat the oven (10 minutes) No separate cooking time for potatoes	Preheat the oven (10 minutes) No separate cooking time for potatoes
(Fuel energy used in baking depends on the type of oven)	Baking: 50–60 minutes, 190°C (for a fan oven, reduce temp by 25°C and time by 5–10 minutes)	Baking: 40 minutes at 220°C (reduce for fan oven)	Oven from chilled: 190°C (gas mark 5), 30–35 minutes. Oven from frozen: 190°C, 50–55 minutes (reduce for fan oven)
Human energy applied in the kitchen:	Skin and debone the fish and cut into chunks. Wash fish and prawns, blot dry. Peel potatoes, cook, then mash with butter and	Fish is already prepared and cut. Simmer frozen prawns and scallops from packaging (usually	Remove sleeve (can be recycled) and film lid (cannot be recycled). Put into preheated oven, remove from

(Continued)

Table 8.1 (Continued)

	hot milk. Make white sauce. Place fish and prawns in ovenproof dish, cover with sauce. Place mashed potato over the top, decorate with a fork. Bake (brush with beaten egg after 30 minutes)	cannot be recycled) with the vermouth in a frying pan (5–10 minutes). Remove prawns and scallops and boil the sauce to reduce it to 2 tablespoons in volume. Arrange everything in the dish, season, add sauce, cover with ready-made mashed potato	the oven at the appointed time, stand to cool. (Container may become flexible when hot)
	Recycle skin bone and peelings as appropriate – e.g. fish stock can be prepared for later; potato peelings could feed chickens, if any	No peelings or cut-offs left to recycle. Recycle packaging where applicable	Recycle sleeve, check local recycling for tray, and put film lid into 'cannot be recycled' waste bin
	Time taken to collect ingredients (est.): approx. 1 hour Preparation time: approx. 1 hour Total time taken: about 3 hours 15 minutes	Shopping time: 10 minutes within weekly shopping trip Preparation time: 20 minutes Total time taken: about 80 minutes	Time taken to select: approx. 5 minutes within weekly shopping trip Total time taken: 40–60 minutes (not a microwaveable dish)
Portions:	Serves 4–6	Serves 6	Serves 2
Nutrition:	Protein, carbohydrates, micronutrients, fat (unsaturated and saturated). Fat and salt levels can be adjusted by the cook, who can reduce the amount of saturated fat by avoiding butter or cheese and keep salt to a minimum	Protein, carbohydrates, micronutrients, fat (unsaturated and saturated). Fat and salt levels depend on what is in the cheese sauce and mashed potato	Per portion: 416 calories, protein 27.6g; carbohydrates 34.3g; sugars 3.2g; fat 18g (of which 10.6g saturates); fibre 3.2g; salt 1.5g

Sources: [a] Creda (n.d.); [b] Smith (2008); [c] packaging of a Morrisons' Fisherman's Pie.

Note: Recipe percentage calculations may not add up to 100% due to rounding.

Cooking decisions and trade-offs

The 'Tale of Three Fisherman's Pies' set out in Table 8.1 is not to suggest that any of the above approaches to putting a meal on the table is superior. What the 'Tale' does is force us to consider the trade-offs involved: enjoyment and availability of time for the cook; the availability (or otherwise) of willing potato-peeling, sauce-making helpers; energy and resource use; ingredient choices; nutrition; and flavour. Delia Smith's 'middle way' reduces both preparation time and sweated labour for the cook by 'delegating' (an economist would say 'outsourcing') the ancillary jobs – vegetable-peeling and sauce-making – to the food-processing industry. This is compensated for with the addition of vermouth and cornichons to give a few tweaks to the flavour. The 'proper' cook might regard the potential loss of vegetable stock and the like as nutritionally wasteful. Those teaching children to cook might regard the use of pre-packaged mashed potato and cheese sauce as a wasted opportunity to practice developing culinary skills. However, the middle way does certainly give the individual more control over the contents of what they are eating than depending entirely on processed food.

The more a meal is prepared from scratch, the more control the cook has over the contents. The health-conscious cook might decide to avoid salt, saturated fats or indeed the trans-fats found in hydrogenised vegetable oil. Avoiding such products is an option for home cooking. Against that, precision in respect of calories, fibre, protein and micronutrients is not available to the home cook. There is more immediately available information per portion on the packaging of the ready meal version of the fish pie. The cook starting from scratch is relying on rules-of-thumb designed to deliver a well-balanced diet designed to allow the human body and brain to grow and function properly.

What, when, how and where we eat affects mind and body

It was Adelle Davis, American nutritionist and writer, who said that one should breakfast like a king, lunch like a prince and dine like a pauper. The traditional English breakfast we have already encountered – of both factory worker and fox-hunting aristocrat – is meat focused, and has high protein content. Davis described experiments in which people's blood sugar was measured after different kinds of breakfast. Unsurprisingly, the forces of economics that pushed the British towards a high-protein breakfast actually led to the most productive worker. We summarise Davis's conclusions in Table 8.2.

The adage Adelle Davis left behind for later generations is most often cited in the context of healthy eating. It suggests that we are not only what we eat. It gives a particular redolence to the idea that we are what, when, why, where and how we eat. The nutritional mix and timing of food consumption through the day has an influence on the energy 'bang for bucks' we extract from food consumed, determining how much of what we eat will spend a minute in the mouth, an hour in the stomach and a lifetime on the hips. Eating well means feeling well. Eating badly can result in feeling under par, and has unwelcome health effects we shall explore in a later chapter. Suffice it to say, nutrition and diet are key concerns in

Table 8.2 Breakfast like a king

Breakfast type	Impact
Coffee only	Low energy levels, irritability, nervousness, tiredness, headaches (Environmentalists never start the day on this sort of starvation diet)
High carbohydrate and sugar, low protein	Inefficiency and tiredness (Environmentalists cycle to work which forces them to eat proper food for breakfast, rendering this diet impractical)
High protein	A sense of well-being; high efficiency (A well-fed environmentalist is a happy environmentalist, if such a concept is not oxymoronic)

Sources: Davis (1979), p. 8; authors.

the kitchen and at the table – something Mrs Beeton was well aware of and thought carefully about when putting together recipes and menus.

We are where and when we eat

Traditionally, breakfast, lunch and dinner are more than opportunities to consume food. They are also social occasions allowing family, friends or co-workers to gather round, catch up and relax. All do not relish such occasions, of course – Winston Churchill and his wife are said to have avoided breakfast to avoid wrecking their marriage. The existence of the 'TV dinner' suggests that some would rather commune with the TV than with other people. Even in countries where lunch is a prized daily occasion, the number of families gathering round a table two or three times a day for meals is rarer than it once was, and the increasing number of single-person households suggests that many meals are likely to be solitary affairs. Solitary eating leads to solo food procurement, and when this is undertaken on the basis of processed or pre-packaged food, it can lead to over-eating (the two portions of fish pie ravenously devoured at the end of a long day) or waste (where the virtue of self-control may come at a cost of more food waste).

We are what we eat – so what on earth are we eating?

The fact is that the consumer cannot readily ascertain whether nutritional content is better or worse when consuming a diet made up mostly of processed food rather than one made up of so-called 'slow food'. The 'Tale of Three Fisherman's Pies' illustrated that it is actually much more work to find out about the nutritional content of a home-prepared meal than for a processed version.

Popular perceptions are that home cooking is obviously best from a nutritional perspective; but this conclusion requires trust in the quality of the ingredients purchased to make the dish. Emotional as this decision may be, it is not entirely irrational.

Visiting the farmers' market to buy fish, potatoes, cheese, and vegetables for the side dish, the queue waiting to buy these food ingredients would stand as testimony to their quality. The stallholder should be able to describe in detail where the fish came from, and how it was bred, and what it was fed upon. Against that verbal assurance we have the problems of adulteration recounted in Chapter 5.

Cooks often work on the basis of a rule-of-thumb, adjusting recipes so that what is available can be used, or to find the right taste or texture. Delia's *How to Cheat at Cooking* is a version of this – she does not only look to minimise effort. Maximising flavour is also an important goal. The great-grandmother of one of the authors showed an absolute disregard for the calorific consequences of adjusting a favourite dessert recipe, reducing the amount of flour and increasing the amount of treacle in order to produce a nice gooey ginger sponge pudding recipe.[8] Considering the likely working regime of her immediate family, it is unlikely many of said calories would have the temerity to hang around on anyone's hips – they were too busily fuelling hard physical work.

The same point applies to the environmental footprint of the dish. Bearing in mind that the lion's share of environmental impact is found at the stage of food procurement and production, the environmentally conscious consumer needs to know about what happened in the supply chain. Food manufacturers and retailers are under pressure from consumers for greater transparency with respect to the food food-chain. When such information is disclosed, reading the label is more easily accomplished than making a trip to the local farm – unless, of course, food is bought from a farm shop (although farm shops will often stock produce from a wider geographic area). The consumer does still have to rely on the label being accurate, which may not always be the case.

Even an energetic search for a recipe book that details the carbon footprints for individual recipes has proved to be fruitless, so far. This might be because there is little demand for such a book – although it might also simply reflect the complexity of the environmental impact of food that this book has attempted to detail. When it comes to controlling environmental impacts, a practical, broad-brush approach tends to be taken in modern-day recipe books. On balance this is a good thing: an environmental footprint can raise as many questions as it answers, whereas a good sound rule-of-thumb can get to the right place. Amanda Woodvine's *Didsbury Dinners: The Low-Carbon Community Cookbook*[9] is, at first sight, disappointing for the cook seeking recipe-by-recipe guidance on the subject of environmental footprints and nutritional balance. However, a more careful reading finds a book organised to allow the cook to use what is in season, alongside a number of sensible rules-of-thumb. Hugh Fearnley-Whittingstall, writing in *The Guardian*, suggested similar rules-of-thumb: buy ingredients locally or seasonally whenever possible; where possible, grow your own vegetables; use gas rather than electricity (because gas is less carbon-intensive and in winter incidental heat does a better job of warming the room); cook several things at the same time – for instance a casserole for use later in the week could be cooked at the same time as the main meal; and where possible use leftovers.[10] (We note the 'middle way' style of cooking or eating ready meals need not preclude efficient use of leftovers – but, the cook has less control over what happens to some of them.)

Other things being equal, the well-established 'sustainable food' rules-of-thumb should lead to a less fuel intensive, less wasteful approach to cooking. None of this is rocket science, and none of it is new. Several of these rules would have been obvious to cooks of previous generations, seeking where possible to maintain the stock, stew-pots and soups designed to eke every last bit of nutrition out of food. Some of us remember our mothers and grandmothers used to work on the basis of a weekly 'baking day' and owned a stack of cake tins (now often found selling second-hand in flea markets) designed to keep the output fresh until it was needed.[11] Of course there were also recipes designed to use stale bread crumbs, stale cake, or sour milk, ensuring that no money or food were wasted.

The discerning reader will by now have spotted the fact that this is a good-news-bad-news story. On the positive side there is no need to spend hours slaving over a hot keyboard, inputting carbon emissions and nutrient values into a spreadsheet whilst stirring the Béchamel sauce with the other hand. On the other hand, following the rules-of-thumb proposed by the supporters of so-called slow (or slower) food requires different working patterns to those followed by many of us. Continuing with the bad news story, the financial credit crunch may well free up enough time for some people to cook from scratch by throwing them out of a job. For all but the most enthusiastic cooks this is unlikely to be much of a consolation for lost employment. For those in employment, the risk is that the financial credit crunch reduces the time available for preparing food.

What this suggests is that the rules-of-thumb described above need to be internalised by those who have the scale to adopt them. The restaurant, school, workplace, hospital and institutional canteen have significant power to influence where, what, how and when we eat in ways that could be positive for both taste and nutrition, but may not always be as things stand.

Eating out

Eating out – what economists call with precision 'food away from home' in all their data – is a different issue. Unless one's house space is so constrained as to reduce a kitchen to nothing, eating out is a choice. It is, moreover, a choice that is closely tied to economics. The economics of eating out is generally the economics of luxury spending. It is also a form of spending that can readily find a substitute. This means that eating out is a trend that is highly sensitive to the economic cycle.

The necessity or desirability of eating away from home starts with the structure of the economy. The United Kingdom saw the development of coaching inns as a means of providing sustenance to travellers in the seventeenth and particularly the eighteenth centuries. This was partly because the suppression of the monasteries created a gap in the market for hospitality, and partly as the early industrialisation of the UK encouraged more communication and intra-national trade. The UK was notable for not having internal trade barriers and customs tolls, in contrast to other countries – even unified countries. Trade and internal communication flourished, and with it the need for sustenance en route. It was not going to be convenient to carry all one's supplies with one while travelling around the country engaged in trade – hence the rise of the inn.

The necessity of eating away from home today continues with the staff canteen – where such entities still exist – or the chains of sandwich shops that jostle for space on the high streets of even relatively small towns. Our working practices encourage eating out. One can take sandwiches to work, of course, but it is less common than once it was. Sandwich sales rose 6 per cent in the United Kingdom in 2012 and 3.25 billion 'commercial' (as opposed to 'amateur') sandwiches are sold in the United Kingdom each year.[12] Why is this? Again we come back to the poverty of time in the household. Single-person households working longer hours, one-and a-half- or two-income households with both adults in some kind of employment – the reduced leisure time is theoretically still compatible with the idea of making sandwiches for work. In practice it is not a process that is encouraged.

This economic drift towards shop consumption increases the amount of money spent on food. The addition is not, of course, an increase in the price of the raw ingredients of a sandwich. The increase is in the cost of the packaging, the cost of the shop premises (with all the associated overheads of heating, lighting and so forth), and of course the cost of labour. That combination takes the sandwich we consume at lunch time further and further away from the concept of food as food – we have added several additional layers of humanity into the process.

The process also lessens the consumer's economic and environmental control of what they eat. Is the ham in the sandwich humanely reared? Locally produced? Organic? Or is it the cheapest available that is commensurate with an acceptable level of taste – particularly if that taste is combined with avocado, brie and grapes (or whatever fantastical combination the retailer has dreamt up under the desire to generate the illusion of gastronomic sophistication). The consumer is unlikely to have much of a say in the matter – there is a choice of foodstuffs presented to them, but the content of each foodstuff is beyond their control. Even the American sandwich shops which allow you to 'Build your own sandwich' are more about an illusion of economic choice. The key choices have already been made for the consumer by the food retailer. How those pre-selected ingredients are combined is of scant economic or environmental significance.

Perhaps nothing is more redolent of the economics of catering dictating our choices than the chicken (the filling of 30 per cent of UK commercial sandwiches). The glamorous lifestyle of a global economist is often dominated by the 'rubber chicken circuit' – a series of (catered) meals at which the economist is required to present their views, but rarely allowed to eat the food. Those lucky enough to hear the economist and to eat at the same time are often served chicken, because it is cheap, versatile, and easy to cook and keep warm (up to a point). The 'rubber chicken' sobriquet is well deserved. In the UK roughly half the chicken that is consumed is used in catering in some form.[13] America slaughters twenty-three million chickens per day (sic).

The economics of catering therefore dictate the economics of farming, and have served to encourage battery-chicken production. The diner at an economics dinner loses control over this process; it may well be that the economics acolytes attending a formal dinner would never dream of purchasing anything other than a free-range, organic chicken for their home consumption. As soon as they are catered to, they lose that element of choice.

In extremis, consumers can wrest control by choosing to boycott a restaurant chain over their choice of food ingredients. This is, however, a relatively rare circumstance. Nevertheless, the consumer can exercise some power to bring about change through the oxygen of publicity.

Box 8.1 **School dinners**

Martha Payne, nine years old in 2012, is the author of the school meal blog called *NeverSeconds*.[14] Her illustrated school lunch reviews are 'direct' on the subject of school meals' taste and nutrition. She built an international following of like-minded bloggers. Her delighted father (an enthusiastic grower of food and able family cook) nevertheless worried about contradictions in the blog. Martha's food preferences were clearly being shaped by forces outside the family home.

Through this imaginative initiative Martha hoped to raise a few hundred pounds to help the charity Mary's Meals feed African children. She could not have foreseen what happened: following a heavy-handed attempt to shut down her website, her story went viral and her blog attracted some seven million website hits.[15] Martha's story addresses many issues at the core of this chapter for it brings together a love of delicious food and a dislike of bad food with present-day concerns about institutional food and nutrition, with the guilty awareness of food insecurity in far-away countries many of us associate with being urged to clear our plates in childhood, with, in turn, the desire to do something about unequal access to good nutrition in less fortunate communities.

Martha's story also of course testifies to the fact that feelings run high on the subject of food. Even if we have enough self-discipline to keep to the principle of eating to live rather than living to eat, the strong link between food and the emotions is hard to ignore. Nowhere is this clearer than in the kitchen and at the table. Home is where the heart is, the kitchen is traditionally the heart of the home. In the experience of the authors all the best parties tend to migrate to the kitchen. And indeed, Martha's story illustrates that an enjoyment of food sufficient for those fortunate enough to know where the next meal is coming from to engage fully with the task of serving up good, nutritious food is at least half the battle when it comes to eating to live well.

There is evidence that the environmental and nutritional issues described above are recognised and some are trying to do something about them. Food produced in the work canteen, a school or university cafeteria, or on planes, trains or boats, these days often has nutritional and environmental labelling, and some of the menus describe the produce as sustainably sourced or as having a low environmental footprint. Nevertheless, speaking in general, environmental and nutritional performance in these contexts is more likely to be driven by economics or operational constraints. Thus, on the plane, biscuits or salty snacks are more likely to be provided than fruit because they weigh less. On the plane or the train, menus will tend to be constrained to what will warm up easily. Costs will tend to be cut as much as possible post the financial credit crunch, when food is delivered bundled up as part of the price of a ticket.

Changing economics and changing consumption

What are the trends in eating at home versus eating away? The aftermath of the global financial credit crunch has generally led to an increase in time poverty for those households that have work. As a result, the consumer is unlikely to eschew the purchased food for their workday lunch. This is a daily necessity. The substitute – home-produced food taken to the office – is considered too expensive in terms of the time required – making sandwiches every night is considered a chore, and it is a chore that can be avoided for relatively little cost. However, when it comes to more serious eating out, the economics of the post-financial-credit-crunch world are quite different.

Properly eating out is a different concept from buying a sandwich for lunch. Eating out in this sense is an obvious luxury item. The decision to eat out is (for most households) an occasional experience, and associated as much with leisure as with the necessity of ingesting (or imbibing) the requisite number of calories per day. The alternative is to eat at home in the evening or at the weekend. The act of eating out entails even more costs to put into the economic chain. Restaurant dining requires larger premises per calorie sold than does takeaway food. It is a more labour-intensive process. The costs of land and labour must be reflected in the cost of the food that is eventually procured by the aspiring gourmand. The very act of cooking food for sale may also be more energy-intensive as restaurants have an incentive to make sure (for instance) meat is well cooked and bacteria-free. The cost of undercooked meat at home is a stomach complaint. The cost of undercooked meat at a restaurant is a stomach complaint, a visit from the health inspector, reputational damage to the business and sometimes financial losses or outright closure.

This, incidentally, is why so many companies' travel policies for their staff are sometimes problematic. Staff travelling on business are often given a *per diem* budget for food, along the lines of teenagers being given an allowance. That budget for food may look generous to someone who is providing their own labour on their own premises. If one is unable to prepare one's food oneself, the additional land and labour costs associated with eating in a hotel or even an airport restaurant make the comparison invalid. The whole allowance may in fact be completely exhausted in purchasing a hotel breakfast, which would cost very little to prepare at home.

These economic costs are also environmental costs. A restaurant meal generally consumes more power than an equivalent meal produced at home (the lights are on in the restaurant regardless of how many patrons there actually are; the ovens in the kitchen are heated in anticipation of customers). In America, restaurants account for almost 16 per cent of the fossil fuel used in the food supply chain, while food prepared at home absorbs 25 per cent.

Eating out as a leisure activity is something that is peculiarly vulnerable to the consequences of the financial credit crunch. Eating out is an obvious luxury in terms of consumer spending. Prior to the financial credit crunch it could also be considered to be a relatively high-frequency leisure activity. That combination is potentially fatal in an age of austerity, particularly when there are ready substitutes to hand. Any high-frequency purchase assumes disproportionate importance in the mind of the consumer, and as they seek to economise it is just such spending that falls prey to the constraints of the household budget.

What has happened has been a classic substitution effect. The expensive meal out is abandoned. By economising on eating away from the home the costs (land cost, serving staff, lighting, ambience and so forth) are cut from the household budget. Of course, the consumer is not likely to fast as an alternative, but to purchase a ready meal from a supermarket and suitable bottle of wine for home consumption. Essentially, the food costs are still the same – most of the preparation is outsourced (as with restaurant eating), the range of meals is not dissimilar to the restaurant, and it is prepared to a consistent quality. The consumer cuts out the extraneous costs, heats at home, puts an appropriate soundtrack onto the iPod and imagines themselves to be having a fine dining experience.

The financial credit crunch has therefore produced yet another economic effect that has environmental consequences. Since the start of 2008, spending in the UK on food away from home has fallen by 8.8 per cent, while food consumed at home has risen 15.4 per cent. The financial credit crunch has changed where we eat, and how we eat, through its impact on consumer psychology. The changing consumer patterns have at least contributed to the ongoing decline in pubs in the UK (there are fewer than 50,000 public houses in the UK compared with over 60,000 in 2000[16]). This may incidentally reduce the environmental consequences of food consumption, although it means that there is a greater onus on controlling the environmental costs of ready meals, as the substitute for external catering.

We should not assume that trends are inexorably broken. It is perfectly possible that the inclination to consume food away from home will return as economic growth recovers. The longer the economy remains anaemic, however, the more ingrained the current more home-focused consumption patterns are likely to become, and the more likely it is that the nexus of environmental and nutritional issues arising from modern food habits will be addressed at home.

This chapter would be incomplete without a mention of the efforts of a small number of imaginative entrepreneurs to engineer a shift in food culture.

Seeking economies of scale – community food

In recent years, awareness of environmental and nutritional issues relating to dishes issuing from the modern kitchen has resulted in community-based social-enterprise approaches to food buying. As an example The People's Supermarket (in London) aims to set up an 'alternative food buying network' by connecting the urban community with the farming community.[17] The Fife Diet was started up in the autumn of 2007 in Scotland by a local Fife man and nineteen other environmental devotees who set out to reduce the carbon footprint of meals.[18] The aim of this network was to eat locally for a year, thereby putting items such as coffee, many teas, wine and chocolate off the menu. It was inspired by the Canadian 'One Hundred Mile Diet'.[19] A common thread in such initiatives is to make it possible to return to wholesome cooking. These attempts to restore more traditional approaches to food provision often means climbing back up a learning curve that was second nature to our ancestors.

Fife Diet members discovered with hindsight, for instance, that the autumn was a bad time to start such an initiative because the opportunity to prepare by stocking up the larder with jams, preserves and pickles was lost. What also tends to become apparent, in the context of such initiatives, is that a modicum of trade is no bad thing. Thus, project members of the Fife Diet have shifted to a compromise (80 per cent of food is now procured within 30 miles). The two learning curve points encountered in the context of the project (maximising seasonality and optimising trade outside the immediate community) demonstrate significant experimental value in such initiatives.[20]

Adapting to change

Innovation has always driven the way our food is cooked and served. Think of the invention of bread, the development of new strains of grain, or more frivolously, the application of blowtorches or liquid nitrogen to some desserts. Some innovations sometimes bring problems in their wake if food knowledge and culture do not keep up with them. Leaving behind traditional cooking methods as a consequence of technological changes (such as the discovery of hydrogenated vegetable oil, the invention of stock cubes, or the discovery of the microwave oven) can mean that hidden folk-knowledge embedded in old-fashioned recipes may be lost. However, this does not have to be the case, thanks to the legions of writers coming up with the ideas, entrepreneurs developing rules-of-thumb, and the imaginative individuals prepared to take the lead on community-based food, introducing economies of scale in so-called slow food. The positive story is that innovation can do a great deal towards the improvement of nutrition, delivering up food good enough to tempt even an economist to breakfast like a nutritional king. In this interconnected age, the forces of fashion, technology, economics, and environmental constraints may (we can hope) accelerate the pace of change towards a more sustainable way of going on.

The economics of consuming food is a synthesis (a ragout, perhaps) of the economics that has brought us to the table in the first place. How we eat, where we eat and what we eat are shaped by economic forces, which in turn impacts the economics of the food supply chain. To disentangle these forces is complex. It is clear, however, that the financial credit crunch has led to a notable shift between eating at home and eating away. This is something that economic and environmental policymakers will need to focus on – for five years after the onset of the financial credit crunch there is an air of permanence about this change.

How, where and what we eat is also shaped by important cultural forces. The question is how economics and culture can be combined to make it possible for nutritional food to be delivered in a sustainable fashion in the modern kitchen. The purpose of all the ingenuity and hard work in evidence in every kind of kitchen is to feed people well. Making things taste good is fun, but with a serious purpose, for inadequate nutrition can undermine the wellbeing of future generations and thus ultimately the wealth of nations. Perhaps because food has become a small part of the household budget in some economies, the importance of good, sustainable, nutritious food has been forgotten. The consequences of this are visible in the global obesity epidemic. The problem facing the government policymaker trying to do something about this is that millions of food-related decisions are taken every day in ways that are not always under the control of those making them. In our view the only reasonably reliable way of influencing such decisions so that, on average, they have positive nutritional and environmental consequences, will be by establishing a sound food culture throughout every kitchen, large or small. Food is a sensitive subject, therefore also attention-grabbing. All kitchens, large and small, need to unite behind delicious, nutritious food. The only way forward for food is education, education, education.

Notes

1 Nabhan (2004).
2 Burnett (1966), p. 180.
3 *Field* (2012).
4 Burnett (1966), p. 3.
5 Watanabe *et al.* (1998).
6 Burnett (1966), p. 242.
7 Smith (2008). See also: www.deliaonline.com
8 Great-grandmother's extra-sticky version of this recipe appears in Gaskell (1925), p. 54:

> Ginger Sponge Pudding (Very Good). 3 oz flour, 2 oz lard, 2 dessertspoons treacle, 1 dessertspoon sugar, 1 egg, a little milk, half a teaspoon baking powder, half a teaspoon ginger. Pour into a well-buttered mould and steam 2 hours.

9 Woodvine (2011).
10 Fearnley-Whittingstall (2010).
11 Smith (1976).
12 British Sandwich Association (2012).
13 Seddon (1989), p. 202.
14 NeverSeconds, at http://neverseconds.blogspot.co.uk/. See also Payne and Payne (2012).
15 Johnson and Hough (2012).
16 Cocco (2012).
17 The People's Supermarket, at www.thepeoplessupermarket.org/home/about-us
18 The Fife Diet, at www.fifediet.co.uk/media/
19 *Scotsman* (2007).
20 Brown (2012).

9 Human health and food

There are three possible parts to a date, of which at least two must be offered: entertainment, food and affection. It is customary to begin a series of dates with a great deal of entertainment, a moderate amount of food and the merest suggestion of affection. As the amount of affection increases, the entertainment can be reduced proportionately. When the affection is the entertainment, we no longer call it dating. Under no circumstances can the food be omitted.
(Judith Martin, *Miss Manners' Guide to Excruciatingly Correct Behavior*)[1]

Food, health and economics – inseparable bedfellows

Health and economics are closely intertwined. Rather obviously, health is big business. Americans spend the equivalent of over 17 per cent of their economy on health, although admittedly the American healthcare system is often considered to be one of the most economically inefficient in the world. But healthcare matters more than as a business per se. A healthy population is more likely to be productive, and productivity is something of the Holy Grail of the economics profession. Fewer days off due to illness, a better-performing workforce when that workforce does show up to work, and (for jobs that require physical exertion) a more energetic workforce; all of this comes from health.

It is therefore obvious that the health of the population is important economically, and at times when economic efficiency has been stretched to the utmost, maintaining that health becomes a matter of national priority. One of the key ways of ensuring health is through the provision of adequate amounts of nutritious food. This is why rationing has traditionally been so important in wartime. The economy has to be producing at its most efficient to sustain a war, and to do that it is important that the population at large receive the optimal quantity of food, of the optimal quality. In the UK the idea of optimal quantities of food in wartime extended to varying the size of the ration of certain foodstuffs according to a crude approximation of need. Pregnant women received a higher allowance of dairy, and those in some industries like mining received a special ration of cheese (if they could not take their midday meal in a works canteen, and yet needed calories).

Quantity and quality of food are the two economic strands that matter. Historically speaking, food was all about quantity. Until relatively recently in human history nutrition was not well understood, and what limited ideas did exist around the concept of a balanced diet were subordinated to the idea of getting enough to eat, at least for the majority of the population. The idea of excess food for the population at large has generally been a utopian dream for most of human history. Developed countries no longer have that particular challenge. Instead it is the excess quantity of food (and the fact that the food is of the wrong quality) that is the problem.

Food, health and the environment – a complex relationship

Seeking to untangle the Gordian Knot of the food–health–environment relationship, it is tempting to rely on the three-part statement of logic known as the syllogism. However, unlike the excellent relationship advice dished out by Miss Manners above, syllogistic statements can be deeply illogical. This happens frequently in the context of sensitive subjects – and both food and the environment happen to be pretty sensitive topics. Take the following, as an example. A growing population means a rising demand for food, which means food production, processing and retailing practices that in aggregate are wrecking the environment. A significant number of people are eating too much food and becoming obese, thereby putting themselves at risk of poor health. If people stopped over-eating this would take significant pressure off the environment as well as improving human health.

Other things being equal, the above statement can only be true if jointly the resolving of the obesity epidemic and the problem of environmental degradation caused by food production were a matter of persuading people to eat less. If this is not the case then this seeming opportunity to kill two birds with one stone – slimming down physically and environmentally at the same time – may be nothing more than a pipedream. That it is indeed a pipedream will be suspected by anyone who has tried to lose weight by going on a diet (ignoring for the moment the broader matter of life plans). As everyone knows who has actually tried it, diets based on calorie reduction tend not to work. Weight may be lost in the short run but, as soon as the dieter lets down their guard, it creeps back on. In a similar vein, the simple relationship between human health and the environment described in the above paragraph might not reflect the real world. We cannot be sure that reducing our total food intake will resolve either environmental degradation or obesity.

Let us consider an alternative syllogism: body weight is controlled by hormones which interact with the sweetness and glycaemic load[2] of food intake to determine fat.[3] A significant number of people are eating a processed-food diet containing large amounts of carbohydrates and fructose which give a sugar rush (known as high-glycaemic-index foods). This diet is causing the consumer to put on a lot of weight. If people shifted to a less processed diet, the obesity epidemic would be resolved.

In this model it is primarily food processing rather than the whole nexus of relationships between agriculture, processing and retailing that lies at the root of the obesity epidemic. As we know, after eight chapters of this book, the sizeable part of the environmental impact of food comes from the agricultural links of the food

food-chain (the first three links of land, animal and vegetable). This is likely to be the case even after accounting for the ways in which the shift towards processed food has changed agriculture. Thus, the consequences for the environment of a transition for those on a diet heavy in processed foods towards a diet focused around high-fibre, low-sugar-rush-inducing foods would be unpredictable.

All this goes to illustrate the impossible challenge for anyone addressing the health–environment–food nexus. Food provisioning, the environment and human beings are each complex systems. Scientists do not yet fully understand each system or its often mysterious relationships with the others. Thus, it may be foolhardy to advance beyond these paragraphs. However, environmentalists will step in where angels fear to tread and economists are willing to predict almost anything.

Occam's Razor tells us to take the simplest solution to the most complex of problems – and food, health, the economy and the environment are clearly pretty complex problems to contemplate. Let us therefore take two big concepts, and examine them economically and environmentally: how much food is consumed; and how good is the food we are consuming? We are basically boiling down the swirling mass of stock arguments to a clear consommé of *quantity* and *quality*.

Quantity, part one – the economics of enough

The relationship between the quantity of food and economic wellbeing is not linear. In a relatively wealthy society it is possible to have malnutrition (insufficient quantity of the right sort of foods) or even the extreme of famine (the lack of food in any form), at a time of relative prosperity. As famine is associated with death, either through starvation or through weakening the body's ability to repel disease, it can be considered the most extreme health consequence of the food cycle. The Irish famine of the 1840s took place at a time when the UK was a relatively prosperous society, and followed on from a period of quite extended prosperity. The problem was the unequal distribution of food at the time, and the British government's concern over food prices and the potential for popular discontent in mainland Britain were it to be seen to be assisting in famine relief through government action.

Generally, famine is now a consequence of human action or inaction, not a consequence of nature. Global transport and food distribution, in a world that produces more than sufficient calories to feed the current population, mean that the extreme of famine will occur through human miscalculation. Food can be flown anywhere in the world within hours, after all. Malnutrition is more prevalent, and perhaps more difficult to control – although one could argue that malnutrition sometimes seems to be the unfortunate consequence of societal choices about income distribution.

Within society, food consumption, health and income have some obvious links when it comes to the quantity of food available. Money enables one to afford food, and as a necessity of life food will be purchased whenever it is possible to do so. The wealthy in Ireland did not starve in the 1840s. Wealthy Sudanese did not starve in the 1990s. The price of food may have risen because of the famine, but they had the means to afford the food. What was happening was the normal rationing mechanism that the pricing mechanism provides. The problem of course is that the rationing mechanism was being applied (in both cases) to something that is essential to human survival. Those without the power to purchase, regrettably, died.

Even in less extreme circumstances the level of food intake will vary with income, and as the quantity of food consumed varies so there will also be variability in the quality of health. John Boyd-Orr published a study of British food consumption and its relationship to health and income (imaginatively entitled *Food Health and Income*) in 1937.[4] He showed that lower-income groups consumed less in absolute terms of nearly every category of food than did those in higher-income groups; bread and potatoes were the exceptions. This difference in the quantity of food consumed, taking place as late as the 1930s and in a society as developed as that of the UK, shows how relatively recent is the idea of food excess as a health issue. To be fair, this is a quantity and quality issue – but in terms of calories consumed from whatever food source, the bottom 30 per cent of British society by income had a below adequate calorie intake by the standards of the day and very definitely by modern standards.

The results of this lower calorie intake were then evident in the health of the nation. A classic device for measuring generic health was to look at the average height of children from different income backgrounds – healthier children will, on average, tend to be taller. There are other measures one could use, of course, but this has the benefit of being relatively simple to collect across a diverse range of income groups, as well as being something that can be compared over different periods in history. What Boyd-Orr showed was that children from lower-income backgrounds were consistently, and noticeably, shorter than children from higher-income backgrounds. The lack of calories was arresting the healthy development of children.

Similar patterns of health are observed in studies of the eighteenth and nineteenth centuries. And, perhaps most tellingly of all, when rationing was introduced into the UK during the Second World War and calorific intake became somewhat more standardised, the differences in height between higher- and lower-income groups started to recede. Clearly, a child who had experienced fourteen years of insufficient food by 1939 was not going to suddenly catch up with their higher-income peers as a result of the introduction of rationing, but over the course of the war the enforced homogenisation of calorie intake that was the consequence of rationing led to less discernible differences in height and health.

The issue went beyond height and physical development. Rickets, bad teeth and nutritional anaemia were all health problems coming from insufficient food in the UK of the 1930s. Of course, this was insufficient food of the right sort (calcium being an important deficiency in the diet of the lower-income groups). Boyd-Orr noted that to get to a healthy diet, the lower-income groups would need to increase consumption of milk, butter, eggs, fruit, vegetables and meat. He somewhat drily observed that these categories of food formed the 'more expensive foodstuffs'.

The set of conclusions Boyd-Orr was drawing over seventy years ago still holds today in some societies. If income levels for some are sufficiently constrained as to limit calorific input, then the aggregate health of the nation will be affected. This has economic costs – either because the economy will have to pay for the treatment of poor health, or because workers will be less efficient as a result of their ill health. In the OECD today, however, it is not malnutrition or famine that forms the food quantity health challenge. Today, the problem is quite the reverse.

Just another wafer-thin mint – eating too much

The British Monty Python film *The Meaning of Life* featured a sketch where a gourmand at a restaurant was pressured into eating 'just another wafer-thin mint' to complete his meal. The diner had no need to increase his calorie consumption (the man was depicted as obese) and had no real desire to eat any more. After token resistance the diner gave into pressure, consumed what was unnecessary and promptly exploded – perhaps the ultimate instance of ill-health resulting from the over-consumption of food. Developed societies are consuming 'just another wafer-thin mint' – excess calories that are not required, purely for the pleasure of eating. While the health consequences may be less explosive than those of the Pythonesque world, they are considerable. Obesity and its related diseases like diabetes are the rapidly expanding health issue of today. Indeed, humanity now has triple the number of people dying of diseases related to obesity than dying of diseases related to malnutrition.[5]

Two points stand out from this simple fact. First, this must be the first time in human history that obesity has exceeded malnutrition as a cause of death. Second, the world has people simultaneously dying of obesity and of malnutrition. Suzanne Collins' bestselling trilogy *The Hunger Games* presented a dystopian society where citizens of the Capitol deliberately cultivated a perverse form of bulimia – vomiting up food at feasts so as to be able to indulge in the pleasure of eating more.[6] At the same time, people in the Districts starved to death. This work of futuristic fiction is not far from the reality of today. Humanity has created a global society where excess and want can kill side by side.

If one lives in a society where income is not a limiting factor on the quantity of food consumed – if everyone can afford to obtain sufficient calories in a day – then the health consequences of food shift effortlessly from physical limitations imposed by underdevelopment to the concerns that surround obesity. This is a significant concern. It has been suggested that obesity is the fastest-growing cause of disease in the world. Again, this is not necessarily just about quantity; it can also be about eating the wrong sorts of foods (quality). The causes of obesity and overweight are several, and complex – genetics, physiology, psychology and culture can all be involved. Nevertheless, we think it must be recognised that, as excess consumption is now possible in a way that it was not in the past, overindulgence has to be considered an economic problem.

Two-thirds of American adults are classified as overweight or obese. Over one-third of Americans are classified as obese.[7] These are precise classifications, not hyperbolic terms of castigation (the calculations are derived from thresholds of body mass for any given height). There is an excessive consumption of calories going on. In Europe the problem is not as large, but it is significant. Moreover, the trend in the newly industrialised societies also demonstrates the tendency to over-consume calories. We see China as an excellent case study. A quarter of the adult population are at least overweight – as China's prosperity has allowed consumption of more and different food.[8] Moreover, urban consumers are more overweight than rural consumers. There are various factors at work in that, no doubt, but one consideration is that the urban consumer will tend to have a higher level of income than will their rural cousin.

Perhaps the most chilling consequence in health terms is that for the first time, a significant number of American children will have a lower life expectancy than their parents because of the negative health impacts associated with obesity.[9] Previously, declining life expectancy was virtually unheard of in developed societies (Russia was an exception, largely because of alcohol-related diseases). In Italy, home of the Mediterranean diet, things are changing. A new generation of children brought up on a different and more processed diet, containing higher levels of saturated fat and sugar, has resulted in rising levels of obesity.

There is also evidence that economic development will trigger a biological process that accelerates obesity. Expectant mothers who do not receive sufficient calories during their pregnancies give birth to children who are more inclined to be obese if the income constraint on calorie intake is lifted. Genetically this is logical – such children are conditioned to store calories whenever they can get them. The health problem from this genetic imperative is that economic development over the course of a generation will completely alter the necessity of storing calories. The next generation are genetically programmed to store fat as an insurance against times of want, when such scarcity is not likely to occur during their lifetime. While the economic progress that removes the income constraint on calorific consumption is to be heartily welcomed, it does potentially come at a price in terms of obesity and overall health in countries that are transitioning in economic terms.

Box 9.1 Fasting oneself clever

Human beings seem to be programmed to eat more than they need. This may be cultural. It may also be rooted in a now-irrelevant survival strategy of the hunter-gatherer, for whom over-indulgence one day was simply making up for short rations the day before. If so, the difficulty most of us experience in constraining our calorie intake unless forced to do so may be deeply rooted in psychology. It is likely this is also deeply rooted in *physiology*, but the good news is that it may not be a one-way street. Scientists have discovered that animals fasting every other day enjoy an extended lifespan and healthier cardiovascular and neurological systems, and blithely suggest that humans can do this too.

> Mark Mattson, Professor of Neuroscience at John Hopkins University, Baltimore, said: 'We have found that dietary energy restriction, particularly when administered in intermittent bouts of major caloric restriction, such as alternative day fasting, activates cellular stress response pathways in neurones'.[10] This regime purportedly brings significant benefits: rejuvenating the brain and improving cognitive powers. And it sounds so much fun, too...

The tipping point of the scales

This then is the problem of economics and calorie consumption. Too little income means too few calories, which means an unhealthy diet (and an economically unhealthy workforce). Once income ceases to be a constraint on calorie consumption, however, the tendency is to over-consume, which means an unhealthy diet (and an economically unhealthy workforce). The happy medium, the balance between too many and too few calories seems to elude us.

What is interesting in economic terms is that once income ceases to be a constraining factor on calorific intake, the relationship between food, health and income reverses. In other words, if income is a constraint on calorific intake then the poor have insufficient food while the rich have sufficient or excess food. In contrast, when everyone can afford to eat, poor people in any given society are more likely to be overweight and the wealthy of that same society are more likely to be healthy. The relatively extreme degree of the inequality of income distribution in the United States may be a factor that has fostered the relatively extreme degree of obesity in that society (the USA has an unusually high proportion of its population with a below-mean income level).

There are several hypotheses as to why this income versus calorie-consumption relationship shifts once the tipping point has tipped. There is a correlation between income and education levels, so it may just be that higher-income groups have a better understanding of the health implications of their diet. Higher-income groups are not prevented by lack of income from exercising in a focused way (personal trainers, gym memberships and so forth do cost money). It could also be that higher-income groups are able to enjoy a wider range of entertainments – pleasure can be obtained from several pastimes. Wholesome food is not necessarily the food that humans are most likely to crave. As a species, we enjoy being bad. But being bad in terms of food quantity and quality will exact an environmental toll.

Quantity, part two – the environmental issue

In 2011 the UK Foresight report described the drivers of obesity as a complex mix of primary appetite control in the brain, the force of dietary habits, the level of physical activity and the 'psychological ambivalence' of people making lifestyle choices. As an example, encompassing all these conditions, the authors know they *should* fuel themselves with fruit as they work on this book, rather than chocolate biscuits. Halva, a confection of ground sesame seeds and honey, would be a bit better than chocolate – in health terms – containing mostly unsaturated fat. However, having halva is still not necessarily healthy; there are higher levels of fat and sugar than are contained in, say, an apple. The rational decision-maker should choose the apple, but the feel-good factor associated with chocolate biscuits or halva is surely better for motivation.

Each of these drivers of obesity is complex in its own right. From the perspective of the environment, perhaps the most important change has been the replacement and supplementation of human energy with energy from other sources – what would be categorised as the level of physical activity, perhaps the lifestyle choice. While this shift has been tremendously civilising in some respects, in others the opposite may be said to be true: the consequent separating of human beings from their natural environment may be an 'obesogenic environment' (a fancy way of saying 'an environment that makes people fat').[11]

Sugar, sugar

We now venture into dangerous territory. Are we eating too much sugar, and would it not perhaps be better to divert sugar production from fuel for the body, to fuel for the engine?

At first sight this looks like a risky path to tread. The conversion of food crops into ethanol may have contributed to the spike in corn prices that led to the tortilla riots of 2007,[12] and, even worse, ethanol-based bio-fuel is no longer regarded as automatically environmentally friendly. When ethanol's impacts are analysed from the field to the exhaust pipe, it cannot always be described as zero carbon. Whether ethanol's carbon footprint is low heavily depends on how it is delivered, in ways that are hard to regulate. Should the growing of crops for fuel displace land formerly used for (non-sugar) food production, this could have profoundly negative consequences for human nutrition. If rainforests were destroyed to facilitate the growing of bio-fuel crops, the object of the exercise would be anything but environmental. All of this simply reinforces the point that *how* things are done can matter a lot more than *what* is done. None of it invalidates the view that many of the calories in sugar are currently being wasted when eaten: those that consume sugar are often consuming too many calories in the first place. Sugar used as a mechanical (rather than human) fuel may not necessarily be a waste. On the basis that not eating too much sugar could be good for human health, burning sugar in a fuel tank could (other things being equal) be the opposite of wasteful.

Average annual sugar consumption per person was twenty-one kilograms worldwide in 2006–10 (with significant regional variation), seven in China, thirty-four in the USA and fifty-six in Brazil.[13] To give some idea of what this means, global consumption of sugar is equivalent to eating twenty-seven small apples per week or putting a daily fourteen teaspoons of sugar into tea or coffee.[14] It is easy to see why sugar consumption can easily skyrocket. (One of the authors of this book has no problem getting through seven cups of tea a day – fortunately without sugar.) Of course, sugar and 'sugars' are not to be confused. The guideline for the total consumption of 'sugars' per day is ninety grams, or forty apples per week. On average we could consume another two apples a day before hitting the guideline limit.

Such high levels of (manufactured) sugar consumption in the diet are a relatively recent phenomenon. Over the past half-century, sugar consumption has grown by some 300 per cent globally.[15] As would be expected, this trend has generated some debate in the field of public health. An article in the weekly science magazine *Nature* observed that, consumed regularly in large quantities, fructose gives rise to a range of chronic, ultimately life-threatening diseases.[16] Faced with such evidence, the rational thing to do would be to consume sugar in moderation. Some would go much further than that: '[If] only a small fraction of what is already known about the effects of sugar were to be revealed in relation to any other material used as a food additive, that material would be promptly banned.'[17]

We think it likely that sugar is over-consumed in urban societies because it is over-available, by dint of being embedded in many processed food items, and on many supermarket checkouts in the form of sweets. In such a context sugar is likely to end up replacing key nutrients and, consumed to excess, can be rightly viewed as having toxic effects: sugar is linked to tooth decay, hypertension, heart problems, pancreatitis, insulin resistance, kidney problems and addiction. The World Health Organization's research on sugar consumption patterns in South Africa found sugar consumption in urban areas to be twice as high as it is in rural areas (12.3 per cent of daily calories vs. 5.9 per cent), and the penetration of carbonated soft drinks to be over ten times as high in urban areas compared with rural areas (33 per cent vs. 3 per cent).[18]

Experience has shown that an effective way to curb consumption of alcohol and tobacco is to curb availability through taxes, and controls on distribution. This is just one way of changing the economics of sugar consumption, but the recent Danish experience shows it does not always work.[19] Research has suggested that a tax of over 20 per cent on the price of foodstuffs would be required to have a discernible impact on consumption.[20] Turning sugar into fuel rather than a food additive could have the effect of curbing consumption by reducing the amount available, thereby bringing a significant health dividend. It may also raise the price of sugar as a foodstuff – mimicking a tax effect. However, such an idea could only be considered after reviewing the potential nutritional and environmental impacts on a country-by-country basis. We think it likely that when calories are hard to come by for reasons of food shortage or economic constraint, or indeed when sugar is needed to store perishables for medium-term use, sugar might turn out to be a lifesaver. The view that sugar, consumed in moderation, can be a valuable component of human diets[21] is likely to be fair enough if all else is equal. However, we note that all else is very rarely equal in the context of food because of the complex mix of physiology, psychology and culture that drives eating patterns.

Turning sugar into fuel on a widespread basis could of course have a number of negative environmental impacts. However, these costs could be outweighed by the health gains. Moreover, to an extent this would depend on a number of other variables. The two most important may be government policy and economics. Let us imagine a world in which cities and working lives are designed to enable us to replace fuel-driven journeys by journeys driven by human energy – on foot or by bicycle. This would have positive effects on human health by increasing the amount of exercise embedded in the day, and might also reduce the demand for fuel. If that happened in wide-enough scale in a sugar-fuelled world we would need less sugar to drive cars – potentially freeing up land to be left as forest land or to grow a different crop.

Returning from the unlikely world of fiction to the world of fact, we contemplate the parlous situation many populations are faced with – an increasingly obese population, bringing with it rapid growth in healthcare costs that governments must be greeting with horror in the wake of the financial credit crunch and its associated fiscal constraints. We urgently need to return to diets containing less fat and less sugar. The environmental relevance of this point lies primarily in the changes consumer demand for this toxic mix has had upon agriculture. However, if eating patterns are seen in the wider context of the environmental footprint of the consumer society, it is clear to see that there are many other indirect environmental costs that might be addressed by a change in consumer behaviour.

The fat of the land

In an earlier chapter we noted that fat and sugar, in combination, should amount to about 8 per cent of a balanced diet, whereas the typical British shopping basket contains 23 per cent in fat and sugar. The quantities are too high. A diet high in saturated fat not only has the obvious effect of causing weight gain – it has other unwanted health effects. This brings us to the topic of cholesterol.

Cholesterol is not all bad – it is naturally present in most body tissues, and plays an important role in metabolism. However, high concentrations of cholesterol in the bloodstream are associated with the build-up of fatty plaques on artery walls, potentially leading to narrowing or blockage – a serious matter when it affects the arteries of the heart. However, there is cholesterol and there is cholesterol; good cholesterol (HDL) is protective of arterial health. It is bad cholesterol (LDL) that is potentially damaging.

The advice to those seeking to lower their blood cholesterol levels (or keep them low) is a diet low in saturated fats (found in butter and cheese, lard and palm oil), and high in fruit, vegetables and wholegrain cereals. Cakes, biscuits and pastries tend to contain so-called trans-fats which (like saturated fat) raise levels of bad cholesterol, whereas unsaturated fats found in vegetable oils, sunflower spreads, nuts, oily fish, and avocados may help lower bad cholesterol.[22] Note the significant overlap between foods that raise bad cholesterol with foods high in sugar. Such foods also tend to be processed. Again it can be claimed that the direct impacts of food processing upon the environment are far less important than the indirect impacts, with health one of those indirect routes.

Quality, part one – the economics of being what you eat (again)

It is reasonably safe to assert that it is not the quantity of food consumed that is the main cause of health problems today, at least in developed economies. Rather, it is the *quality* of food that is consumed, which means quality as to its nutritional value. We ingest the wrong sorts of foods to an excessive degree, and it is that which creates the health problems we have today. The wrong *quantity* of the wrong *quality* – our distinctions are starting to merge into one another – and the consommé of food health is acquiring the opacity of vichyssoise.

A healthy diet is 'everything in moderation'. Reasonable amounts of a wide range of foodstuffs. Information and education encourage us all to consume 'target' amounts of foodstuffs. British supermarkets obligingly publish on their product packaging what a 'typical' portion of a certain food will produce as part of the 'guideline daily allowance'. The 'five-a-day' mantra for fruit and vegetables is widely known, widely understood – and yet the introduction of something so readily comprehended has not led to a surge in consumption of fruit and vegetables. The government's efforts to raise the quality of our food intake seem to have been widely disseminated and then just as widely ignored.

There seems something very odd in this. The dieting industry, which is all about monitoring and controlling the food that we consume, is a multi-billion-dollar industry worldwide. In the UK, consumers spend over two billion pounds on dieting in a year. In the United States, one of the most obese nations in the world, consumers spend over sixty billion dollars a year on the products of diet companies – and that is in a world where it is increasingly common to pursue a policy of 'self-dieting' (buying 'diet sodas' and so forth), aided by free diet websites. From an economic point of view, if people are prepared to spend so much on controlling what they eat, there is a huge (economic) value in exercising that control. Sensible eating has a discernible worth. Against this there are two counter forces that drive us to put the wrong food into our mouths. These can be thought of as 'desire' and 'distance'.

The economics of diet and desire

Humanity likes all the wrong things. To paraphrase P.G. Wodehouse, anything that is any fun is immoral, illegal, or fattening – and of the three, the third option tends to be the easiest to achieve (and generally speaking the most socially acceptable). Products that are high in sugar or saturated fats tend to be sought because they taste nice. Such products produce a physical reaction – a sugar high, for instance – which the body then starts to crave. The sugar high is in fact the release of dopamine in the brain – a chemical reaction that is similar to that produced by drug addiction.[23] (One of the authors, for instance, developed a coke habit at university. Not the white powdered variety, but the soft-drink variety – the combination of caffeine and sugar high became seriously addictive.)

As we remove the absolute income constraint from calorie intake, and create a situation whereby people can afford food, there is a tendency to cling to the wrong sorts of food as a form of recreational pleasure. George Orwell's *The Road to Wigan Pier* summarised this with a certain patrician distain:

> When you are unemployed, which is to say when you are underfed, harassed, bored, and miserable, you don't want to eat dull wholesome food. You want something a little bit 'tasty'. There is always some cheaply pleasant thing to tempt you. Let's have three pennorth of chips! Run out and buy us a twopenny ice-cream![24]

Orwell – writing around the same time that Boyd-Orr was conducting his surveys of food and income – had picked up on a problem that was also evident in Boyd-Orr's statistics. Once a society has reached a certain level of income, food is a cheap source of entertainment – a means of alleviating (temporarily) the dull monotony of life. Palatability and ease of effort effortlessly triumphs over nutrition. In the absence of other entertainment, food can be relied upon as means of stimulating pleasure. We shun raw carrots and wholemeal bread in favour of biscuits or buttered toast. Orwell's observed desire for something 'a little bit "tasty"' is what we know today as comfort eating.

The addictive nature of such products is something that food producers rely on. This is not to say that the food producer is standing in darkened corners of nightclubs offering small plastic bags of icing sugar in exchange for used bank notes. However, food producers want people to purchase their products (that is, after all, the *raison d'être* of the food producer). If food producers cannot promote the healthful properties of their food, they can promote the potential enjoyment of the taste of their products. Confectionery is sold as fun, as an indulgence, occasionally as something that is part of a glamorous and sophisticated lifestyle. It would be absurd to promote confectionery as something healthy or as a necessary part of one's diet, so gratification and pleasure is the obvious marketing strategy. (One of the authors believes chocolate is, actually, necessary.)

The health consequence of such gratification and pleasure has led to some extreme consequences. Between the First and Second World Wars, a working-class woman would often have all her teeth pulled for her eighteenth or her twenty-first birthday. The reason was that the diet of the working class encouraged tooth decay (an obvious health problem prevalent in more-developed economies). The parents of the unfortunate young woman hoped to increase her eligibility in the marriage market. A woman with a complete set of false teeth is a woman who will not cost her husband anything in terms of dentists' bills. The alternative would be to adopt a healthier lifestyle, of course, but that was not a course of action that appeared to be given much consideration.

The economics of diet and distance

The other reason we eat the wrong foods is the distance that now exists between the consumer and the food that they eat. 'Distance' in this sense is not the physical distance, at least not really. It is the fact that the food we eat is not food, but a highly processed industrial product that emerges at the end of a very long manufacturing chain. Modern consumers are bad at controlling what they eat because they have very little control over what they eat in the normal sense.

The American television series *Supernatural* dedicated a whole season to a story arc that was based on an attempt to drug the entire population of the United States (and ultimately the world). The device through which this domination of humanity was to be accomplished was through putting drugs into high-fructose corn syrup. The use of fructose is so ubiquitous in processed foods that it would be virtually impossible for anyone other than a wholefood fanatic or organic-only consumer to avoid its consumption. This is the point. The consumer is almost powerless in their ability to control their fructose intake, or indeed the intake of any other food-like substance, if they buy processed food. The antagonists of the *Supernatural* season, the Leviathans, aimed to reduce the population of North America to a state of placid obesity through doses of corn syrup (in order to consume said population; Leviathans presumably have no concern about the fat content of their own diet). The subtext regarding the real-world American diet is not especially subtle – the hidden meaning of many television programmes is never terribly far below the surface.

The problem for the health-conscious consumer is the difficulty of controlling what types of food they actually consume, when something like fructose corn syrup is so ubiquitous. The consumer preparing a meal from scratch at home, using only raw ingredients, has a certain amount of control as to the content of the meal. If you bake your own bread, you can control how much salt is in it (for example). If you buy bread, be it from an artisan baker, an in-store bakery or from a large-scale food producer, the salt content decision has been taken away from you and is dictated in an arbitrary fashion. The consumer is given a range of salt content options, perhaps, but it is a finite range. The consumer of processed food, who has outsourced the preparation, has to accept the content of the food that they are sold. While they may be able to choose one food product or another on the basis of the fructose content or salt content, the choice of processed food rarely comes down to a single measure. Choosing on the basis of fructose also may mean having to compromise on saturated fat content, sodium content, or on some other aspect of the meal.

Frustrating this is the hidden nature of the contents of processed foods. Superficially, salad is good for you. A chicken salad (admittedly with 'crispy' chicken) from a multinational fast-food chain can however provide a third of one's recommended daily fat intake, almost a quarter of the recommended cholesterol intake, and over a third of the recommended salt intake. This is a salad for goodness sake! A cheeseburger from the same chain has fewer calories, lower fat levels, and lower sodium levels.[25] The consumer who has been drilled into believing that 'five-a-day' of fruit and vegetable products is the foundation of good health could be led astray by not understanding the components of the processed food that they are consuming. Parents who persuade their children to eat vegetables by covering them in sugar, otherwise known as 'tomato sauce', focus on the vegetables not on the addition that the sauce brings to the diet.

Tomato sauce is categorised by the British government as a high-salt, high-sugar product. Nearly a quarter of tomato sauce is sugar according to the label on many makes.

As already mentioned in the chapter on processing, there is clearly a link between the amount of processed food that is consumed and the instance of obesity in a society. Indeed, it is possible to determine a relationship between the intensity of microwave ownership and the instance of obesity. This is not because microwaves somehow increase the calorific content of the food that they reheat: microwaves have been the subject of many health scares over the years, but enhancing cholesterol is not one of them. The problem is that microwave ownership encourages the consumption of highly processed foodstuffs. One can put a raw potato into a microwave and turn it into a jacket potato, but one can also put in a pre-processed ready meal like a lasagne – containing fructose, saturated fats, and a wide range of other ingredients. Use of the microwave also, of course, gives instant gratification of the desire to consume food – remember those microwavable chips that are ready in moments. It reduces the time cost of preparing food, and that time saving will tend to increase the consumption. One could, in essence, characterise a microwave society as a society that has built a pro-obesity infrastructure.

The distance between food in its raw state and the consumer is compounding the health problems of modern society, and this process is encouraged by the economics of a post-financial-credit-crunch world. Time-poor consumers will tend to prioritise the immediate problem (lack of time) over the potential for longer-term problems (poor health in the future). There is even the risk of an internal compromise that is little more than self-deception; 'a ready meal now, but I will go to the gym when I have more time'. The problem is that government action and moral suasion are unlikely to make a significant difference to the decision process of the consumer. The 'five-a-day' mantra has been about as successful in persuading people to eat more healthily as was the Brown Bread Act of 1800,[26] forcing bakers to sell only wholemeal-based loaves. Confronted by the change in diet, the population of 1800 rioted and the act was repealed. George Orwell's *The Road to Wigan Pier* observed the considerable distrust that working-class families had for wholemeal and brown bread. The five-a-day concept of modern times has not as yet provoked riots or even necessarily distrust, but it has produced a form of civil disobedience or wilful disregard (or perhaps self-delusion – the 'fruit' in a bar of 'fruit and nut' chocolate should not perhaps be considered one of the five items of 'five-a-day').

Quality, part two – a healthy environment means a healthy body

The nutritional content of plant-based foods depends on the quality and composition of the soil in which they are grown. A rich soil is productive, and productive land obviates the need for the agricultural equivalent of urban sprawl. A higher crop yield per acre is the agricultural equivalent of a high-rise tower block. This underscores an absolutely critical point: sound (agricultural) land is simultaneously better for the environment and good for human health. Looking after the land so as to encourage sustainable agricultural productivity without encroaching on or degrading the environment may thus turn out to be one of the best possible investments human beings could make.

It is possible to have enough to eat, or even too much to eat, and yet to be undernourished as a consequence of soil content. If key micronutrients are not present in sufficient quantities in the soil those key micronutrients will then be absent in the plant (which may or may not affect the health of the plant), and those key micronutrients will then be absent from any food derived from the plant (animal or vegetable). The risk of micronutrient deficiency can be minimised if the population has access to a varied diet; if micronutrients are missing in one food item the body may be able to absorb them elsewhere. In well-off countries, food supplements are also available on the shelf in every chemist's shop for the 'worried malnourished', and some food companies have developed so-called 'functional foods' designed to deliver a specific benefit such as improved digestion or mental alertness.

In developing countries, variety in the diet and key minerals in the soil may both be missing along with the wherewithal to afford luxuries such as food supplements. When this is the case malnutrition is still a threat even when there is sufficient *quantity* of food. Such malnutrition risks weakened immunity to disease, higher childhood mortality, lower educational attainment, and lower economic productivity.[27]

Key micronutrients are added to food as it passes through the production process as a matter of course in wealthier countries. The question is whether this is the optimal stage in the food food-chain for them to be added. Focusing on and improving plant nutrition in such a way as to make sure key nutrients get to the plant through the root, perhaps as an additive to fertiliser, could turn out to be more effective or more equitable. In developing countries, equitable access to micronutrients could turn out to be a powerful policy instrument from the perspective of human health and economic development.

Box 9.2 **Adding variety to the diet with the mealworm**

A casual traveller in Peru came across *suri*. A row of these creatures, grilled, on a bamboo skewer, looks vaguely shrimp-like. Fully cooked they are glossy and pale golden in colour, and are a highly prized local delicacy. Yet *suri* is just clever branding. They are, in fact, a worm that bores its way through the species of tree in which it resides – the agave. The agave worm is not unique in being edible. Worldwide there are at least 1,400 edible species of insect, of which the most numerous are beetles; ants, bees and wasps; and grasshoppers, cockroaches and crickets.[28] According to Julieta

(Continued)

> *(Continued)*
>
> Ramos-Elorduy, ants taste sweet and nutty, agave worms taste like kidney beans, and crickets and grasshoppers absorb the taste of the sauce in which they are cooked. But, enough of taste, what about health? Many species of insects are an excellent source of protein – anywhere between 30 per cent and 70 per cent on a dry-weight basis.
>
> From an environmental perspective, it is likely that the development of a much more insectivorous human and animal population would have good and bad consequences. It is likely that next to nothing is known about environmental demands of insect husbandry. Insect-eating in hunter-gatherer mode as currently practised in Latin America and Australia is likely to be of low impact from an environmental perspective. Industrialising production would inevitably have environmental costs. However, the addition of a meaningful insect-based segment to the food industry would be good for human and animal health, and might also diversify resource usage, giving greater choice in respect of the agricultural feed-stock portfolio.
>
> We cannot leave this section without pointing out that such a segment already exists. Millions of mealworms are shipped daily by specialist firms, to be fed to garden birds and pets.[29] According to David George Gordon (author of *The Compleat Cockroach*) they also appear in the form of culinary delicacies. (Mealworms reportedly contain 46 per cent protein, 25.3 per cent fat, 6.7 per cent fibre.)[30] Mealworm omelette, anyone?

Meat – what it means for the environment and human health

Meat consumption gave our ancestors access to a nutritious diet, and meat continues to be an important part of a balanced diet for many people. The benefits of chicken soup as nourishing food are deeply rooted in some cultures – think of the well-known book series *Chicken Soup for the Soul* (which is not about food – here chicken soup is a metaphor for spiritual nourishment). However, the pressures of a constrained environment (such as the limited availability of land required for meat production) and economics mean that meat eaten in large quantities by a growing human population tends to rely increasingly on factory farming. This form of farming does provide affordable protein. However, this form of meat production is generally considered detrimental to animal welfare.[31] The environmental consequences of factory farming in terms of emissions to land, water and air are not *inevitably* negative – it depends very much on how things are done. The consequences for human health may turn out to be negative, even as protein increases in the diet. This is because food is not just food, from a health perspective.

The health effects of meat produced on the factory farm go beyond food. Hence, mega-herds of cows or pigs housed in close proximity to each other can create the perfect conditions for some diseases to flourish,[32] a situation that potentially affects human beings in two ways. First, the regular application of antibiotics to suppress the development of disease may lead to antibiotic resistance in humans, making it difficult to treat some illnesses.[33] Second, bacteria or viruses present in large flocks and herds may be able to jump the species barrier, potentially infecting human beings with diseases some may find hard to fight off. Human ingenuity may be able to come up with new vaccines or other strategies in time to fight off this problem but unfortunately the adaptability of viruses and bacteria knows no bounds. Thus, the brief encounters between human beings and animal flu witnessed in recent years may turn out to be little more than minor skirmishes in a new war against disease, in which technology struggles to keep up with biology. If the aim of factory farming is to facilitate access to affordable nutrition, but the costs include poor animal welfare and a potentially significant new disease burden for humans, the question is whether such agricultural intensification is a self-defeating exercise.

Trade, food health and the environment

It is a combination of global trade and the cultural melting-pot that has helped to create rich and varied developed-country diets. The value of global trade in agricultural products alone is estimated to be well over 500 billion dollars.[34]

In the absence of food trade, many regions of the world would struggle to provide themselves with a sufficient and balanced diet as their populations expand. Autarky is simply not the answer to the problem of feeding nine billion people by 2050. The production shares of key food categories such as meat, dairy, vegetable oils, and sugar are rising in the developing world.[35] From the perspective of development economics this is good news. It suggests that regions of the world that have historically been the most likely to suffer food insecurity (with all of the health risks this entails) are becoming more food secure. From the perspective of the environment the trend is bad news, for meat and dairy products are environmentally costly. However, for the moment, we leave the bad-news story to one side and consider the good-news story.

The risk of inconsistency in food quality and safety in such a large trading system led to the creation of the *Codex Alimentarius* in 1963.[36] This was jointly established by the United Nations' Food and Agriculture Organization, the World Health Organization Food Standards programme and the Codex Alimentarius Commission with the aims of protecting the health of the consumer as well as ensuring fair trade. The importance of good food standards in smoothing trade flows cannot be underestimated – without trust, global food markets would be unable to operate. Codes such as this are thus supportive of food security as well as food safety. The scope of the Codex is wide, covering everything from genetically modified crops to pesticides to food contamination. The three main scientific committees of the Codex focus respectively on food additives, pesticide residues and microbiological risk assessment. Although not the main aim of the Codex, it is nevertheless very clearly connected to the environment. In particular, what happens in the environment will have a direct impact on food safety. Good practice in agriculture will be protective of human health and the environment alike because it addresses issues such as microbiological risk and pesticide residues early on in the food food-chain. Thus, as well as being good for food security, global food trade has the potential to be good for the environment, too. As usual, it is not what is done but how it is done.

Food processing and health

The industrialisation of food processing has two environmentally related consequences for human health. The first is that the nutritional content of processed food may not be the same as the nutritional content of so-called 'slow food' because of micronutrients lost along the way. The second problem is that what the manufacturer puts into the recipe may not be what the home cook would put into the recipe – this is variation on the economic concerns of distance. Most home cooks would not be keen on the idea of replacing natural vitamin E with synthetic vitamin E (an unknown quantity in terms of its nutritional impact), or injecting beef protein or butter fat into chicken. Those replacing home-cooked food with a diet of industrially produced food may inadvertently do exactly that, with potentially significant changes to the quality of their diet. The recent media storm over horsemeat introduced into processed food in the UK and Ireland is a good example of the problems of control (although many cultures have no problems with eating horse, of course, and it is a relatively healthy meat to eat – the issue is not what was introduced into the food food-chain, but the fact that it was introduced without the consumer being aware).

Governments tend to obsess about nutrition in diet – for good economic and environmental reasons. This obsession at least allows economists and environmentalists to gorge themselves on a veritable smorgasbord of statistics. In the UK, official statistics suggest that the consumption of substances such as riboflavin, iron, magnesium, calcium and potassium was in excess of recommended levels. However, the consumption of some nutrients had fallen between 2007 and 2010 – vitamin B_6, potassium and zinc, calcium and folate.[37] The question is whether this trend has continued, for, if it has, it would suggest that the financial credit crunch has caused some people to 'trade down' the nutritional content of the shopping basket, decreasing fruit and vegetables and moving to (cheaper) processed foods. Later surveys report that the evidence is 'showing downward trends', but this evidence is not yet strong enough to suggest that the fall is attributable to consumers cutting key food groups in order to save money.[38]

The economic and environmental consequences of food and health

In perhaps two generations we have gone from a state where insufficient food was the main global health concern, to one where excess food of the wrong sort is the main health concern. This is not to dismiss the fact that malnutrition and even famine exists in some parts of the world, but the rise of affluence in many parts of society has tipped the balance towards too much rather than too little food as the dominant health problem for a majority of the global population. A third of the world's population was deemed overweight in 2008.[39]

The damage, economically speaking, comes in three ways. First, society is wasting food. We will explore this in more detail in the next chapter, but for now let us simply recall the money spent on diet remedies in the UK or the USA. This is wasted money and wasted economic resources, because the diet industry is just correcting a problem that did not need to exist in the first place. The efforts of the diet industry are wasted effort – wasted economic resource if you will. Those efforts or resources could be applied more profitably elsewhere if there were a little forethought on the part of the consumer.

Second, there is the cost of treating diseases related to obesity. Anything from tooth decay to diabetes can be included in this (along with the cost of cosmetic surgery treatments like stomach bands and liposuction). These are diseases that are generally preventable and whose presentation can often be directly linked to a poor diet. One could then add to the list those diseases that are exacerbated by poor diet. This might include mental health issues (depression, for instance) or allergies. Stretching the chain of causation a little further, issues like alcoholism could be included.

What is the economic cost of this 'unnecessary' medical treatment? It is hard to quantify. Some diseases will have multiple causes, and something as complex as the human body will have complex maintenance issues. However, with a third of Americans classified as obese, and American healthcare costing the equivalent of 17 per cent of the US economy, one could make a very crude case that up to 6 per cent of the US economy is taken up with tending to food health issues. In other words, obesity in America could be considered roughly as big as a problem in economic terms as is the budget deficit.

Such numbers must be considered as purely indicative. However, the market for diabetes care is estimated to reach 114.3 billion dollars in 2016.[40] And this is just the cost of *treating* a health problem that is often (though not always) preventable through changes in diet.

The final economic cost of food and health is the loss of productive capacity that ill-health creates. A worker that is subject to illness not only incurs an economic cost in terms of treatment. While that worker is being treated, they are not working. Time off for illness is a loss to the economy. If they are 'under the weather' at work – lethargic either physically or mentally, for instance – potential production is lost. Thinking about a wartime economy might help to frame the importance of this. A wartime economy is one that is fighting for its survival, and which needs to be as efficient as possible – hence the phrase 'fighting-fit'. An overweight workforce is not fighting-fit.

Sound agricultural land is better for the environment and produces food that should be better for human health. Given the importance of soil quality in the production of food with adequate micronutrients, looking after the land in such a way as to facilitate environmentally sustainable agricultural output may be one of the best possible investments human beings could make. Similarly, in developing countries, equitable access to micronutrients could turn out to be a powerful policy instrument in economic and health terms.

If factory farming is pursued to increase humanity's access to affordable nutrition, but the costs include poor animal welfare and potentially significant new disease risks, the question is whether such agricultural intensification is a self-defeating exercise. A better balance between food groups in the diet (including things we are culturally unused to) may be the answer. Putting people in developed economies back in control of how they get and prepare their food, by giving them the time and the means to do it, could reduce the extent to which we depend on non-human energy for daily activities. This would be positive for health and the environment. However, so simple an idea in theory might require significant changes to the way we live and work if it were ever to be implemented in practice.

Notes

1. Martin (1979).
2. Foster-Powell et al. (2002).
3. Taubes (2011).
4. Boyd-Orr (1937).
5. Adam (2012), citing the WHO's Global Burden of Disease study.
6. Collins (2008).
7. Weight-control Information Network (2012).
8. Popkin (2008).
9. Former Surgeon General Richard Carmona, cited in American Heart Association (n.d.).
10. Leake (2012).
11. Foresight Programme of the UK Government (2011b).
12. BBC (2007).
13. Koo and Taylor (2012), p. 9, Table 1.
14. Assuming a teaspoonful of sugar contains four grams, and a small apple about fifteen grams.
15. Lustig et al. (2012).
16. Ibid. Sugar is composed of two sugars in roughly equal measures – fructose and glucose.
17. Yudkin (2012), Kindle Location 152.
18. World Health Organization (2003).
19. In Denmark a fat tax was abandoned just a year after it came into law because of the heavy burden of paperwork for companies, and the ability of consumers to pop across the border to obtain fatty, sugary comestibles untaxed.
20. Economist (2012).
21. Food and Agriculture Organization of the United Nations (1997).
22. Similar advice appears on many websites. See for example National Health Service (n.d.).
23. MacPherson (2008).
24. Orwell (1937).
25. McDonalds, at http://nutrition.mcdonalds.com/getnutrition/nutritionfacts.pdf.
26. Technically, the 'Making of Bread, etc. Act 1800' (41 Geo. III c 16). Millers were only allowed to produce wholemeal flour, in response to the poor harvest of wheat in 1799.
27. See, for example, Welch (2002).
28. Ramos-Elorduy (1998), p. 4, Table 1.
29. Gordon (1998), Chapter Six.
30. Analysis by Woodson-Tenent Laboratories, cited by Gordon (1998), p. 56.

31 We are well aware that some of our readers will disagree with this comment and others will think we do not make enough of it. A full exploration of the arguments on both sides of this topic would require an entire book.
32 We should be careful not to assume this is always the case – the instance of disease and medication amongst free-range chickens is higher than it is amongst battery chickens, as we saw in Chapter 4.
33 Barton (2000).
34 Figure for the year 2003, see Food and Agriculture Organization of the United Nations (n.d.).
35 OECD-FAO (2012).
36 See www.codexalimentarius.org
37 DEFRA (2012a).
38 DEFRA (2012b).
39 Howard (2012).
40 Transparency Market Research reported on www.prneswire.com on 1 November 2011.

10 Food waste

CHIEF JUSTICE: Your means are very slender, and your waste is great.
FALSTAFF: I would it were otherwise, I would my means were greater, and my waist slenderer.

(Shakespeare, *Henry IV, Part 2*, I.ii, 140–141)

Waste is the end, but also the beginning of the topic of food policy and the environment. It is the end because it is the natural conclusion of the food food-chain. It is the beginning, because waste – at least organic waste – can be an input at the start of the food food-chain. Compost is a fertiliser every amateur gardener is familiar with, and it enhances (potentially) the yield of the land which formed the first link in the food food-chain of this book. But waste is also the beginning of a book like this because waste is the area where economists and environmentalists can come together in a joyous harmony of opinion.

Remarkably, economists and environmentalists often disagree with one another – the co-authorship of this book being the exception that proves the rule (possibly because the authors hardly ever meet face to face). Economists are looking for the optimal way of improving the standard of living. An economist's focus tends to be on the pricing mechanism as a rationing system or as a means of discovering consumer preference, but in using this mechanism they run the risk of offending the environmentalist's medium-term objectives. However, waste is an area of common ground. Economists dislike waste because it represents an unnecessary loss of economic resources. Environmentalists dislike waste because it represents an unnecessary loss of environmental resources. Minimising waste across the food food-chain is therefore something that both the economist and the environmentalist can applaud.

This does not mean that there will be complete harmony about the best *way* to reduce waste, of course. Economists are still likely to favour market-based solutions, although in that context environmental concerns are recognised as an area of occasional market failure that will require regulations or some other non-market force to correct. How environmentalists see the matter may vary. Some will take a strict normative view of the matter and recommend a strict regime of rules and regulations. Others might suggest a balanced combination of market forces and rules. Whichever approach is taken, disharmony will arise because food waste is very often a behavioural issue. Attempts to control behaviour can quickly become political, especially in the context of a sensitive matter like food.

Falstaff's attitude to authority and waste, expressed above, gets right to the heart of human behaviour, then as now. Thumbing his nose at the powers that be, represented in the Chief Justice, through the joking reference to his large waistline, he refuses to recognise the criticism implicit in 'waste', instead giving voice (for a modern audience at least) to the impossible dream of being rich and slim. This psychology may chime with the cultural environment in wealthier countries, but, for anyone suffering the effects of dearth or famine, then or now, there is no funny side to Falstaff's dietary profligacy. Indeed, the early performance history of *The Merry Wives of Windsor* (said to have been written around 1597 to give Falstaff a new lease of life at the request of Queen Elizabeth I) may have been influenced by the mood of a population suffering the environmental conditions of the so-called Little Ice Age. England suffered five years of bad harvests and hunger in the 1590s,[1] and these conditions seem to have deferred the first appearance of the play at its intended venue, Windsor, until harvests improved, food prices dropped, and it became acceptable to laugh at waste (and Falstaff's waist) once again.[2]

It is unlikely that the residents of early modern England were in ignorance about where their food came from, but highly likely that many had suffered the ignominy of not knowing where the next meal was coming from. Thus, waste would be avoided at every stage of the food food-chain. These days, in the developed world at least, the conception of waste tends to focus on the very end of the food food-chain. The mental image of someone scraping a plate of half-eaten food into a bin or jettisoning a product that is past its 'sell-by' date tends to dominate our concept of waste. This is not too bad a proxy, in fact. In the developed world it is the later stages of the food food-chain that tend to be more wasteful, and it is the personal interaction with food and food waste that is most likely to remain emblazoned on the consumer's mental retina. Economically, this also makes the waste of food product a form of waste that is perhaps easier to tackle. The consumer is acutely aware of the waste that they are undertaking, and in times of economic austerity (when the economic costs of waste appear heightened) the consumer will tend to be sensitive to this form of waste.

However, as this book has hopefully articulated across the preceding chapters, both in economic terms and in environmental terms there is a great deal that goes on before the food reaches the plate. There is economic and environmental waste at every link in the food food-chain. Controlling that waste is important. It may well be that the consumer, in choosing to minimise waste at the end of the food food-chain, will make economic choices that create either economic or environmental waste higher up the food food-chain. Indeed, one of the issues with waste in the concept of food is that it is extremely unlikely in a modern society that we can reduce waste all along the chain. There will inevitably be a trade-off: we must accept a degree of waste or inefficiency in one link of the chain in order to mitigate waste or inefficiency in another link. The trick is to take decisions that minimise waste in total, without obsessing about waste in one link in the chain to the detriment of waste elsewhere.

182 Food waste

Waste, in every sense of the word, runs through all the stages of the food food-chain discussed in these pages. In agriculture, water, soil and fertiliser are used wastefully, and land and water sometimes laid waste by food production; modern meat husbandry and fish harvesting both waste and lay waste the environment. The twenty-first-century food distribution system – transport, wholesaling and retailing – wastes resources and encourages people to throw away food and indeed to throw away human health. Waste, in the context of twenty-first-century food, is thus a serious matter. In the context of the scenario diagrams of earlier chapters it can be described as a 'lose–lose' situation, for it is bad news from the perspective of economist and environmentalist alike.

However, the human psychology represented by Falstaff and overlaid upon Figure 3.1 illustrates the difficulty of reducing waste (Figure 10.1). The treehugger scenario of an earlier chapter is all too easily associated with repentance – sackcloth and ashes. Falstaff would vote for its opposite – 'new silk and old sack'[3] (drink) – every time. Using resources efficiently (doing more with less) translates, other things equal, to a better match between infinite desires and limited resources, but given the Falstaffian desire to make less effort to get to a better place, the optimal is all too easily configured as an impossible dream. Waste reduction – forced upon people by market forces and the financial (not the environmental) credit crunch, or seemingly autocratic environmentalists urging people to repent their wicked ways – is simply no fun. If Falstaff were alive today we hazard a guess that he would see tree-huggers as Chief Justices to be flouted or ignored, and would not be unduly concerned by food waste – whether in the form of food sent to landfill or food over-filling his stomach.

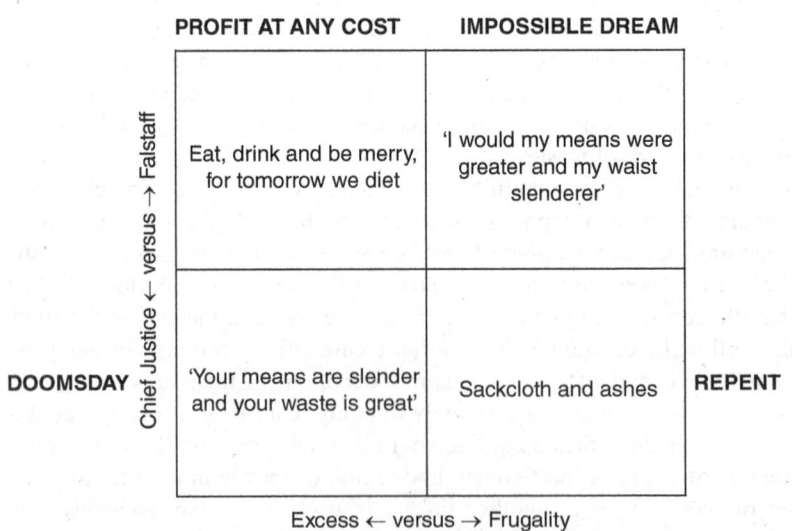

Figure 10.1 The Falstaffian approach to food waste.

In the twenty-first century, the topic of food waste very often hits the headlines in the press. Reading the headline statistics, one might think that all it would take is for the world to return to a simpler food food-chain. In the OECD countries, we learn that each *consumer* disposes of between 95 and 115 kilograms of food a year, while in South Asia this number is between six and eleven kilograms of food.[4] Similarly, United Nations' numbers suggest that in Europe and North America consumers throw away between one-and-a-half and two times the body weight of an average adult in food per year.[5] However, waste is not just a Western habit. India also loses around twenty-one million tonnes of wheat a year (which is the wheat output of Australia, basically) as a result of poor storage. Waste is a common problem – the difference is where it is located in the food food-chain.

The UK Institution of Mechanical Engineers estimates that, annually, food wasted in global markets lies anywhere between 30 and 50 per cent of all food produced, and that between 1.2 and 2 billion tonnes of food never reaches its intended destination. Mind-boggling though these numbers are, they do not take into account all of the waste elsewhere in the system. Thus, it seems clear that if the food-waste issue could be even only partly remedied in some of the dimensions described, this could amount to significant environmental and economic gains. However, it also seems clear that there is no silver bullet. Even leaving aside the problems of Falstaffian psychology, the fact is we are dealing with an entire system of waste, briefly set out in Table 10.1.

Food security and food waste

The extent to which any given country or society is 'food-secure' (defined as having consistent access to affordable, good-quality, nutritious food for the population at large) is likely to be determined by the prevailing mix of economic development, climate and culture. Hence, regular weather volatility together with food wasted in transit owing to logistical inefficiency is likely to be a regular cause of food insecurity in developing countries. In contrast, for developed countries, food security is only likely to be encountered for such reasons in extreme situations. The more relaxed people are about food security, the less they are likely to care about food waste, as the FAO's regional food-waste numbers demonstrate. Attitudes can, however, change quite rapidly even in the face of a modest challenge to food security.

Such a challenge, in the form of the volatile weather patterns experienced in the UK in 2012, is a good example. Here, very wet conditions followed a period of drought, significantly reducing agricultural production. It cannot be said, strictly speaking, that food security was a problem in this context – after all the UK trades food in global markets and has the wherewithal to import in the event of a local shortfall. This, bar wartime disruption, has been the case since the nineteenth century. Nevertheless, we note the significance of this point in the context of this chapter: 2012 was the year in which food waste was used to make good a food shortfall. Specifically, the 'ugly vegetable', formerly consigned to the scrapheap or ploughed back in to the field on the basis of its appearance alone,

Table 10.1 Summing up – waste in the food food-chain

Area	Waste
Agriculture – mineral	Water and fertilisers are often inefficiently used
Agriculture – vegetable	Crop protection chemicals need to be used in increased quantities in the context of monocultures
Agriculture – animal	Meat production delivers a poor return in terms of productivity and is environmentally costly
Food processing	Food processing can help protect perishables; however, this benefit is offset by the over-eating that processed food seems to encourage
Transport	Transport gets food to where it is needed. The lack of adequate facilities results in food waste in developing countries. Car journeys to shop for food may be used to excess
Food retailing and wholesaling	Promotion and packaging designed to sell food in bulk may encourage over-eating
	Processed food saves time but at a cost of potentially less healthy diets and higher environmental impacts
Cooking pot and table	Cooking know-how in the average household is low, so leftovers are more likely to be thrown away than used up. This wastes the resources used to produce the food, and entails an opportunity cost of nutrients not consumed. Feeding food scraps to animals is increasingly uncommon
Health	The obesity epidemic in some parts of the world with several million undernourished people in other parts of the world reflects wastefully used food and wastes healthcare resources
Food waste	Much food waste goes to landfill rather than being recycled

Source: Authors.

was suddenly in fashion on the supermarket shelf. Perhaps the next food-culture shibboleth to be challenged will be the oft-wasteful sell-by date.

Global food systems and food security

Short-run volatility in agricultural production driven by the weather is a salutary reminder of the vulnerability of *global* food systems to changes in the climate. Although global trade usually provides a cushion against food insecurity in this context, the food commodity price shocks that sometimes follow from supply shocks in agriculture can lead to a food-security problem for the less well-off in relatively wealthy countries. The importance of affordability may be forgotten by the better-off for whom food is a small part of the annual budget, but higher prices for food staples can rapidly become a political issue when forcing people to go without essential nutrients. It should never be forgotten that the soundness of the global food trade on which many countries depend for food security depends in turn upon the sound functioning of developing-country food systems, and this, in turn, depends on a decent global environment, defined as the sum of the many local micro-environments on the planet. Damaged ecosystems in developing countries will affect food prices in wealthier regions through the medium of global markets. Thus, investing to avoid waste in the food food-chain can be seen as the responsibility of food businesses dependent on food trade no matter where based.

For the consumer the far-flung food food-chain may be out of sight and out of mind. However, there are powerful arguments to suggest that the food processing and retailing industries should not let the consumer forget. Human physiology leans towards over-eating as an insurance policy. If it is not clear where the next meal is coming from, it is only prudent to have fat reserves to draw on. Ironically, however, over-eating, which can be seen as a form of short-term food security, is also a risk to food security when repeatedly indulged in. One of the consequences of a fundamentally wasteful food food-chain is reduced food security owing to the depletion (through over-use) of environmental resources that will be needed to grow food in the future. It is unlikely that all food waste can be avoided (because of the perishable nature of food), and it is unlikely that any given reduction in food demand arising from any reduction in food waste would translate to a similar reduction in production on the supply side. Nevertheless, given the scale of food waste and the unavoidable conclusion that this is putting pressure on ecosystems on a global basis, there is little doubt that food security could be at least somewhat improved by food-waste avoidance.

Food waste and culture

The desirable outcome is that consumers should be as careful about food waste in developed countries as they are in developing countries. Food thrown away per head in developed countries should simply not be ten to sixteen times higher than it is in developing countries. Developing countries play an important part in global trade, and in the supply chains of firms trading in better-off nations. Developed-country waste thus has a bearing on developing countries. On the basis that economics has delivered this result it is unlikely that economics can be relied on to sort it out. Cultural change is needed. It needs to become unacceptable for the well-off to throw so much food away. Avoiding food waste will not prevent the vagaries of the climate from affecting agricultural production in such a way as to produce years of lean between the years of fat. Similarly, if less food were thrown away it does not necessarily follow that it could be redistributed to those in dearth, nor that such food might be stored against a rainy day. However, the resources freed up by the reduction in volume required to feed the same number of people could, with a little imagination, be engineered to facilitate an increased investment in food storage and delivery logistics. The collection by some airlines of spare change that cannot easily be converted back to home currency – crumbs from the table of the better-off for reinvestment in education – may be a good analogue for food.

A different collection and conversion system would be needed for food, but, given the system-wide wastefulness in evidence in food procurement, production, distribution, preparation and consumption, there are plenty of opportunities to reinvest a few crumbs along the way. In the next few paragraphs we recap on key points for the food food-chain, considering the concept of waste, link by link.

Waste and land

Around half of the useable land on the planet is dedicated to agriculture in some form. Most of the rest is part of the environmental ecosystem in some way. In spite of the popular image of a planet overrun by urbanisation (like some version of Coruscant in *Star Wars*, where the entire planet was a city), humans occupy relatively little of the planet's surface in the form of dwellings and industry. Human dominance of the landscape comes from the need to eat.

How does land waste occur? In economic terms, land is wasted if it is used inefficiently. Land should yield the highest possible economic rent – and economic rent means pretty much what it sounds like. If one could earn a higher rate of return for using the land for some other purpose, then it is the right thing to change the use of that land ('right' in this sense meaning 'economically right'). In terms of economic efficiency, land use can be distorted by government subsidies. Subsidising ethanol production in the United States, or the excesses of the European Economic Community (now the European Union) Common Agricultural Policy in the 1980s led to an economically inefficient use of land. Farmers had incentives to grow crops that the economy did not want because of a misguided attempt to stabilise the market, to produce energy, or perhaps simply in response to the lobbying power of interest groups. Of course the decision to use land in a certain way may mitigate waste later on in the food food-chain (transport waste being the example that leaps to mind), but it still produces economic waste.

The other form of waste in land is something that excites economists and environmentalists alike, which is the waste of resources required to make land productive – fertilisers. Fertiliser is the agricultural equivalent of a perpetual-motion machine (sort of). Every unit of energy used in the manufacture of fertiliser which is subsequently absorbed by a crop of wheat or barley will generate three units of energy in the form of that crop (additional energy input comes from solar power, but that is free in both economic and environmental terms and so can be ignored).[6] Note that this is about the fertiliser absorbed by the crop – there may be inefficiency before that. As already noted in Chapter 2, China has around 30 per cent efficiency in its application of fertilisers to enhance the fertility of land. In other words, 70 per cent of applied fertiliser never goes into the crop, and has to be considered waste in its purest (or perhaps its most impure) form. This waste appears as nitrogen run-off, causing damage to the environment. It represents wasted economic effort, in particular with regard to the energy that will have been used in its manufacture.

So profligate a process of waste is seems unnecessary. In fact around half of all the nitrogen that is leached into the world's soil (and is not taken up by the plant, and is therefore wasted) comes from Chinese agriculture.[7] Agriculture in the United Kingdom is far more efficient in its use of fertiliser, with over 95 per cent finding its way to the plant. The economic solution seems obvious – introduce UK farming techniques into China and waste will be slashed.

Of course the problem is the practicalities of this. UK agriculture is efficient because it is large scale. The global positioning satellite technology tells the farmer in the cockpit of their agricultural machinery how much fertiliser to apply to that specific square metre of soil. The Chinese farmer tending to their smallholding could not even begin to conceive of doing this. This sort of efficiency leap would require a revolution in land ownership, a huge population shift, changes in education, massive investment – this is a change that would take a generation at least. Environmentally, we probably do not have a generation. But at least it goes to show that technology can provide a solution, just as long as we look out for unwanted environmental consequences along the way.

Waste is not always waste

Land misused, or put to the wrong use, or moved to a new use to provide for wasteful food usage is land wasted. In particular, a good soil is a fragile resource and needs to be looked after with care. Related resources such as fertiliser, water and crop-protection can be used far more frugally than they are through better targeting. The so-called Green Revolution was not exactly a waste of water because more water led to productivity gains, as a consequence of the technology-based shift towards agricultural intensification. Nevertheless, the question is whether these productivity gains could have been delivered in some other way. Constrained resources tend to have the impact of whetting the human intellect to find ways of dealing with them through technology. Had water been less readily available as new seed technology developed, we can speculate that the Green Revolution might have evolved down a different path.

Sometimes, agricultural practices that look wasteful are the reverse. And practices that are efficient from one perspective are wasteful from another. Hence, land left fallow might be regarded as a wasted resource from a purely economic perspective, but fallow periods during which the soil is allowed to recover are critical to productivity in agriculture. In this book we have described meat production as a wasteful approach to food procurement, from the perspective of the environment. From the perspective of human physiology this is not altogether true of course. Human beings have looked to put food on the trencher, plate or table that can be used efficiently by the human digestive system.

Waste and vegetables

Waste in the production of vegetables starts with waste of water and pesticides. These are the two big exogenous inputs into modern agriculture after fertiliser. Historically, it was a little broader than that – the random scattering by medieval peasants, rather than the precision planting by the modern farmer's plough and seed drill once meant that valuable seed grain was wasted. Even in developing economies, however, precision in planting has obviated much of that waste.

Water poses its own specific challenges. It is very difficult to price water in many societies because, of course, water is a necessary condition for human existence. While it is easier to put a price on water for commercial purposes (and agriculture is commercial), any passing through of water costs in the form of higher food prices will bring its own political concerns. Moreover, many legal systems give water rights based on the ownership of land around streams and rivers. Farmers, as owners of land, will also have 'ownership' of water, or at the very least the right to draw a quantity of water.

Around 40 per cent of all grain grown worldwide requires irrigation. However, much of irrigation is inefficient. At its very worst, open ditch irrigation, which is very prevalent in the paddy fields of Asia, can waste half the water. Open ditches encourage evaporation, fairly obviously. Even more sophisticated irrigation systems that spray from above tend to be inefficient in that the water does not go to the plant but is broadcast over a relatively wide area. It is an aquatic version of the medieval peasant scattering seeds, and is surprisingly prevalent today. The most efficient irrigation system is, unsurprisingly, quite common in those parts of Africa where water has an obvious value derived from its scarcity. This irrigation is commonly known as 'drip irrigation', as water is dripped right to the root of the plant. Readers of Alexander McCall Smith's writings on Botswana will know that a system of string can provide this irrigation. British gardeners are often familiar with the idea of a 'leaky hose' buried under the plants.

The problem with managing this water waste is that it requires investment, and re-education for farmers who have been used to flooding fields, and whose forebears in all probability flooded those same fields for generations before. However, with water becoming a limiting factor for crop growth in many parts of the world, avoiding waste in this area is going to become more and more economically important.

The pesticide issues around efficiency are similar to those encountered with fertiliser and land efficiency. The technology to apply pesticides in as efficient a manner as possible does exist, and is widely used in developed economies. However, in emerging markets the structure of agriculture does not lend itself to this form of efficiency. This means that for any crop that is not subjected to pest control (even with organic alternatives) part of the harvest will be wasted to disease or predators. The alternative is an inefficient and generally indiscriminate application of pesticide or herbicide, much of which will miss its target, and the waste from which could create wider environmental problems.

There is an alternative to this static interpretation of waste in plants, which is to change the plants themselves. It is worth saying from the outset that this need not entail genetic modification in the laboratory – cross-breeding and selective breeding have been part of farming history for over two millennia (albeit somewhat haphazard until the last thousand years or so). Breeding wheat that is short brings all sorts of efficiencies. The literary-named 'Hobbit' variety of wheat puts 50 per cent of its biomass into the grain (which is the bit to be eaten), compared with only 30 per cent on older varieties. It has, fairly obviously, a shorter stalk (and stalk is in food terms pretty much all waste). Moreover, because it is shorter it responds better to nitrogen fertiliser – taller varieties keep growing and then fall over. The question is whether consumers will purchase genetically modified foodstuffs, and survey after survey has indicated that they will not (at least in Europe). Ignoring the fact that selective breeding is genetic modification in the field, however, economists have conducted their own field work which suggests that consumers will be prepared to purchase genetically modified food if the price is right (which basically means cheaper, of course). This could be important if inefficiencies in food production lead to higher food prices in the face of rising global demand. Consumer aversion to genetic modification could fade.

The final issue with waste and vegetables is more of an emerging-economy problem than it is for the OECD economies. The problem of storing crops is something that has tested human ingenuity almost from the emergence of the pastoral community. The threats are basically rot or mildew or some other form of natural decay, and animals like mice and rats. (As an aside, 'saddle stones' that now form a common ornament in country gardens in the UK have nothing to do with saddles. The stones, which are shaped like giant mushrooms, were used to lift grain stores off the ground and prevent rodent infestation. Rats could climb up the vertical 'stalk' of the saddle stone, but could not navigate the horizontal underside of the 'head' of the saddle stone, and so could not gain access to the granary.)

The problem in many emerging markets is that the storage of crops at or near the metaphorical farm gate (before processing is undertaken) can be wasteful. Estimates suggest that up to 80 per cent of Vietnam's rice crop is lost, as is 45 per cent of China's crop.[8] Damp grain that becomes mildewed or rots, or storage that is not protected from vermin, is a big part of this process. Of course more efficient storage may entail other costs – drying grain to prevent decay or temperature-controlled storage for fruit. The energy used to prolong the storage life of these crops is an economic and environmental cost. However, even basic improvements in storage techniques in emerging markets could achieve much in minimising the amount of food waste – after the economic cost of an initial investment in the necessary infrastructure.

Waste and animals

There are those who contend that the whole business of animal husbandry is wasteful. They do have a point. Considering how much energy goes into rearing a cow and how little of that energy translates into actual beef (5 per cent of the energy winds up as edible meat), one could make a case that animal husbandry is just waste on a large scale. Against that, there is the rather obvious point that human beings tend not to thrive on a diet of grass, while a cow (or a sheep) will. If growing grass is the most efficient use of land (for instance, hill farming) then animal husbandry is likely to be the most efficient option.

If we assume that meat is still going to be consumed, at least to some extent, then controlling waste must be about making sure that the type of meat that is reared is economically optimal. There are two related ways this can be achieved. First, in terms of land use, pork and chicken are the more efficient forms of meat. Waste of land can be contained. However, such a pursuit of economic efficiency may lead to uncomfortable choices for the consumer. In economic terms and in environmental terms (from a pure resource perspective) battery chickens are preferable. The mortality rate of free-range hens, prior to the 'desired' mortality of killing the hen for meat, is 10 per cent. So 10 per cent of the resources applied to free-range poultry is economically and potentially environmentally wasted resource. The mortality rate of a battery chicken is 3 per cent. Moreover, free-range hens (as categorised by UK regulations) are more resource-intensive. Free-range hens are more susceptible to disease, and require more drugs to keep them healthy than their caged peers. From an *efficiency* perspective we should eat battery chicken if we chose to eat chicken at all. From an economics perspective the moral qualms that surround such a diet encourage waste. The environmentalist would argue that cheaper food, other things equal, encourages more consumption and more throwing away – both forms of waste. Thus, without a full Life-Cycle Analysis, we do not know which system is more efficient in an all-round sense.

Second, farmers can make sure that the right sorts of animals are reared. Producing the captive barrage-balloon-shaped pigs of the eighteenth century would be an economic and an environmental waste. Porcine fashion has changed, at least as regards consumption. The fat of the animal is wasted in modern society. Through selective breeding or some other form of genetic modification the farmer can produce animals that maximise the attributes consumers want (lean meat, for instance) and minimise the attributes that are not needed. Breeding programmes can also help minimise the risk of disease (early death being a very visible form of economic waste). What is important is that the meat satisfies the desire of the consumer, otherwise there will be waste. However, there is an important caveat, for not all of the consumer's demands may be reasonable.

Meeting the demands of the consumer

In some societies the only regularly available food is animal based. For everyone else, there is arguably no need for a well-balanced diet to include meat every day. Reducing the proportion of planetary bio-production that is dedicated to meat production could significantly reduce resource waste. Moreover, lower production volumes could have an impact on how meat is produced (for instance rendering large factory farms less necessary). Such change in production processes, returning to less intense animal husbandry, could in turn have a significant knock-on impact on the extent to which meat production degrades the environment.

The obvious solution to the meat problem will not be new to our readers. Omnivores could simply reduce the number of times they eat meat per week. Technology may be able to help. Enzymes that improve the digestive efficiency of animals may one day routinely reduce the amount of land needed to produce animal feed. Farming units that use every scrap of biological material (e.g. animal waste to produce electricity to run operations) could take the pressure off other parts of the environment. However, the effect of such changes is likely to be marginal if the volume of food consumption continues to rise. What is needed is a strategy of reducing the amount of land per head assigned to agricultural production and (thence) food consumption.

Putting the two strategies (volume control and technologically driven efficiency) together could amount to a significant brake on the size of the food-driven human footprint. This would mean a reduction in the pressures on the environment. In short – we suggest that there is no escape from the need to consume less meat per head in some regions of the world.

Waste and processing

Processing creates waste in the act of processing but also in the output. The waste in processing is perhaps more immediately obvious. Raw food that is rejected on purely aesthetic grounds, or mass food-processing techniques that discard what an individual may retain, create a degree of waste. Added to this the process of processing can entail the use of economic resources that would not be required if the food was processed in the home. The oven chips derived from potatoes blasted by jets of steam to strip them of their skins will take a lot of energy to prepare (steam at pressure being energy-intensive). A potato-peeler-wielding individual requires none of this level of energy. However, this form of waste is probably not the key problem. The food processor has an economic interest in making their production as efficient as possible, in economic and generally in environmental terms. There are limits – pressure jets will almost certainly always be used in preference to potato peelers in chip manufacture – but if economic costs can be minimised in the processing of food then profits can be made. However, the act of processing food then generates waste beyond the factory gate. One could argue that processed food is designed to encourage waste.

A generation ago, 'leftovers' were a whole culinary subcategory. Delia Smith's *Complete Cookery Course*, first published in 1978, dedicates an entire chapter to the recycling of leftover food.[9] An American, married to a British husband, wrote with an air of complete bemusement that 'some of my husband's favourite desserts have stale white bread as a major ingredient'.[10] The idea of recycling leftover food was born out of economic thrift combined with the cultural memory of rationing in the war years.

The concept of minimising food waste through reusing leftover food has been challenged by several factors. The cultural memory of the war years has naturally faded. Food is a smaller part of the household budget today. Jamie Oliver, the chef of choice for Generation Y, gave *no* space to the use of leftovers in his 2000 edition of *The Return of the Naked Chef*.[11]

Alongside these budget and cultural factors, the rise of processed food is undoubtedly an important part of the practice of cooking with leftovers falling into disuse. Recycling a joint of meat that was roasted on a Sunday is perhaps an obvious thing to do – the meat could go into rissoles, it could be served cold with a salad, or it could even become the basis of a pie. Saving a third of a frozen lasagne that has been microwaved is less obvious – what does one do with a third of a lasagne? A third of a lasagne cannot readily become a component to any other dish. Moreover, the manufacturer, with an eye to the ever present threat of litigation, is likely to warn explicitly somewhere on the packaging that the lasagne cannot be reheated once cooked. Indeed, one could question why one would save stale bread to make a dessert today; bread pudding comes in plastic packaging and a box that says it 'serves two' – what has stale white bread to do with desserts in the age of processed food?

If the food we buy is the processed finished product, rather than the ingredients (economic subcomponents) of a finished dish, then the versatility of the food that we buy is reduced and the likelihood of waste increases. Clearly, some processed food can be recycled – the bread pudding can be made with stale shop bread as well as stale home-made bread. Cold takeaway pizza left over from the night before is a staple breakfast food for many a university student. But these are the exceptions, not the rule. Processing reduces the choices available to the consumer when it comes to managing waste. The economic forces that push consumers towards the consumption of processed food similarly push consumers into the uneconomic behaviour of wasting that food.

Waste in food processing and packaging

Packaging can, in the right circumstances, avoid food waste, for it contains and preserves the contents in the right conditions for a longer life on the cupboard shelf. When the reverse is true this may be for one of two reasons, one relating to the food itself, and the other to the packaging. In respect of the contents, the amount packaged may not be optimal in relation to the amount likely to be used by the time it needs to be used, and the consumer is forced to throw bad food away. In respect of packaging there can simply be a lot more of it than is needed, using resources such as fibre or plastic that must then be disposed of, and cannot always be readily recycled.

Waste in transport and logistics

Transport and logistics can lead to food and energy wastage if there is too little of the relevant infrastructure and food rots before it can be moved from the farm to market. Even if there is sufficient provision for the storage and transport required to take food to where it is needed, food efficiently stored and transported can still be inefficiently used. Sometimes efficient operation of transport and logistics systems requires a minimum level of throughput which can result in the delivery of more produce than is needed. Inefficiency in transport thus includes the problem of sending too much food through the transport system – defined as more than is needed by the end user. Economics (for instance in the form of high fuel prices) can take care of this second problem. The first problem – an insufficiency of transport and storage – tends to arise in developing countries when food perishes en route because it is transported in the wrong conditions or there is simply no means of getting the food to market. Here, economics cannot help – politics must intervene.

However, in the context of food transport neither of these problems takes centre stage in the media, which are after all trying to sell newspapers and blogs. Economically speaking, waste and transport may be one of the things that bring an economist and an environmentalist into conflict. Waste and transport has attracted a lot of attention in recent years because of the concept of 'food miles'. For those that follow the black art of public relations this is a fantastic concept. Food miles are easy to understand, easy for the consumer to mentally picture (distance is something we can generally process very easily), and easy to identify. 'Food miles bad, local good' has an elegant Orwellian simplicity to it. And yet economists really cannot be brought to care too much about this.

The problem is that transport is a relatively small part of the economic cost base for food distribution. One could justify local food purchases out of a desire to preserve local skills, maybe (specialist cheese-making, perhaps?), although in economic terms if there is no demand for the product in the absence of a food miles campaign, the product is probably not efficient to produce. (As discussed above, efficiency isn't everything.) One could make a justification on the grounds of food security, certainly. The externalities of things like preserving the countryside through an active farming community can also be considered. But, at the end of the day, the economist looks askance at the idea of food miles as a guide to waste control.

Why is this? Well, the problem is that in seeking to minimise food miles one may create economic and environmental waste elsewhere along the food food-chain. A national, even an international food distribution system does consume resources, but it can also ensure that other resources are more efficiently used. The classic example is that it is more economically and environmentally efficient to grow a tomato in Spain and fly it to the UK during the winter months than it is to grow a tomato in the UK for domestic consumption. Winter tomato production in the UK requires the fruit to be pampered and cosseted in heated glasshouses with labour-intensive attention; this is not really an optimal method of production. Spain's natural comparative advantage (to use the economic jargon) that comes from its climate obviates the necessity for any of this. But it goes beyond the production. Having an advanced transport system for food allows supermarkets to have 'just in time' supplies. The supermarket does not need to overstock food, because if supplies are running low the food transport network can replace the food quickly. Not overstocking means less food is disposed of.

To give an example of this, in the UK, 46 per cent of potatoes grown to be sold as potatoes (i.e. not processed into oven chips, etc.) are never in fact sold – they are rejected at some point in the food food-chain. However, only 5 per cent of potatoes are wasted at the store level – most of the waste occurs earlier. The store is a relatively economically and environmentally efficient link in the food food-chain because the transport process means that potatoes are not displayed for very long in the suboptimal conditions of a supermarket vegetable aisle – instead they are stored off-site in more suitable conditions, and bussed in to the supermarket as required.

If we accept that transport is going to take place, then economists and environmentalists can agree that making the transport of food as efficient as possible is mutually beneficial. There are some interesting options here. Transporting concentrated product to rehydrate close to the consumer is one option. Minimising packaging, which allows more food to be fitted into a lorry (or other mode of transport), and which reduces the weight per calorie carried, will make transporting food more efficient. Something so simple as replacing canned food with the same quantity of food in rectangular cartons will increase the quantity of food that can be carried (the packaging company Tetra has estimated that such a move could reduce the number of lorries required to transport a given quantity of food by around 55 per cent).

Transport – the last mile

Transport is everywhere in the food food-chain. The round-trip car journey for the weekly shop undertaken by so many is fundamentally wasteful from the perspective of fuel usage, and other resources required for the construction of the average car (which is, with apologies to car lovers) a heap of metal, plastic and glass doing nothing at all most of the time. If the weekly shop can be combined with other activity (for instance in combination with the journey home from work), it will be less wasteful of fuel. Even better, those lucky enough to be able to walk easily to the supermarket, market or other shops on a higher-frequency basis probably end up spending no more time on shopping than those who do the big weekly shop, and they are less likely to waste food, being able to buy just what is needed.

Unfortunately, in practical terms, shopping frequently on foot can be hard for most people to do. For one thing, we all need to earn a living, and our working patterns are not always under our control. Thus, to fit food shopping around work is at the heart of many decisions to shop by car. The Internet may be changing this, at least to an extent. Shopping by Internet for a weekly or less frequent delivery and supplementing this with small trips for perishable items is likely to be more efficient from an energy use perspective – for the delivery van driver may be able to optimise the route to keep fuel use per delivery low. With fuel prices high enough, the economic incentive could even be in place to elicit such behaviour from the consumer. However, in difficult economic times, this may be offset by the possibility that lower-cost food retailers seeking to offer food at low prices to their customers find themselves less able to offer nice-to-have services such as food delivery.

Waste in wholesale and retail

We think that waste at the retail sector can be thought of as arising out of two motives. First, there is waste because the retailer rejects food. Second, there is waste because of the consumers' buying patterns cause waste. The UK Foresight report, similarly, suggests that food waste in the UK is driven by three factors: the supply chain, procurement and messaging, and consumer behaviour.[12] Although the food retail sector is not the best-qualified sector to deal *directly* with food waste, it is highly likely that this sector could have a significant impact on food waste by acting as a catalyst for avoiding food waste. The sector could help change behaviour: by changing supply chain contracts to be more flexible with respect to variability in agricultural production; by shifting away from wasteful practices in retailing; and by giving the consumer more access to information.

A retailer would, however, argue that waste in retail procurement practices and waste because of consumer-buying patterns are related – consumers wish to buy carrots of a particular appearance, for example, and so carrots that do not win in the vegetable beauty parade will not be stocked by retailers because they are not what the consumer wishes to buy. In practice, it is more complicated than that, as the consumer is rarely given the chance to express their opinion – and the consumer's preference for the appearance of food may well change over the course of the economic cycle or as their personal economic circumstances change.

So what does this mean in practical terms? Up to one-third of the UK's vegetable crop is not harvested because it fails the retailers' vegetable beauty contest. That means 30 per cent of the land used for vegetable growth for human consumption, with proportionate amounts of fertiliser applied and of the energy used to produce fertiliser, is wasted. Some fertiliser may be reclaimed if the crop is ploughed back in, but this is hardly an efficient process in either economic or environmental terms (unless, perhaps, the crop is a legume like turnips; remember Turnip Townshend and his nitrogen-replenishing tactics).

The economist might argue that there are two options available to minimise this waste. Consumers could be given an incentive to buy misshapen carrots through lower prices. This has actually been tried in the UK with some success during the economic downturn. The alternative is to use aesthetically unappealing but otherwise sound foodstuff in processed food. No one really cares what a carrot looked like if it is sold in the form of carrot soup. The environmentalist would argue that Mother Nature might have something to say in the matter. She threw a spanner in food retail supply chains in the UK in 2012. This was the year of the ugly vegetable. Contract standards had required the rejection of slightly misshaped fruit and vegetables for the supermarket shelf. Confronted by a supply shortfall, these standards were abandoned. The alternative would have been substantially higher prices. However, unless the weather patterns experienced in 2012 repeat themselves over a number of years *or* a cultural change leads the consumer to demand a continuation of ugly fruit and vegetables, this change is unlikely to last. Nevertheless, the point remains that this could be a good moment to move for such a change.

Environmentally it also makes sense to encourage a shift away from wasteful retailing practices such as bundling (e.g. buy one, get one free), heavy discounting of bulk purchases, or indeed jumbo-sized packages (although such packages do minimise packaging). Dealing with this issue may be harder than it looks. In the aftermath of the credit crunch the cash-constrained consumer may eschew bulk buys in favour of purchasing smaller amounts – if so, the problem is solved. On the other hand, the need to economise may propel some consumers towards larger packages, and an attempt to remove the opportunity to bulk-buy cheap food in the middle of a financial credit crunch could turn out to be a political hot potato.

Beyond this the food retailer could potentially help the consumer make better use of all food that is taken home from the shop by making labels clearer and providing information on packaging, or in the store, with demonstrations designed to fill the gap in home economics education. This would not require a major change – fishmongers and butchers are well known for furnishing the customer with preparation and cooking advice, and this also happens at specialist counters in some supermarkets. Cookery know-how is also readily available in the media. The question is whether cookery programmes are food-waste aware. As 2013 opens we do not see consistent encouragement to use leftovers as a matter of routine in the context of cooking programmes on TV or in other media, nor for that matter in cookery books.

Waste in the kitchen and at the table

In the efficient kitchen nothing would be wasted. Vegetable peelings would be fed to chickens or pigs, or perhaps composted to help grow future vegetables. The parts of the animal not eaten as dishes in themselves would be used to make soups, stocks and gravies. Cooking liquids would be saved in the stock-pot and recycled through the very same soups and gravies. Elizabeth Acton, writing in her enticingly entitled *Modern Cookery for Private Families* of 1856 was very upfront about this. At the start of her book she lectured:

> It may be safely averred that good cookery is the best and truest economy, turning to full account every wholesome article of food, and converting into palatable meals what the ignorant either render uneatable or throw or way in disdain.[13]

True, she later went on to detail a recipe for truffles boiled in champagne, which might strike some as a little incongruous with the idea that she was advocating the 'best and truest economy', but the intention was good.

Modern cooking habits, driven by the desire to save time, give no scope for such an approach. However, to return to some of the oldest, most old-fashioned yet still best-loved recipes is to rediscover this culture of frugality is not dead, thus, reviving frugality in the kitchen may not be as impossible as it seems. Raymond Blanc, for instance, describes *pot-au-feu* as the 'most celebrated' dish in France. It could not be simpler to make and, since it is made in a single self-contained pot, all of the juices are consumed in the dish. The only item discarded is the fat skimmed off the top. It is a relatively fuel-efficient dish since the meat is very slowly cooked (in a casserole on the stove-top) for three-and-a-half hours. Other ingredients, including the vegetables, are added to the same pot for a further half hour.

This delightful, nutritionally complete, repast (let us not insult it by calling it anything so dry and dusty as efficient but it is exactly that) is served with mustard and, of course, a French baguette. 'You can feast on this dish for three days', declares Raymond Blanc.[14] With the addition of a covering of mashed potato and parmesan cheese, leftovers from *pot-au-feu* can be used to make a cottage pie – better known in situ as the classic dish *hachis Parmentier*. Thus, this dish is embedded in the culinary tradition of making delicious dishes from leftovers – and letting no morsel go to waste.

Thus, it can be seen that it is scandalous that the scraping of the plate into the bin is the epitome of food waste in the developed world. However, leaving aside the idealistic approach to food preparation described above, it must be admitted that in the modern kitchen the cooking pot has the potential to create more waste than the slop bucket alone suggests. Waste here can be classified under two headings: waste of uneaten food; and waste in food preparation.

The waste of uneaten food is not really about scraping the plate. For the consumer at home, waste of uneaten food is largely about disposing of food that is past its 'use-by' date. The use-by date may well have done more to generate waste in the developed world than any other concept. Food that is in fact still fresh, nutritious and edible is jettisoned because of a conservative assumption as to the likely day on which that food will become less fresh, or less nutritious. Even if the conservative assumption is correct, the food is often still edible. The fact that we have a generation who have lost the olfactory and tactile senses required to test the edibility of food is worrying.

In the United Kingdom it is estimated that the food thrown away by households represents the energy equivalent of 20 per cent of all cars on the UK's roads. The vegetables thrown away in the United States are the equivalent of 26 per cent of Sub-Saharan Africa's total vegetable supply. Several factors have conspired to bring us to this point. Processed food in pre-determined package sizes, which cannot readily translate into 'leftover' dishes are part of it. So are supermarket promotions that suggest 'buy one, get one free' or some variation thereof, which encourage over-purchase and then subsequent waste.

The shift in favour of convenience stores and daily shopping may go some way to reduce the 'use-by' waste problem. Buying food on a daily basis naturally minimises the waste. However, there is a displacement in this process because, as we observed in Chapter 7, moving to daily convenience-store shopping may increase the waste associated with packaging, transport and so forth.

For caterers, food waste is also a potential problem. This is less likely to be about use-by dates, though they exist on catering packs as much as consumer packets. Instead, the caterer is likely to over-order food to ensure that the restaurant does not run out of an advertised dish (or too many advertised dishes). To do so would be to undermine the reputation of the restaurant. Some caterers are estimated to throw away a third of their food purchases uneaten.[15] Of course, this may depend on the catering style. A kebab van patently does not throw away the rotating spit of meat that forms the basis of the kebab at the end of the day. A fast-food restaurant with a high footfall of eager diners thronging through its doors every day will be able to sell today's chips tomorrow, as they are stored frozen and cooked on demand. A pub that serves frozen food to its customers is less vulnerable to the waste of time-limits. But for many caterers serving fresh food on a daily basis, waste is something that is included in the price of the meal.

The other form of waste and the cooking pot comes with the cooking pot itself (or with the heating of the cooking pot). Cooking can often mean overcooking. In some countries, for instance, hotels will refuse to serve a cheeseburger 'rare' for fear of litigation should food poisoning ensue (economists tend to be connoisseurs of hotel cheeseburgers; along with French onion soup it is the only thing one can dependably find on the night room-service menus of the world's hotels). The meat is overcooked from the perspective of the consumer, to prevent the small risk of an upset stomach. In the home, reheating processed food in a conventional oven may be a wasteful use of energy – the average family oven being far larger than a supermarket ready-meal for one would really warrant. Daily shopping may leave large fridge-freezers running while empty – or empty bar a bottle or two of white wine and similar necessities. The energy consumption continues because the consumers' cooking infrastructure (fridge, freezer, oven) is associated with bygone consumption patterns.

Eating habits and food waste

It is tempting to conclude that modern living and working patterns have led to the situation described in the above paragraphs in which the minimum of time is allocated to food procurement and preparation. However, we see it as more likely that ingrained ways of dealing with food and prevailing cultural norms can make it difficult for things to change. Food is, after all, a sensitive subject – and (even leaving aside the problem of allergies) people are capable of refusing to eat perfectly good nourishing food items, preferring to let them go to waste, on the basis that they are simply not used to eating them. The mention of one of the namesake dishes of Antoine Auguste Parmentier, above, reminds us that in eighteenth-century France, people who were starving to death would nevertheless not eat anything as disgusting as the lowly *pomme de terre*. It was, after all, animal fodder and, as part of the diet, would weaken those who consumed it. Moreover, it would have unwanted environmental impacts, being naturally ruinous of the soil. Parmentier used every possible tactic he could think of to improve the reputation of the potato. He used science – he wrote *Inquiry into Nourishing Vegetables That at Times of Necessity Could be Substituted for Ordinary Food* (1773). He was a past-master of communications: he prevailed upon the King and Queen of France to wear a potato flower in their buttonhole and hair, respectively, at the King's birthday party. However, the killer strategy (this man was well versed in human psychology) was to put a small field of potatoes growing in poor soil under guard. The locals obligingly decided something under guard was worth pilfering, and the rest is history.[16]

Imagination and innovation regularly result in new approaches to food procurement. Changing eating habits even to the extent of introducing a new staple food can seem impossible – for instance it is unlikely that insects will become staples in countries where they are not already regularly eaten, though there may be more hope for them to become more environmentally friendly ways of feeding fish or farm animals.[17] However, the French history of the potato reminds us that cultural change in food on an unimaginable scale is not an impossible dream. Other pieces of potato history – such as the Irish potato famine – remind that overdoing something (such as monocultures in agriculture) can also lead to waste of human life, livelihood and food resources on an equally unimaginable scale. In the context of food (and related) waste avoidance, balance is as important as it also happens to be in the diet.

Waste in human health

Not getting enough to eat is well known to have adverse health consequences. Eating too much is a waste of food that could have gone to someone who needs it more and it is wasteful in two respects. When entire populations eat too much, a portion of the resources and labour that go in to food production are wasted. The over-consumption of food (often combined with consuming too much of the wrong kinds of food and not enough of the right ones) is wasteful from the perspective of human wellbeing. Over-eating wastes the resources used at every stage of the food food-chain (agriculture, processing, transport, retailing and cooking). Using the same natural resources to produce empty calories is a waste of natural resources, and at the same time wastes one of the most important resources each of us has – our health.

Moreover, when human beings become ill as a result of eating too much this puts a burden on health services and gives rise to unwanted healthcare costs. Food that is wasted in the sense that it would have been better left uneaten thus leads to further waste in the form of unnecessary consumption of healthcare resources.

Ill-health is thus economically wasteful on several levels. Essentially, economic resources are misallocated either in causing ill-health, or in remedying its consequences, or as a result of ill-health if that ill-health has arisen from preventable causes like obesity.[18]

The most visible demonstration of economic waste in health is obesity itself. The additional weight carried around represents the consumption of unnecessary calories. The economic (and environmental) effort that went into creating those calories in the first place, along with all the economic and environmental effort that took those calories from the farm gate to the plate, or restaurant, or kebab van, or pub were wasted from an economically optimal point of view. As we observed in the preceding chapter, two-thirds of Americans are overweight[19] and other countries such as China appear to be catching up rapidly, which means that significant numbers of people have, in effect, wasted food by consuming unnecessarily.

There is a slightly grey area in economics, if we assume that people take pleasure in eating even when eating more than they should. This pleasure has (strictly speaking) an economic value and it is possible to argue that excess consumption is still optimal if it gives enough pleasure to the consumer. However, this Utilitarian standpoint is somewhat dangerous, and can quickly lead to a justification for destructive drug addiction – heroin gives pleasure which has an economic value. Given the chemical reaction triggered in the human brain by the consumption of sugar,[20] the analogy is not inappropriate.

So what is the economic value of the waste represented by a spare tyre around one's midriff? It is hard to be precise, but problems with precision have never stopped economists before. Dietary guidelines suggest men should eat 2,000 to 3,000 calories per day depending on their level of physical activity. Allowing for underestimation of actual consumption and a relatively sedentary lifestyle, it is not unrealistic to suppose that there is consumption of 20–25 per cent more calories than are actually needed.

If we take a large food market as an example to gain an idea of scale, America's domestic food sales were worth 1.16 trillion dollars in 2012 (including eating out). If 20 per cent of that is going to produce unnecessary fat, then we can argue that over-eating costs America 232 billion dollars per year. That is almost 750 dollars per person, per year in wasted spending on calories. Considering the speed with which other nations may be catching up in the calorie consumption stakes, the global economic costs could be considerable.

To this economic waste, actual and potential, we can then add the actual and potential cost of treating preventable diseases that are the result of people being overweight or obese, or having an inappropriate diet. This is a wide range of issues – everything from cosmetic surgery through to tooth decay, via diabetes, heart disease, and liver damage.

Controlling waste

So how can waste be minimised? Clearly, if waste is a significant problem, seeking to minimise waste along the production chain to the consumer would be economically and environmentally optimal. With up to half the world's food wasted in some form, it seems clear that control of waste could solve any potential problem about how to feed the projected increase in the world's population over the next thirty years. Nine or ten billion people? Bring it on. The world produces enough food to feed that many people today.

It is also important to recognise that waste is still waste. The compost bin may be the best way of disposing of broccoli that is past its sell-by date, but that is still a form of waste (for all that it is recycled back into the start of the production chain). If the broccoli was not consumed, the economic and environmental resources that were applied to growing it, harvesting it, transporting, packaging and retailing it, along with the costs of storage, were all wasted. It makes for fairly expensive compost. Where waste is waste, because it was inedible in the first place (egg shells, banana skins and the like) then compost is, of course, the preferred option. Even here we should not assume that the basic recycling of waste is the best option. The Tottenham Pudding of the Second World War was a mix of organic waste from bakers, shops and households that was fed to pigs. This sounds like the exemplary sort of recycling that we should all wish to see – a return to the halcyon days of yesteryear when the cottage pig was fed on household scraps. The reality was somewhat different. The use of Tottenham Pudding as a feed promoted diseases amongst the pig herd of the United Kingdom because it was not properly sterilised. Recycling food waste in an inappropriate manner resulted in waste higher up the food food-chain.

Wartime examples have been cited in this book several times, but with good reason. Wartime is an instance of extreme pressure on resources, when efficiency in all things is necessary to help promote the defence of society. How a society reacts in wartime is a good example of what an economy can accomplish in terms of efficiency *in extremis*. The First World War saw food waste declared a crime in the UK, with fines and even prison terms for such heinous acts as feeding a St Bernard dog a steak. The efficiency of the UK's rationing system in the Second World War has often been cited as an instance of how an economy can manage its resources. It is worth observing in passing that the UK's rationing system during the 1940s was a combination of government regulation and market forces. The pricing mechanism was a part of rationing, as much as the books of coupons.

It is unrealistic to assume that society today would accept the degree of government interference that wartime rationing requires. That does not mean that we cannot have some degree of government involvement, however. Indeed, given the political prioritisation of food that we have seen as a recurring theme throughout this book, it is perhaps inevitable that there will be more politics on our plates in the future. Bald regulation at the consumer level is unlikely to work (we would be back to the complete failure of the nineteenth-century Brown Bread Act). However, an intelligent regulation across the food food-chain – and it must be holistically applied – could bring about meaningful and intelligent reductions in waste. The challenge for politicians is to ignore the siren voices of populism and to implement regulation where it can do most good, not where it can be most readily understood. Focusing on food miles and ignoring 'sell-by' dates is not the way to go.

Conclusion

This chapter is a key chapter for this book. It suggests that waste avoidance points to several actions that could be taken to help with the feeding of a still-growing human population sustainably. Wasting less will immediately and directly take pressure off the environment. This is of course not the only answer. In absolute terms, reducing waste will not entirely resolve the problem of population growth – a subject for an entirely different book and requiring a vigorous debate of population ethics. However, there is an urgent need to buy time. Although waste avoidance does not, for the most part, require complex technology, food-related waste avoidance might buy enough time to allow research and development to come up with technologies designed to procure food more sustainably before significant parts of the world hit environment limits. Just because the Green Revolution was not the perfect answer does not mean that technology cannot help – the important point is that the Green Revolution was not conceived within a mind-set of avoiding resource limits. An economist would say it was developed with operational (rather than Pareto) efficiency in mind. An environmentalist would point to the existence of planetary limits that were ignored or not known of by those involved at the time. A Waste-Nothing Green Revolution is needed, and here, we should waste none of the resources at our disposal – particularly not the ultimate resource of human ingenuity.

After ten chapters of careful consideration of each link in the food food-chain, it is time we turned our attention to policies and actions that could make the chain stronger – in economic and environmental terms.

Notes

1 The term 'Little Ice Age' usually refers to the cooler global climate between roughly 1550 and 1800. Evidence of temperature fluctuation through this period has been found in glacial fluctuation, with glacial 'maxima' from time to time. As an example, in northern Norway, paleo-climatologists identified a Little Ice Age 'culmination' (glaciation gradually rising to a peak then falling) between 1590 and 1620. See Grove (2008), Kindle Location 2475.
2 Kinney (1993), p. 228.
3 *Henry IV, Part 2*, 1.ii, 197–198.
4 Tetra Pack (2012), p. 23.
5 Europeans and Americans throw away between 95 and 115 kilograms of food per year; African and Asian consumers do better, ditching only 6–11 kilograms (Food and Agriculture Organization of the United Nations 2012c). An average adult weighs 62 kilograms and an average American adult 82 kilograms according to the London School of Hygiene and Tropical Medicine (cited in Quilty-Harper 2012).
6 Seddon (1989), p. 61.
7 McWilliams (2009), p. 79.
8 Institution of Mechanical Engineers (2013), p. 2.
9 Smith (1978).
10 Lyall (2008).
11 Oliver (2000).
12 Foresight Programme of the UK Government (2011a).
13 Cited in Burnett (1966), p. 184.
14 Blanc (2012).
15 Institution of Mechanical Engineers (2013).
16 This paragraph draws upon Reeves (1997).
17 We note that the elephant on the page may be insect welfare. This book is too short to dig into this topic but we acknowledge that in making this suggestion we may be raising a number of issues, and are unaware (as non-entomologists) of environmental constraints.
18 In saying this, we recognise that not all forms of obesity are self-inflicted or preventable.
19 Weight-control Information Network (2012).
20 On the addictive powers of sugar, see Allday (2013).

11 Conclusion

> In my end is my beginning.
>
> (Mary Queen of Scots)

With this final chapter we come full circle in more than one sense: our final words focus on food waste, for waste is the place where food policy must begin. Preventing waste in the food food-chain, as we observed in Chapter 10, is the area where economist and environmentalist can agree. Neither side likes food waste. Food waste, composted or otherwise digested, has historically made its way back into the food food-chain through the soil. We say 'historically' because the natural cycle that used to drive food provisioning is often broken up by the intervention of industrial processes in evidence in several pieces of the food food-chain. Food waste that ends up in landfill has been ejected, perhaps permanently, from the cycle, taking wasted nutrients with it. Food waste that goes into the composting bin might foster new growth – potatoes or cabbages or roses – at a later date. Thus, picking up the subject matter of Chapter 10 to drive our conclusions, we arrive where we started our exploratory journey on the food food-chain, modern agricultural systems permitting.

The theme running through this book at every stage is that waste – or rather, waste avoidance – holds a very important key to sustainable food provision in the context of the looming environmental credit crunch. In this brief concluding chapter, we consider potential solutions to the problem of waste at each stage of the food food-chain, as reflected in the chapters in this book. The book title suggests this book is about 'food policy'. It would be truer to say that it is about the place for policy in a wider mix. We must acknowledge that policymakers cannot simply legislate change in people's eating habits, and expect their diktats to be obeyed; history is littered with examples of impotent attempts by rulers to achieve goals that might nevertheless be desirable. Cultural change tends not to arise from 'policy'. However, policy can help create the conditions that foster cultural change.

What we suggest over the remainder of this chapter is a series of possible solutions to the challenges that run up and down the food food-chain. Many of these policy ideas face practical problems in implementation. However, if even some are implemented they could combine with cultural change to present a more optimistic, economically and environmentally sustainable future for food. We do not suggest who should take these suggestions forward because several organizations will often need to be involved.

Agriculture – mineral

Avoiding wastefulness in the context of land is challenging because the land endowment that supports food provisioning is global. A global 'land-use' oversight body could help reduce land degradation, but only if enough buy into it. The failure of international cooperation on the issue of food trade does not, perhaps, raise one's hopes in this regard. What is really needed is a cultural change at the level of national politics, such that system resilience is regularly considered as a policy goal. That could achieve a desirable global outcome, almost by accident. For developed countries, such a stance would urge some investment in developing-country food systems such as land stewardship, and soil stewardship. Such a change could also be supportive of new markets – such as virtual water markets.

Box 11.1 Raw material inputs – mineral

Water and fertilisers are often inefficiently used.

- A holistic policy perspective on the global land endowment and economic assessment of comparative environmental advantage are needed.

The importance of soil stewardship in particular and land stewardship in a broader sense may be under-appreciated.

- Foster soil science.
- Create a global land-use change oversight body with the remit of assessing strengths and weaknesses in land use, with a focus on food and fibre resources, and the assets that underpin them such as biodiversity.
- Target infrastructure investment, e.g. funding for developing-country use of satellite technology to control fertiliser application and funding for efficient irrigation.
- Adopt the idea of system resilience as an input to food trade policy.

Agriculture – vegetable

The main risks to sustainable agriculture for non-animal products appear to arise from the scale of production needed to feed large numbers of humans. Industrialisation of the production of many crops has led to increased chemical use as well as inefficient use of water. Biodiversity is critically important to sustainable food provisioning and yet amongst policymakers biodiversity is not well-understood or necessarily thought of as having intrinsic value. The question mark over the future of pollinator populations ('where have all the bees gone?') can be seen as symbolic of potentially systemic risks to agriculture posed by modern agricultural systems.

> **Box 11.2 Raw material inputs – vegetable**
>
> *Crop protection chemicals need to be used in increased quantities in the context of monocultures.*
>
> - Establish raw ingredient traceability throughout the local and global agricultural supply chains. (Note that the practical challenges might force supply chains to become shorter or less complex, thus improving their potential resilience.)
> - Foster R&D across a broad range of seed and plant technologies to establish a diverse pool of varieties and traits and an insurance stock of others.
>
> *Much water is wasted in irrigation.*
>
> - 'Price' embedded water according to food materials' provenance.
> - Develop sound (well-regulated) virtual water markets.
> - Foster experiments in 'system-wide' approaches such as 'permaculture', e.g. establish a competition, the 'permaculture' prize to be awarded for the best innovation in the field, open to communities, universities or collaborations. Part of the prize could be an injection of funding into the top three projects. This might have human capital-related side effects, encouraging a new generation into farming.

Agriculture – animal

Meat is expensive, whether from an environmental or economic perspective, and eating less of it would be good for human health in some communities. A requirement for greater transparency in respect of its provenance would probably put up costs, thus allowing the forces of economics to constrain consumption. However, a cultural change is almost certainly a necessary condition for a shift in consumption patterns.

> **Box 11.3 Raw material inputs – animal**
>
> *Meat production delivers a low return in terms of productivity and is environmentally costly.*
>
> - Reduce meat consumption by encouraging cultural change (focusing on health, perhaps). A mix of measures may help – regulation, or promoting the health benefits of meat substitutes. Taxing some forms of meat may
>
> *(Continued)*

(Continued)

  assist economic forces, but universal tax is unlikely to be politically feasible given the social aspiration generally associated with meat eating.
- Establish regulation that allows consumers to trace the sources of all animal produce and make provenance transparent to the consumer by labelling.
- Properly assess large-scale factory farming, taking into account all definitions of efficiency. Use regulation to determine the extent to which animal welfare should play a role in advanced economies.

Transport

Transport is hard to come to grips with in the context of food. However, too much of it appears to encourage greater wastefulness in the food food-chain in a general sense. It is possible that eating food produce out of season all of the time (as a matter of preference rather than necessity) encourages wastefulness by separating people from any sense that food availability depends on nature.

Box 11.4 Transport

Transport gets food to where it is needed. The lack of adequate facilities results in food waste in developing countries.

- Use public information campaigns to increase consumer awareness of the environmental costs of (for example) eating foodstuffs out of season.
- Change urban planning to allow more local food growing such as orchards and allotments.

Car journeys to shop for food are used to excess.

- Use planning regulation to achieve a more balanced mix of smaller accessible retail outlets (including farmers' markets) and supermarkets.
- Review business, property and other taxation systems to ensure that there is no bias towards out-of-town retailers.

Processing

Processed food arrived because of economic and cultural change. This book suggests that the well-balanced diet should not be dominated by processed foods which have the effect of disenfranchising the consumer from dietary choice.

Changes to the role played by processed food in Western diets, in particular, could come from many directions, some (like taxes on fat and sugar) government led, but others might be community led, and still others by a greater understanding of the impact of some processed foodstuffs on the human body.

Box 11.5 **Food processing**

Food processing can help protect perishables. However, processed food reduces consumer control of diet and may encourage over-consumption of certain forms of food.

- Tax sugar and fat (with the potential effects of diet substitution by the consumer and/or the stimulation of innovation in the corporate sector).
- Support the efforts of network organisations facilitating industry co-ordination on the issue of food waste, such as such as WRAP (Waste and Resources Action Programme).
- Consider policies that encourage alternative uses for sugar, for instance, as fuel – accepting that this will raise the price of sugar as a foodstuff (thus acting as a supplementary mechanism to fat and sugar taxes).

Processed food seems to be over-dominant in the diets of those who are time-poor and the financially constrained.

- Increase scientific research into the impact of processed food on the human body (also relevant to health).
- Encourage (directly and indirectly) new community structures such as the Transition Network, which encourages the self-organisation of 'Transition Towns' around initiatives that foster resilience and low environmental footprints in lifestyles.

Retailing and wholesaling

Many of the issues we discuss in this book are well known to the food retail sector and some of the things we suggest are already in evidence. Nevertheless, we think that information about nutritional contents and provenance could be vastly improved. The lack of such information seems to be attributable to the scale of the industry and its complexity, which was, in turn, driven by economics. It is likely that significantly improved information flow would change the economics. It is also true that consumers will become indifferent if presented with too much information in too many conflicting forms. 'Five a day', 'Global Daily Allowance', calorie content, fat content, 'traffic light' labelling can present a bewildering range of options. Consistent labelling may be as important as comprehensive labelling.

> **Box 11.6 Retailing and wholesaling**
>
> *Promotion and packaging designed to sell food in bulk may encourage over-eating.*
>
> - Redesign food packaging and further improve food labelling.
> - For seasonal foodstuffs, indicate when in season alongside produce on shelves or on the label.
>
> *Processed food saves time but at a cost of reduced food know-how, potentially less healthy diets and higher environmental impacts.*
>
> - Establish a consistent 'good food' rating system for retail outlets in which points would be lost for junk-food prominence or positioning for impulse buyers, and points gained for balance and quality.
>
> *The average developed-economy shopping basket contains far too much fat and sugar at the expense of healthier food categories.*
>
> - Encourage a fat-and-sugar for fruit–vegetables–bread/rice/potatoes swap in the shopping basket, perhaps by redesigning store layouts.
>
> *Shopping by car removes exercise from daily regimes.*
>
> - Extend voluntary efforts to reduce packaging waste.
> - Note that changes discussed under Transport might result in changes to market structure potentially supportive of changing food consumption habits.

Cooking pot and table

A recurring theme in this book is the ability of the financial credit crunch to change food consumption habits. As consumers are sensitive to the price of things that they purchase regularly, and as real disposable incomes fall or rise more slowly, the desire to practice economy in the kitchen is increasing.

We have already encountered the idea that rules-of-thumb work better than detailed rules for low-carbon cooking. So it is with cooking well on a tight budget. The rules-of-thumb here appear to be: cook it yourself, from scratch (ready meals are a lot more expensive); keep meat to a minimum; liven-up recipes with herbs and spices; and allow occasional treats. This 'recipe' of rules contains the ingredients for healthy, environmentally friendly eating no matter what the (financial or environmental) budget.[1]

> **Box 11.7 Cooking pot and table**
>
> *Cooking know-how in the average household is low, so leftovers are more likely to be thrown away than used up. This wastes the resources used to produce the food, and entails an opportunity cost of nutrients not consumed. Feeding food scraps to animals is increasingly uncommon.*
>
> - Empower the consumer to take good decisions from all perspectives – economics, environment and nutrition – in as many ways as possible, including:
>   - using the power of education and the media, and ultimately even influence urban design to encourage home food preparation;
>   - using education to promote awareness of which foodstuffs are in season, in the manner of Mrs Beeton.
> - Capture the economic and environmental impact of experimental and innovative community initiatives (such as the Fife Diet) in food procurement and consumption, either by supporting university research, or by having regional government bodies or the private sector sponsor selected initiatives as pilot tests for policy measures of the future.
> - Fund scientific research into diet and nutrition, across the full range of physical and social sciences.

Health

Health is arguably the most important thing any of us have. Throwing it away is a waste of life. This is surely the most powerful argument for making sure people have access to a well-balanced nutritious diet. Food as a source of health and wellbeing is enshrined as a human right in Article 25 of the Universal Declaration of Human Rights. Food as a human right is more usually thought of in situations where people are starving. It could perhaps be usefully applied to the consequences of excess fat and sugar, too. Prevention is better than cure, not least because resource availability and quality for food-related health problems will be higher if fewer have need of it.

> **Box 11.8 Health**
>
> *The obesity epidemic in some parts of the world and millions of undernourished people in other parts of the world reflects wastefully used food, and wastes healthcare resources.*
>
> *(Continued)*

(Continued)

- Invest in land and soil stewardship to produce positive all-round health impacts (minerals in vegetables come from minerals in the soil).
- Adjust the regulations governing urban design – make walking or cycling for short journeys (including high-frequency food shopping) easier.
- Rethink job structures to give people more control over food preparation. (Not a policy as such – perhaps something like 'Ensure that tax and health and safety legislation does not discriminate against flexible working practices, which may address some of the time-poverty issues that have in turn encouraged the shift towards processed food consumption'.)
- Once again – tax sugar and fat.
- Governments should influence the food choices that are available in schools and hospitals (where it has direct control) – although it should be noted that in the absence of education and cultural change this may lead to consumer rebellion.
- Invest in prevention through education. Follow up via the health services, as a matter of course, alongside vaccination programmes and other regular events such as blood donation or dental check-ups.

Food waste

The pressures of the financial credit crunch have the potential to bring economics into the picture for food waste. Food wasted is money wasted. Of course, if food is cheap, this matters very little. If food has been too cheap in a structural sense and this is changing, then the economics of food waste may come to matter a lot more. Thus, economics may have greater power to constrain waste than they do currently. The UK horsemeat scandal is a timely example of what goes wrong when the environment (the root cause of shortages that put up raw material prices) collides with the financial credit crunch (which squeezes the whole food food-chain and can potentially bring along the temptation to cut corners). The shock of the systemic nature of the horsemeat problem – which keeps on popping up in unexpected places months after the first discovery – has the potential to be a catalyst for change in some food food-chains.

Box 11.9 **Waste**

Food is wasted because of behaviours higher up in the food food-chain.

- Avoid food waste by discouraging over-purchasing – perhaps easier said than done. Research may be needed into what shapes the food-mix in the consumer basket – is it price, packaging, positioning on the retail shelf?

Much food waste still goes to landfill rather than being recycled.

- Develop accessible community systems for recycling food waste, e.g. food to energy.
- Fund scientific research into the use and disposal of perishables (and the organic material they contain) across the range of social and physical sciences.
- Campaign for cultural change so that 'throwing away' is not the first thought, replaced by a culture of using-up. Accelerate new labelling technology so that the sell-by date can be supplanted by a more accurate indicator.
- Precedents for cultural campaigns include anti-waste drives in wartime. High-profile chefs have campaigned on healthy food in schools – we would encourage them to do the same for leftovers.

Running through the food food-chain, from the physical to the intangible, from pip to plate to waste bin, we have explored the web of connections and feedback loops running through food. As we suspected, the culture of food drives aspects of food consumption patterns, but perhaps in a far richer sense than we initially suspected. Culture and social structure – nature, genetics, history, science, and tradition – drive good food, defined as food that is nutritious, balanced and good to eat. They help shape the all-important body of human knowledge underpinning each stage of the food food-chain. Culture and social structure hold the keys to making a large portion of food waste a thing of the past. The opportunity to change the way we procure, prepare and consume food before the environmental credit crunch hits home must not be wasted. It's time to make waste history.

Note

1 Clay (2013).

Bibliography

Adam, S. (2012) 'Obesity killing three times as many as malnutrition', *Daily Telegraph*, 13 December
Addison, P. and Crang, J. (2010) *Listening to Britain*, The Bodley Head, London
Allday, E. (2013) 'Dr. Robert Lustig crusades against sugar', *San Francisco Chronicle*, 1 January
American Heart Association. 'Overweight in children', website updated 16 January 2013. At www.heart.org/HEARTORG/GettingHealthy/Overweight-in-Children_UCM_304054_Article.jsp
Astor, V. and Murray, K. A. H. (1932) *Land and Life: The Economic National Policy for Agriculture*, Victor Gollancz, London
Bacon, C. M., Mendez, V. E., Gliessman, S. R., Goodman, D., and Fox, J. A. (Eds) (2008) *Confronting the Coffee Crisis: Fair Trade, Sustainable Livelihoods and Ecosystems in Mexico and Central America*, The MIT Press, Cambridge, MA and London
Barton, M. D. (2000) 'Antibiotic use in animal feed and its impact on human health', *Nutrition Research Reviews*, 13, 279–99
BBC (2007) 'Mexicans stage tortilla protest', 1 February, *BBC News* website, News.bbc.co.uk/1/hi/6319093.stm
BBC (2012) 'Brazil's congress approves controversial forest law', *BBC News Latin America and Caribbean*, 28 April. At www.bbc.co.uk/news/world-latin-america-17851327 (accessed on 4 May 2012)
Beeton, Mrs. I. M. (2012) Mrs Beeton's *Book of Household Management* (Kindle Edition, Public Domain book, first published as a bound edition in 1861)
Beeton, Mrs. I. M. (n.d.) *Family Cookery*, New Edition, awarded to Amy Hudson (née Casson), grandmother of one of the authors, for five years' full attendance at Steeton Wesleyan Sunday School
Beveridge, W. H. (1928) *British Food Control*, Oxford University Press, Oxford
Black, M. (1985) *Food and Cooking in 19th Century Britain*, English Heritage, London
Blanc, R. (2012) 'Recipes. Pot au feu'. At www.raymondblanc.com/RECIPES/October-2012-Pot-au-Feu (accessed on 27 January 2013)
Blouet, B. W. and Luebke, F. C. (Eds) (1979) *The Great Plains: Environment and Culture*, University of Nebraska Press, London
Boizot, C., Robin, J-M. and Visser, M. (2001) 'The demand for food products: An analysis of interpurchase times and purchased quantities', *The Economic Journal*, 111, 391–419
Bowles, N. (2005) *Nixon's Business*, Texas A&M University Press, College Station, TX
Boyd-Orr, J. (1937) *Food Health and Income: Report on a Survey of Adequacy of Diet in Relation to Income* (2nd edition), Macmillan and Co., London

Brears, P. (1985a) *Food and Cooking in 16th Century Britain*, English Heritage, London
Brears, P. (1985b) *Food and Cooking in 17th Century Britain*, English Heritage, London
British Brands Group (2007) *Consumers' shopping wants and UK grocery retailing*, 18 July. At www.britishbrandsgroup.org.uk/upload/File/BBG%20Needs%20research%2077.pdf
British Sandwich Association (2012) 'The sandwich: A tasty cause for celebration 250 years on', 14 May. At www.sandwich.org.uk/information_centre/general/press_releases/2012/the_sandwich_a_tasty_cause_for_celebration_250_years_on.shtml
British Standards Institution (BSI) (2011a) *The Guide to PAS 2050: 2011, How to carbon footprint your products, identify hotspots and reduce emissions in your supply chain*, BSI, London
British Standards Institution (BSI) (2011b) *PAS 2050: 2011, Specification for the assessment of life cycle greenhouse gas emissions of goods and services*, BSI, London
Brown, A. (2012) 'Scots family reveal they live their life only eating food produced locally', *Daily Record*, 13 September. At www.dailyrecord.co.uk/lifestyle/health-fitness/family-use-fife-diet-as-their-food-1322121
Burnett, J. (1966) *Plenty and Want: a Social History of Diet in England from 1815 to the Present Day*, Thomas Nelson and Sons, London
Carpenter, S., Caraco, N. F., Correll, D. L., Howarth, R. W., Sharpley, A. N. and Smith, V. H. (1998) 'Nonpoint pollution of surface waters with phosphorus and nitrogen', *Issues in Ecology*, No. 3, summer. At http://cfpub.epa.gov/watertrain/pdf/issue3.pdf
Clark, G., Huberman, M., and Lindert, P. (1995) 'A British food puzzle 1770–1850', *The Economic History Review*, 48(2), 215–237
Clay, X. (2013) 'My 49p lunch with a girl called Jack', *Telegraph Weekend*, 2 March
Cocco, F. (2012) 'Are pubs faring well, or are they bidding farewell?', 2 November. At farewell?http://fullfact.org/factchecks/18_pubs_closing_per_week_camra_bbpa-28582
Cohen, D. (2011) 'Grow your own meat', *BBC News, Technology*, 24 October
Collingham, L. (2011) *The Taste of War: World War Two and the Battle for Food*, Allen Lane, London
Collins, S. (2008) *The Hunger Games*, Scholastic Press, New York
Colquhoun, K. (2007) *Taste: The Story of Britain Through Its Cooking*, Bloomsbury, London
Cordain, L., Eaton, S. B., Sebastian, A., Mann, N., Lindeberg, S., Watkins, B. A., O'Keefe, J. H. and Brand-Miller, J. (2005) 'Origins and evolution of the Western diet: Health implications for the 21st century', *American Journal of Clinical Nutrition*, 81(2), 341–354. At www.ajcn.org (accessed on 29 July 2012)
Country Life (2010) 'Who is responsible for obesity?', *Country Life*, 29 September
Country Life (2012) 'The Country Life Olympics', *Country Life*, London, 11 July
Creda (n.d.) *The Cook Book*, designed for use with a Creda Circulaire fan oven, Creda, Stoke on Trent
Cutler, D., Glaeser, E. and Shapiro, J. (2003) 'Why have Americans become more obese?', *Journal of Economic Perspectives*, 17, 93–118
Daily Mail (2007) 'So are chips the new health food?', *The Daily Mail*, 13 March
Davis, A. (1979) *Let's Eat Right to Keep Fit*, Unwin Hyman, London
de Leo, F. (2000) 'The environmental management of packaging: An overview', *Environmentally-friendly Food Processing* (edited by Mattsson, B. and Sonesson, U.), Woodhead Publishing, Cambridge, pp. 130–153
Department for Environment, Food and Rural Affairs (DEFRA) (2012a) *Food Statistics Pocketbook 2012*, Crown Copyright, London

Department for Environment, Food and Rural Affairs (DEFRA) (2012b) *Family Food 2011*, Crown Copyright 2012. At www.defra.gov.uk/statistics/foodfarm/food/ (accessed on 16 December 2012)
Department for Transport (2009) *The Air Freight End-to-End Journey: An Analysis of the End-to-End Journey of Air Freight Through UK International Gateways*, Department for Transport, London
de Vries, J. (2008) *The Industrious Revolution*, Cambridge University Press, New York
des Abbayes, C., Schultze, A. and Jaussaud, E. (2009) *Towards a Greener Retail Sector*, European Commission (DG ENV) and BIO Intelligence Service, 070307/2008/500355/G4
Donovan, P. and Hudson, J. (2011) *From Red to Green? How the Financial Credit Crunch Could Bankrupt the Environment*, Earthscan, London
Ecological Society of America (n.d.) *Ecosystem Services Factsheet*. At www.esa.org
Economist, The (2012) 'The nanny state's biggest test', *The Economist*, 15 December. At www.economist.com/news/special-report/21568074-should-governments-make-their-citizens-exercise-more-and-eat-less-nanny-states
Edwards-Jones, G., Plassmann, K., York, E. H., Hounsome, B., Jones, D. L. and Milà i Canals, L. (2009) 'Vulnerability of exporting nations to the development of a carbon label in the United Kingdom', *Environmental Science and Policy*, 12(4), 479–490. At www.oecd.org/tad/envtrade/42930889.pdf
Fairlie, S. (2010) *Meat – A Benign Extravagance*, Permanent Publications, East Meon
Farmers Guardian (2008) 'Bread market is changing, so should wheat growers worry?', *Farmers Guardian*, 20 June
Fearnley-Whittingstall, H. (2010) Hugh 'Hugh Fearnley-Whittingstall's climate-friendly recipes', *The Guardian*, 9 October. At www.guardian.co.uk/lifeandstyle/2010/oct/09/climate-friendly-recipes-fearnley-whittingstall
Field, The (2012) 'The big breakfast', *The Field*, December, 100–101
Fisher, M. (2009) *The Silver Darlings*, Theatre review, His Majesty's, Aberdeen, *UK Guardian*, 8 September
Fisher, M. C., Henk, D. A., Briggs, C. J., Brownstein, J. S., Madoff, L. C., McCraw, S. L. and Gurr, S. J. (2012) 'Emerging fungal threats to animal, plant and ecosystem health', *Nature*, 484, 186–194
Food and Agriculture Organization of the United Nations (n.d.) 'Codex and the international food trade'. At www.fao.org/docrep/008/y7867e/y7867e08.htm
Food and Agriculture Organization of the United Nations (1997) 'Is sugar "pure white and deadly?"', in *Proceedings of the Fiji/FAO 1997 Asia Pacific Sugar Conference*. At www.fao.org/docrep/005/X0513E/x0513e07.htm (accessed on 30 December 2012)
Food and Agriculture Organization of the United Nations (2009) *Agribusiness Handbook: Red Meat*, FAO Investment Centre Division, Rome
Food and Agriculture Organization of the United Nations (2011a) *The State of the World's Land and Water Resources for Food and Agriculture: Managing Systems at Risk*, Summary Report, FAO, Rome. At www.fao.org/docrep/015/i1688e/i1688e00.pdf
Food and Agriculture Organization of the United Nations (2011b) *The State of Food Insecurity in the World*, FAO, Rome
Food and Agriculture Organization of the United Nations (2012a) *Energy Smart Food at FAO: An Overview*. At www.fao.org/docrep/015/an913e/an913e00.htm
Food and Agriculture Organization of the United Nations (2012b) 'Road to Rio: Improving energy use key challenge for world's food systems', 14 June. At www.fao.org/news/story/en/item/146971/icode/

Food and Agriculture Organization of the United Nations (2012c) 'FAO, partners, urge greater push to reduce food losses and waste', 13 June, Rome. At www.fao.org/news/story/en/item/147427/icode/ (accessed on January 20 2013)

Ford, W. C. (1882) *Dear Food*, The Bradstreet Press, New York

Foresight Programme of the UK Government (2011a) *The Future of Food and Farming: Challenges and Choices for Global Sustainability*, Final Project Report, The Government Office for Science, London

Foresight Programme of the UK Government (2011b) *Tackling Obesities: Future Choices – Project Report* (2nd edition), The Government Office for Science, London

Foster-Powell, K., Holt, S. H. A. and Brand-Miller, J. C. (2002) 'International table of glycaemic index and glycaemic load values: 2002', *The American Journal of Clinical Nutrition*, 76(1), 5–56. At http://ajcn.nutrition.org/content/76/1/5.full (accessed on 29 July 2012)

Fox, T. and Vorley, B. (2004) 'Concentration in food supply and retail chains', Working Paper, August, International Institute for Environment and Development (IIED) and the UK Department for International Development (DFID) London. (This is a discussion paper only; it does not represent DFID or UK Government policy.)

Foxcroft, L. (2011) *Calories and Corsets: A History of Dieting Over 2,000 Years*, Profile Books, London

Franklin, T. B. (1948) *A History of Agriculture*, G. Bell and Sons, London

Gardner, B. L. and Rausser, G. C. (Eds) (2002) *Handbook of Agricultural Economics, Volume 2A, Agriculture and its External Linkages*, Elsevier Science, Amsterdam

Gaskell, M. M. (Ed.) (1925) *A Yorkshire Cookery Book* (5th edition), Sanderson & Clayton, Wakefield (first published 1916)

Gautier, C. (2008) *Oil, Water and Climate*, Cambridge University Press, Cambridge

Gerbens-Leenes, W. and Nonhebel, S. (2005) 'The influence of consumption patterns on the use of agricultural resources', *Appetite*, 45, 24–31

Gilbert, N. (2012) 'African agriculture: Dirt poor. The key to tackling hunger in Africa is enriching its soil', *Nature*, 483(29 March), 509–642

Glasgow Herald, The (1952) 'New Argentine meat contract agreed', *The Glasgow Herald*, 20 December. At http://news.google.com/newspapers?nid=2507&dat=19521220&id=oEFAAAAAIBAJ&sjid=hlkMAAAAIBAJ&pg=2978,4760672

Goddard, N. (1988) *Harvests of Change: The Royal Agricultural Society of England 1838–1988*, Quiller Press, London

Golding, W. (1954) *Lord of the Flies*, Faber and Faber, London (paperback edition 2005)

Gonzalez-Diaz, L., van den Berg, F., van den Bosch, F. and Gonzalez-Andujar, J. L. (2012) 'Controlling annual weeds in cereals by deploying crop rotation at the landscale scale: *Avena sterilis* as an example', *Ecological Applications*, 22(3), 982–992

Gopnik, H. (2011) *The Table Comes First*, Quercus, London

Gordon, D. G. (1998) *The Eat-a-Bug Cook Book*, Ten Speed Press, Berkeley

Grossman, L. (1996) *The World on a Plate: The History and Mystery of the Food We Eat*, BBC Books, London

Grove, J. M. (2008) *Little Ice Age*, Routledge, Taylor & Francis e-Library, London and New York

Guillette, E. A. (1998) Handbook case study: 'Pesticide exposure and childhood development in the Yaqui Valley'. At www.chemicalbodyburden.org/hb_cs_mexico.htm (accessed on 21 February 2013)

Hall, A. D. (1910) *Fertilisers and Manures*, John Murray, London

Hamerschlag, K. and Venkat, K. (2011) *Meat Eater's Guide to Climate Change and Health, Lifecycle Assessments: Methodology and Results*, Environmental Working Group (www.ewg.org) and CleanMetrics Corp

Hansard (1963) Questions to the Minister for Agriculture, Fisheries and Food from Denys Bullard MP in the House of Commons on 22 July, *Hansard*. At www.theyworkforyou.com/debates/?id=1963-07-22a.1028.5

Hardin, G. (1968) 'The tragedy of the commons', *Science*, 162(3859), 1243–1248

Hickman, M. (2010) 'Excessive meat-eating "kills 45,000 each year"', *The Independent*, 19 October

Høgaas Eide, M. (2000) 'Life cycle assessment (LCA) of industrial milk production', *International Journal of Life Cycle Assessment*, 3, 15–20

Horrell, S. and Oxley, D. (2012) 'Bringing home the bacon? Regional nutrition, stature and gender in the industrial revolution', *Economic History Review*, 65(4), 1354–1379

Howard, C. (2012) 'The big picture', *The Economist*, 15 December. At www.economist.com/news/special-report/21568065-world-getting-wider-says-charlotte-howard-what-can-be-done-about-it-big

Hudson, K. (1972) *Patriotism with Profit*, Hugh Evelyn, London

Hudson, W. H. (1936) *A Shepherd's Life*, J. M. Dent and Sons, London

Institute of Grocery Distribution (2012) *Convenience Retailing Market Overview*, 8 August. At www.igd.com/our-expertise/Retail/Convenience/3369/Convenience-Retailing-Market-Overview/

Institution of Mechanical Engineers (2013) *Global Food: Waste Not, Want Not*, Institution of Mechanical Engineers, London

International Fertilizer Association (2012) Data on world fertiliser consumption. At www.fertilizer.org (accessed on 16 June 2012)

Jacoby, H. G. (2000) 'Access to markets and the benefits of rural roads', *The Economic Journal*, 110, 713–737

Johnson, S. and Hough, A. (2012) 'Martha's a legend in her own lunchtime', *Daily Telegraph*, 16 June

Jones, A. (2001) *Eating Oil: Food Supply in a Changing Climate*, Sustain and Elm Farm Research Centre. At www.sustainweb.org/publications/?id=98

Karlsson, H. (2011) 'Seasonal vegetables: An environmental assessment of seasonal food', Dissertation, Norwegian University of Life Sciences

Kelbie, P. (2008) 'Back from the brink: Herring fishermen hail conservation success', *The Observer*, 23 November

Kinney, A. F. (1993) 'Textual signs in the *The Merry Wives of Windsor*', *The Yearbook of English Studies*, vol. 23, Early Shakespeare Special Number, pp. 206–234

Koo, W. W. and Taylor, R. D. (2012) *2012 Outlook of the US and World Sugar Markets, 2011–2021*, Agribusiness and Applied Economics 692, April, Centre for Agricultural Policy and Trade Studies, Department of Agribusiness and Applied Economics, North Dakota State University

Law, M. T. (2003) 'The origins of state pure food regulation', *The Journal of Economic History*, 63, 1103–1130

Lawrence, F. (2004) *Not on the Label: What Really Goes into the Food on Your Plate*, Penguin Books, London and New York

Leake, J. (2012) 'The fast way to long life: Starve every other day,' *Sunday Times*, 19 February. At www.thesundaytimes.co.uk/sto/news/uk_news/Science/article874728.ece

Leigh, G. J. (2004) *The World's Greatest Fix: A History of Nitrogen and Agriculture*, Oxford University Press, Oxford

Leith, W. (2002) 'The secret life of chips', *The Observer*, 10 February
Levy, J. (2012) *Freaks of Fortune: The Emerging World of Capitalism and Risk in America*, Harvard University Press, Harvard, MA
Lovelock, J. (2006) *The Revenge of Gaia*, Allen Lane, London
Lustig, R. H., Schmidt, L. A. and Brindis, C. D. (2012) 'Public health: The toxic truth about sugar', *Nature*, 482(2 February), 27–29
Lyall, S. (2008) *The Anglo Files: A Field Guide to the British*, W.W. Norton and Company, New York
McBroom, P. (1999) 'Meat-eating was essential for human evolution, says UC Berkeley anthropologist specializing in diet', News Release, University of California, Berkeley, 14 June. At www.berkeley.edu.news.media/releases/99/legacy/6-14-1999a.html (accessed on 17 June 2012)
McCarthy, C. (2007) *The Road*, Picador, London
Mackenzie, A. (1946) *The Highland Clearances* (2nd edition), Alexander MacLaren and Sons, Glasgow
McKie, R. (2008) 'How the myth of food miles hurts the planet', *The Observer*, London, 23 March. At www.guardian.co.uk/environment/2008/mar/23/food.ethicalliving (accessed 19 September 2012)
MacPherson, C. (2009) 'Back to basics: The 15-year search for sustainable crop protection', *On Campus News*, 24 April. At http://news.usask.ca/archived_ocn/09-apr-24/index.php
MacPherson, K. (2008) 'Sugar can be addictive, Princeton scientist says', *News at Princeton*, 10 December. At http://www.princeton.edu/main/news/archive/S22/88/56G31/index.xml?section=topstories
McWilliams, J. E. (2009) *Just Food*, Little, Brown and Company, New York
MarketLine (2012) *Global Food Retail*, 23 July. www.marketresearch.com/MarketLine-v3883/Global-Food-Retail-7077247/ (accessed on 7 October 2012)
Marshall (1797) *The Rural Economy of the West of England*, P. Wogan, P. Byrne, J. Rice, & J. Moore, Dublin
Martin, E. W. (1955) *The Secret People: English Village Life After 1750*, The Country Book Club, London
Martin, J. (1979) *Miss Manners' Guide to Excruciatingly Correct Behavior*, W.W. Norton, New York
Matson, P. A. (Ed.) (2012) *Seeds of Sustainability: Lessons from the Birthplace of the Green Revolution*, Kindle Edition, Island Press, Washington, DC
Mattsson, B. and Sonesson, U. (2003) *Environmentally-friendly Food Processing*, Woodhead Publishing, Cambridge, England
Mauser, W. (2008) *Water Resources: Efficient, Sustainable and Equitable Use* (English translation), Haus Publishing, London
Mazoyer, M. and Roudart, L. (2006) *A History of World Agriculture, from the Neolithic Age to the Current Crisis* (Transl. J. H. Membrez), Earthscan, London and Sterling, VA
Millennium Ecosystem Assessment (2005a) *Ecosystems and Human Well-being: Synthesis*, Island Press, Washington, DC
Millennium Ecosystem Assessment (2005b) *Ecosystems and Human Well-being, Full Report*, Vol. 1, Chapter 28 (Synthesis), Island Press, Washington, DC
Millstone, E. and Lang, T. (2008) *The Atlas of Food*, Earthscan, London
Mollison, B. (1988) *Permaculture, a Designers' Manual*, Tagari Publications, Tyalgum, NSW
Moomaw, W., Griffin, W. T., Kurczak, K. and Lomax, J. (2012) 'The critical role of food consumption patterns in achieving sustainable food systems and food for all', United Nations Environment Programme Discussion Paper, Paris

Nabhan, G. P. (2004) *Why Some Like it Hot: Food, Genes and Cultural Diversity*, Island Press, Shearwater Books, Washington, DC

National Archives, The (2006) *Brinestain and Biscuit: Recipes and Rules for Royal Navy Cooks 1930*, The National Archives, London

National Health Service (n.d.) 'Lower your cholesterol', NHS online fact sheet. At www.nhs.uk/Livewell/Healthyhearts/Pages/Cholesterol.aspx

Nedwell, D. B., Murrell, J. C., Ineson, P., Reay, D. S., Radajewski, S., McNamara, N. and Morris, S. (2003) 'Microbiological basis of land use impact on the soil methane sink: Molecular and functional analysis', in *Genes in the Environment: 15th Special Symposium of the British Ecological Society* (edited by Hails, R. S., Beringer, J. E. and Godfray, H. C. J.), Cambridge University Press, Cambridge, pp. 150–166

Nonhebel, S. (2007) 'Energy from agricultural residues and consequences for land requirements for food production', *Agricultural Systems*, 94, 586–592

Noussair, C., Robin, S. and Ruffieux, B. (2004) 'Do consumers really refuse to buy genetically modified food?', *The Economic Journal*, 114, 102–120

OECD-FAO (2012) *Agricultural Outlook 2012–2020*, OECD and the Food and Agriculture Organization of the United Nations

Oliver, J. (2000) *The Return of the Naked Chef*, Penguin, Harmondsworth

Ortiz-Monasterio R., J. I. (2002) 'Nitrogen management in irrigated spring wheat', FAO Corporate Document Repository. At www.fao.org/documents/en/detail/148174 (accessed on 21 February 2013)

Orwell, G. (1937) *The Road to Wigan Pier*, Penguin Books, London (reprinted 1989)

Packard, V. (1961) *The Hidden Persuaders*, Penguin Books, London

Park, J. (2009) 'Tesco carbon footprints milk', *Packaging News*, 18 August. At www.packagingnews.co.uk/business/tesco-carbon-footprints-milk/

Payne, M. and Payne, D. (2012) *Never Seconds*, Cargo Publishing, Glasgow

Peacock, F. C. (Ed.) (1978) *Jealott's Hill: Fifty Years of Agricultural Research 1928–1978*, Imperial Chemical Industries, Bracknell

Penman, J., Gytarsky, M., Hiraishi, T., Krug, T., Kruger, D., Pipatti, R., Buendia, L., Miwa, K., Ngara, T., Tanabe, K. and Wagner, F. (Eds) (2003) *The IPCC Good Practice Guidance for the Reporting of Greenhouse Gas Emissions from Land Use, Land-Use Change and Forestry*, The Intergovernmental Panel on Climate Change and the Institute for Global Environmental Strategies (IGES), Kanagawa

Peterman, K. (2012) 'First carbon-neutral coffee takes center stage at UN climate conference', *The Blog: Huffpost Green*, 6 December. At www.huffingtonpost.com/keith-peterman/first-carbonneutral-coffe_b_2249340.html (accessed on 17 February 2013)

Popkin, B. M. (2008) 'Will China's nutrition transition overwhelm its healthcare system and slow economic growth?', *Journal of Health Affairs*, 27(4), 1064–1076

Population Reference Bureau. (n.d.) www.prb.org/pdf12/2012-population-data-sheet_eng.pdf (accessed on 16 February 2013)

Porteous, C. (1948) *Pioneers of Fertility*, Fertiliser Journal, London

Purcell, R., (1997) 'Potential for small-scale irrigation in Sub-Saharan Africa: The Kenyan example', FAO. At www.fao.org/docrep/W7314E/w7314e07.htm (accessed on 16 September 2012)

Quilty-Harper, C. (2012) 'The world's fattest countries: How do you compare?', *Daily Telegraph*, 21 June. At www.telegraph.co.uk/earth/earthnews/9345086/The-worlds-fattest-countries-how-do-you-compare.html

Ramos-Elorduy, J. (1998) *Creepy Crawly Cuisine: The Gourmet Guide to Edible Insects*, Park Street Press, Rochester, VT

Ratcliffe, S. (Ed.) (2011) *P. G. Wodehouse: A Life in Letters*, Hutchinson, London

Reardon, T. and Gulati, A. (2008) *The Rise of Supermarkets and Their Development Implications: International Experience Relevant for India*, IFPRI Discussion Paper 00752, International Food Policy Research Institute, New Delhi. At www.ifpri.org/sites/default/files/pubs/pubs/dp/ifpridp00752.pdf

Reeves, J. (1997) *The Potato Cookbook*, Pelican Publishing Company, Gretna

Rickert, E. (2005) 'Environmental effects of the coffee crisis: A case study of land use and avian communities in Agua Buena, Costa Rica' (a thesis submitted in partial fulfilment of the requirements for the Masters of Environmental Studies Program) The Evergreen State College, December. archive.org/details/Ricket_EVE_MES_Thesis_2005 (accessed on 28 September 2012).

Savage, S. (2011) 'Sustainable wheat production through intensification', *Sustainablog*, 25 May. At www.sustainablog.org/2011/sustainable-wheat-production-through-intensification/ (accessed on 21 February 2013)

Scherr, S. J., McNeely, J. A. (2007) *Farming with Nature: The Science and Practice of Ecoagriculture*, Kindle Edition, Island Press, Washington, DC

Schwartz, H. (1986) *Never Satisfied: A Cultural History of Diets, Fantasies and Fat*, The Free Press, New York

Scotsman, The (2007) 'They call it the Fife-plan diet', *The Scotsman*, 30 October. At www.scotsman.com/news/scottish-news/top-stories/they-call-it-the-fife-diet-1-697479

Scott, R. (2012) *Bread Made Easy: Delicious and Simple Handmade Artisan Bread*, Volume 1, Kindle Edition, Rosemary Scott

Seddon, Q. (1989) *The Silent Revolution: Farming and the Countryside into the 21st Century*, BBC Books, London

Shakespeare, W. (1998) *Love's Labour's Lost* (editorial matter by H. R. Woudhuysen), Arden Shakespeare, London

Shakespeare, W. (2007) *King Henry IV, Part 2* (editorial matter by A. R. Humphreys), Arden Shakespeare, London

Slavin, P. (2012) 'The Great Bovine Pestilence and its economic and environmental consequences in England and Wales, 1318–50', *Economic History Review*, 65(4), 1239–1266

Smith, A., Watkiss, P., Tweddle, G., McKinnon, A., Browne, M., Hunt, A., Treleven, C., Nash, C. and Cross, S. (2005) *The Validity of Food Miles as an Indicator of Sustainable Development*, DEFRA, London

Smith, D. (1976) *Frugal Food*, Coronet Books, Hodder and Stoughton, London

Smith, D. (1978) *Delia Smith's Complete Cookery Course*, Ebury Press, London

Smith, D. (2008) *Delia's How to Cheat at Cooking*, Ebury Press, London

Song, M. and Hwang, S. (2000) 'Recycling food processing wastes', in *Environmentally-friendly Food Processing* (edited by Mattsson, B. and Sonesson, U.), Woodhead Publishing, Cambridge, pp. 205–217

Stead, J. (1985) *Food and Cooking in 18th Century Britain*, English Heritage, London

Steinfeld, H., Gerber, P., Wassenaar, T., Castel, V., Rosales, M. and de Haan, C. (2006) *Livestock's Long Shadow. Environmental Issues and Options*, Food and Agriculture Organization of the United Nations. At ftp.fao.org/docrep/fao/010/A0701E/A0701E00.pdf

Stephens, S. (2011) *Wastwater and T5*, Methuen Drama, London

Stuttgarter Zeitung (1985) 'Zum Wohl, Glykol: Skandal brachte Umdenken in der Weinindustrie', *Stuttgarter Zeitung*, 9 July. At http://content.stuttgarter-zeitung.de/stz/page/951412_0_9223_-9-juli-1985-zum-wohl-glykol-.html (accessed on 25 March 2013)

Sykes, F. (1944) *This Farming Business*, Faber & Faber, London

Tanaka, D. L., Liebig, M. A., Krupinsky, J. M. and Merrill, S. D. (2010) 'Crop sequence influences on sustainable spring wheat production in the Northern Great Plains', *Sustainability*, 2, 3695–3709

Taubes, G. (2011) *Why We Get Fat and What to Do About It*, Anchor Books, New York

Taylor, A.-L. (2012) 'Rise of the "semi-vegetarians"', *BBC Food*, 25 August, online: www.bbc.co.uk/food/0/19294585 (accessed on 17 February 2013)

Tetra Pak (2012) 'Thème: Pertes et gaspillage alimentaires', *Tetra Pak Magazine*, No. 101

Thirsk, J. (1984) *The Rural Economy of England*, The Hambledon Press, London

Thompson, F. (1939) *Lark Rise*, University Press, Oxford

Thompson, H. (2012) 'War on weeds loses ground', *Nature*, 485, 430

Times, The (2012) 'Fabio is auctioned for record £126,000 in bull market', *The Times*, London, 21 February

Tischner, U. and Kjaernes, U. (2010) 'SCP in the agriculture and food domain', in Tischner, U., Sto, E., Kjaernes, U. and Tukker, A. *System Innovation for Sustainability – Case Studies in Sustainable Consumption and Production, Food and Agriculture 3*, Greenleaf Publishing, Sheffield, pp. 6–44

Tischner, U., Sto, E., Kjaernes, U. and Tukker, A. (2010) *System Innovation for Sustainability – Case Studies in Sustainable Consumption and Production, Food and Agriculture 3*, Greenleaf Publishing, Sheffield

Tukker, A., Huppes, G., Guinée, J., Heijungs, R., de Koning, A., van Oers, L., Suh, S., Geerken, T., Van Holderbeke, M., Jansen, B. and Nielsen, P. (2006) *Environmental Impacts of Products (EIPRO). Analysis of Life Cycle Environmental Impacts Related to the Final Consumption of the EU-25*, European Commission Directorate General, Joint Research Centre

United Nations Environment Programme (2012) *Global Environmental Outlook – GEO_5*. At www.unep.org/geo/geo5.asp

Vaitheeswaran, V. V. (2012) *Need, Speed, and Greed, How the New Rules of Innovation Can Transform Businesses, Propel Nations to Greatness, and Tame the World's Most Wicked Problems*, Harper Business, Kindle Edition Location 1269

Waste Watch (2008) *Packaging*, information sheet. At www.wastewatch.org.uk/data/files/resources/12/Packaging_Aug-08-FINAL-CKT.pdf

Watanabe, F., Abe, K., Fujita, T., Goto, M., Hiemori, M. and Nakano, Y. (1998) 'Effects of microwave heating on the loss of vitamin B_{12} in foods', *Journal of Agricultural and Food Chemistry*, 46(1), 206–210

Weight-control Information Network (2012) *Overweight and Obesity Statistics*, National Institute of Diabetes and Digestive and Kidney Diseases. At win.niddk.nih.gov/statistics

Welch, R. M. (2002) 'The impact of mineral nutrients in food crops on global human health', *Plant and Soil*, 247, 83–90

Wohlmeyer, H. and Quendler, T. (Eds) (2002) *The WTO, Agriculture and Sustainable Development*, Greenleaf Publishing, Sheffield

Woodham-Smith, C. (1962) *The Great Hunger: Ireland 1845–9*, Hamish Hamilton, London

Woodvine, A. (2011) *Didsbury Dinners: The Low-carbon Community Cook Book*, Didsbury Dinners, Manchester

World Health Organization (2003) 'Populations with high sugar consumption are at increased risk of chronic disease, South African researchers report', *Bulletin of the World Health Organization*, 28 August. At www.who.int/bulletin/releases/2003/PR0803/en/ (accessed on 30 December 2012)

World Health Organization (2012) 'Obesity and overweight', Fact Sheet 311, May. At www.who.int/mediacentre/factsheets/fs311/en (accessed on 4 August 2012)

World Wildlife Fund for Nature (2012) *Living Planet Report 2012*, WWF, Gland, Switzerland. At wwf.panda.org/about_our_earth/all_publications/living_planet_report/2012_lpr/

Yoo, S., Baranowski, T., Missaghian, M., Baranowski, J., Cullen, K., Fisher, J. O., Watson, K., Zakeri, I. F. and Nicklas, T. (2006) 'Food-purchasing patterns for home: A grocery store intercept survey', *Public Health Nutrition*, 9, 384–393

Yudkin, J. (2012) *Pure, White and Deadly: How Sugar is Killing Us and What We Can Do to Stop It* (with a new introduction by R. H. Lustig), Penguin Books, London

Zielinski, S. (2012) 'Are we headed for another dustbowl?', smithsonian.com, 16 November. At www.smithsonianmag.com/science-nature/Are-We-Headed-for-Another-Dust-Bowl-179667051.html

Index

Note: references to figures, tables and boxes are in **bold type**. References to notes are indicated by page number, followed by 'n' and the note number.

Acton, E. 196
Adam, S. 163n5
additives 93–4
adulteration 94–5
agricultural credit cycle: measures to combat 8
agricultural economics: scope of 2
air freight: food transport 109–10
Allday, E. 200n20
allotment.org.uk **115**
animal farming: disappearance of fish stocks 65; disease control **76**, 77, 80, 81; drivers of consumption 64, 67, 69; ecosystem, and 81; environmental concerns with meat 68, 69, 73, 174; fat, economic value of 63–4; feed conversion considerations 71; financial credit crunch, effect of 81; free-range animals 78, 79; greenhouse-gas emissions 71, **72**, 72; human health 67, 68, 77, 174–5; intensification 70, 71, 78, 79, 174–5; laboratory meat 78; meat economics 65–7, 68; milk quotas **74–5**; milking technology 76; policy ideas 205, **205–6**; scope of 63, 64, 71; selective breeding 73–4, 75, 77, 80, 81; systems–based meat production 79–80; technology used to improve efficiency 76, 77, 78, 80, 81; waste 72–3, 189–91
Austen, J. 85, 141
autarky 40

Bacon, C. 50n4
Barton, M. 175n33
BBC 26n5, 58, 70, 166n12
Beeton, I. 32n13, 90, **91**, 120, 128, 129, 130, 150

biodiversity losses 57–8
Blanc, R. 196
Boyd-Orr, J. 162, 170
bread-making 91, **91**; Brown Bread Act (1800) 172; carbon emissions 96; transport 112–13
breakfasts 142, 149, **150**
British Brands Group 123n6
British Sandwich Association 153n12
British Standards Institution 104n3, **104**, 105n4
Brown, A. 157n20
Brown Bread Act (1800) 172
Burnett, J. 5, 106n5, 121n2, 141n2, 143n4, 146n6, 196n13
'buy one, get one free' (BOGOF) principle 126–7

calorific threshold for survival 14
Carmona, R. 164n9
Carpenter, S. 58n20
China: food retail industry 4–5
chips: consumption of **87**
cholesterol levels 168
'Civilisation at Risk' 10
Clay, X. 208n1
Cocco, F. 156n16
Codex Alimentarius 175, 176
coffee crisis 50–51
coffee processing: waste **97**
Cohen, D. 78n24
Collins, S. 29n10, 163
Colquhoun, K. 67n7, 95n15
comfort eating 170
community food 156–7
complexity of food 3, 4, 5

Consumer Price Index (CPI) 143–4
consumers: food consumption patterns, changes in 17–18; frequency of purchasing food 14, 194, 197; irrational behaviour of 14–15; levels of expenditure on food 14; sensitivity to prices 15; transport 114–17; *see also* retailing and wholesaling
cooking *see* eating
Cordain, L. 89n6
Country Life 76
Creda **147–8**
credit: concept of 6
crop rotation 32–3, 59
cultural change: need for 128–30, 185, 198–9, 203, 211
Cutler, D. 88n2, 93n12

Davis, A. 149, **150**
de Leo, F. 137n26
de Vries, J. 121n3
deforestation: consequences of 26
DEFRA 128n15, 130n19, 131n22, 131n24, 176n37, 176n38
dehydrated foods 113
Department for Transport 109n6
Department of Health 130n20
des Abbayes, C. 123n8, 138n27
Dickens, C. 1, 24, 66
diet: globalisation, effect of 175; need for variety 42–3, 44
dieting industry 169
disease control **76**, 77, 80, 81
Donovan, P. 5n3, **46**, 46, 114n14
DuPont 126, 127

eating: community food 156–7; eating in / eating out 140; education, need for 158; financial credit crunch, effect of 156, 157; habits shaped by history, culture and genetics 140, 158; health issues 158; kitchen and home waste 196–8; policy ideas 208, **209**; technological innovation 157; urbanisation 142–3; 'what, where, when, why and how' 139; *see also* eating at home; eating out
eating at home: breakfasts 142, 149, **150**; constraints of 142–3, 144–6; cooking decisions and trade–offs 149; economic structures 142–3; Fisherman's Pie, ways of cooking 146, **147–8**, 149; health issues 149, 150; hierarchies 140–41; income inequality and eating inequality 141; industrialisation 142; inflation inequality 143–4; rules-of-thumb approaches to cooking 150–52; solitary eating 150; technological innovation 145; 'time-is-money' economics 146
eating out: control over what is eaten 153–4; economic and environmental costs 154, 155, 156; school meals **154**; structure of the economy 152–3; time poverty 155
'eatwell plate' 130
Ecological Society of America 49n3
economic content of food products 4, 5, 17
Economist 167n20
ecosystem services: importance of 10–12
Edwards-Jones, G. **109**
environmental credit crunch: concept of 6–7, 9; groups affected 16
environmental shocks: impact on individual countries 43, **44**, 44
European Crop Protection Association 55

'factory farming' 78, 79, 174–5, 178
Fairlie, S. 35, 67n10, 72n19, 80n27
'fallowing' 32
Falstaff, J. 180, 181, 182
famine 51, **51**, 161; prevention of 9
Farmers Guardian 113n9
fasting **164–5**
fat: consumption of 168; economic value of 63–4
Fearnley-Whittingstall, H. 151
Federation of Bakers 113n10
feedback loops 8
fertilisers: use of 33, **33–4**, 34–5, 36, 37, 186, 187
fertility: crop-rotation 32–3; 'fallowing' 32; fertilisers, use of 33, **33–4**, 34–5, 36, 37; improving the nitrogen content 31–2; yield, and 31
Field 142n3
Fife Diet 157
financial credit crunch: consequences of 12–13, 18
Fisher, M. **54n9**
Fisherman's Pie: ways of cooking 146, **147–8**, 149
'five-a-day' 169, 172
food availability: least-developed economies 44, **45**
food consumption patterns: changes in 17–18

food crunch 5
'food food-chain': notions of 2
'food miles' 102, 114, 193
food price shocks: impact on individual countries 43
food processing 83, 100; additives 93–4; adulteration 94–5; availability of foodstuffs 89, 92; bread-making 91, **91**; chips, consumption of **87** ; coffee processing **97**; consumers' need for reassurance 88, 89, 95; content of food 89, 94; economic structures in society, effect of 85, 86, 87, 88; economics of 83–4; energy use 98; environmental impact 96; health issues 92, 93, 176; high–GI foods 90; industrialisation of 84; market structure 99–100; micronutrients 90; packaging 95, 96, 98, 192; policy ideas 206–7, **207**; quantities of consumption 92–3; rise of factory processing 84; standardisation 97–8; technology use 99; waste 96–7, **97**, 98, 191–2
food security 39–40; autarky 40; consequences of a financial and an environmental credit crunch 40; efficiency of food production 40; incentivising production of otherwise imported foods 40; land and water resources 20; threat of 13, 40, 106–7; waste, and 183, 184, 185
Food Standards Agency (FSA) 95
food standards in international trade 175–6
Ford, W.C. 1
Foresight Programme of the UK Government 61n24, 166n11, 194
Foster-Powell, K. 89n7, 160n2
Fox, T. 127n13
Franklin, B. 32
free-range animals 78, 79
fungal infections **54–5**

Gaskell, M. 151n8
Gilbert, N. 34
Glasgow Herald 74n21
globalisation: diets, effect on 175; effect of 1; environmental impact of global food trade 108–9, 175–6; globally optimal food supply 108; productivity and resilience-related benefits of international trade 10, 107; transport, and 107–10
Glycaemic Index (GI) 89–90

Golding, W. 83n1
Gonzalez-Diaz, L. 59n22
Gordon, D. G. **174n29**
grasslands, role of 29
green beans: transport of 109, **109–10**, 110
Green Revolution **17**, **38**, 187, 201, 202
Grove, J. 181n1
guano 7, **33**, **34**
Guillette, E. **38**
Gulati, A. 127n14

Hamerschlag, K. 71n18, **72**
Hansard **76n22**
Hardin, G. **31**
Hickman, M. 67n9
high-frequency shopping 14, 194; consequences of 134–6, 197; decline of 120–23, 128; limits to 134; return of 133–4
Høgaas Eide, M. 99n22
Hough, A. **154**
Howard, C. 177n39
Hudson, J. 5n3, **46**, 46, 114n14
human health: economics of 159–60, 176–7; food–health–environment relationship 160–61, 177–8; policy ideas 209, **209–10**; retailing, and 130–31; waste, and 199–200; *see also* quality of food eaten; quantity of food eaten
Hwang, S. 97n19

importance of food 1
impulse buying 125, 126, 127, 136
income inequality: proportion of income spent on food 143–4
inflation inequality 143–4
insects: edible species of insect **173–4**
Institute of Grocery Distribution (IGD) 131n23, 134n25
Institution of Mechanical Engineers 189n8, 197n15
Intergovernmental Panel on Climate Change **23**
International Fertilizer Association 35n18
internet shopping 136, 138, 194
Irish potato famine 51, **51**, 161

Jefferies, B. **56**
Johnson, S. **154**
Jones, A. 114n12
Jowett, B. 54

Karlsson, H. 116, **116**
Keats, J. 42
Kelbie, P. **65n4**
Kingsmill 96
Kinney, A. 181n2
Kjaernes, U. 61n28
Koo, W. 166n13

Lancet 94
land: agricultural conversion, effect of 28–9; competing uses of 22; consequences of changing land use 29; deforestation, consequences of 26; demands for land use 21, 22; economic consequences of land use 22, **23**; economic resonance of 20–21; economic returns 21; ecosystem consequences of land use 22, **23**; environmental classifications of land use 22, **23**; grasslands, role of 29; limits to changing land use 25–6; policy ideas 204, **204**; quality of food 172–3, 177–8; ratio of human environmental resource use against the availability of resources 24, **24**; urbanisation, effect of 28; waste 186–7; wetlands, conversion of 27, **27**, 28; *see also* yield on land
Lang, T. 89n5
Lawrence, F. **91**, 92, 114n11
Leake, J. **165n10**
Leigh, G. **33n15**, 36n20
Life-Cycle Analysis 102, 115, 119; Publicly Available Specification (PAS) (2050) 104
Lovelock, J. 11
Lustig, R. 167n15
Lyall, S. 191n10

McBroom, P. 68n11
McCall Smith, A. 188
McCarthy, C. 45, 63, 64
McDonalds 171n25
McKie, R. 115n16
MacPherson, C. **55n14**
MacPherson, K. 169n23
McWilliams, J. 9n4, 53n7, 80n28, 103n2, 187n7
MarketLine 127n12
Marks & Spencer 124
Martin, E. 88n4, 121n4
Martin, J. 159
Matson, P. **38n22**
Mattson, M. **165**

Mattsson, B. 99n22
Mauser, W. 66n6
Mazoyer, M. **17n10**
mealworms **174**
micronutrients 90
milk: cost elements 3–4; milk quotas **74–5**; milking technology 76
Millennium Ecosystem Assessment 11–12, 15, 16
Miller, A. 6
Millstone, E. 89n5
Milton, K. 68
Mollison, B. **27n7**

Nabhan, G. P. 140
Nature 167
Nedwell, D. 28n8
Nonhebel, S. 73n20

obesity 163–4, 165; drivers of 165–6, 172; economic consequences of 177; 'obesogenic environment' 166
OECD–FAO 175n35
Oliver, J. 191
'One Hundred Mile Diet' 157
orange juice production: environmental impacts of transport 104, **104**, 105
Ortiz-Monasterio, R. 39n23
Orwell, G. 76, 170, 172

packaging: food processing 95, 96, 98, 192; retailing 137
Packard, V. 126n10
Park, J. 96n17
Parmentier, A. 198
Payne, D. **154**
Payne, M. **154**
Penman, J. 22n2
People's Supermarket 156
pest control 54–5, 59–60; waste, and 188
Peterman, K. **97n21**
plant health: economic / environmental divisions 52; pest control 54–5, 59–60; weed control 52–4
plant nutrition 172–3
politics of food pricing 15, 144
pollinators, avoiding the loss of 58–9
Popkin, B. 164n8
Population Reference Bureau 44n2
potatoes: consumption of 198–9; Irish potato famine 51, **51**, 161
processing *see* food processing
Purcell, R. **110n8**

quality of food eaten: agricultural land 172–3, 177–8; desire 169–70; dieting 169; 'distance' 170–72; edible species of insect **173–4**; 'five-a-day' 169, 172; food processing, impact of 176; food standards in international trade 175–6; health, and 169; meat consumption 174–5, 178
quantity of food eaten: cholesterol levels 168; economic consequences of overconsumption 177; and economic wellbeing 161, 165; fasting **164–5**; fat 168; income levels and (in)adequate consumption 161–3, 165; overconsumption and health problems 163–4, 165, 166; processed food 92–3; sugar 166–8
Quendler, T. 61
Quilty-Harper, C. 183n5

Ramos-Elorduy, J. **173n28**
Ratcliffe, S. 67n8
Reardon, T. 127n14
'red diesel' 103
Reeves, J. 198n16
Repton, H. 21
resilience: globalisation, and 10, 107; importance of 9–10
retailing and wholesaling: 'buy one, get one free' (BOGOF) principle 126–7; China's food retail industry 4–5; consumers' desire to economise 131–3; cultural change 128–30; environmental impacts 123–4; ethical / environmental purchasing decisions 131; health issues 130–31; high-frequency shopping, consequences of 134–6; high-frequency shopping, decline of 120–23, 128; high-frequency shopping, limits to 134; high-frequency shopping, return of 133–4; impulse buying 125, 126, 127, 136; industry concentration levels 127–8; internet shopping 136, 138, 194; overconsumption 125–7; packaging 137; policy ideas 207, **208**; retailers' influence over consumer choices 127; supporting local produce 138; waste 124, **125**, 125, 194–6
Rickert, E. 50
Roudart, L. **17n10**

Savage, S. 60
school meals **154**
Scotsman 157n19

Scott, R. **91**
seagulls **56**
seasonality in food production **115**, 115–16, **116**, 119
Seddon, Q. 79n26, 153n13, 186n6
Senior, N. 54
Shakespeare, W. 138, 139, 180
Silver Darlings **64–5**
'slash-and-burn' agriculture 30
Smith, D. 146, **147–8**, 151, 152n11, 191
snow geese **56**
soil degradation 57
solitary eating 150
Sonesson, U. 99n22
Song, M. 97n19
sowing and harvesting seasons: UK **115**, 115
Steinbeck, J. 55
Stephens, S. 11
Stuttgarter Zeitung 94n13
sugar: consumption 166, 167, 168; nutritional and environmental impacts of sugar production 166, 167, 168
'swidden agriculture' 30
swine fever **76**

Tanaka, D. 61n26
Taubes, G. 160n3
Taylor, A.-L. 78n25
Taylor, R. 166n13
technology: animal farming 76, 77, 78, 80, 81; cooking food 145, 157; food processing 99; inequality of effects of advances in agricultural technology **17**; risk management, and 8, 9; water delivery 39; yield of land, improving 38–9, 61
Tetra Pack 183n4
Thirsk, J. **27n6**
Thomas, G. **110**
Thompson, F. 101
Thompson, H. 61n27
Times 71n16
Tischner, U. 57n17, 61n28, 70n14
'Tottenham Pudding' 72, 200–201
Townshend, C. 32, 57
Transparency Market Research 177n40
transport 101; air freight 109–10; bread 112–13; consumers, and 114–17; dehydrated foods 113; economic and environmental issues 105, 117, **118**, 118–19; extent of food transport 103–4, 105; factory to retailer 110–12; farm to factory 105–7; 'food miles' 102, 114,

193; globalisation 107–10; green beans 109, **109–10**, 110; Life-Cycle Analysis 102, 104, 115, 119; orange juice production and environmental impacts of transport 104, **104**, 105; policy ideas 206, **206**; 'red diesel' 103; seasonality in food production 115–16, **116**, 119; sowing and harvesting seasons (UK) **115**, 115; waste, and 192–4
Transport 2000, UK 114n13
Tukker, A. 123n7
turnips 32

United Nations: Environment Programme **65n5**; Food and Agriculture Organization 20, 24, 36n20, **43**, **45**, 53n6, 71n15, 71n17, 88n3, 167n21, 175n34, 183n5
urbanisation: eating habits 142–3; land use 28
US Dairy Export Council 97n20

vegetable-based foods 42; biodiversity losses, avoiding 57–8; breeding 60–61; crop rotation 32–3, 59; economic price of veg mechanics 49; ecosystem trade-off matrix for grain markets **46**, 46; environmental costs of veg mechanics 49–52; importance of 45; Irish potato famine 51, **51**, 161; maximising the yield of crops 45, 46; plant health 52–5, 59–60; plant nutrition 172–3; policy ideas 204, **205**; pollinators, avoiding the loss of 58–9; potatoes, consumption of 198–9; precision in arable farming 48; shift to capital-based arable farming 47–8; soil degradation, avoiding 57; sustainable approaches to agriculture 56, 61; waste 187–9; water stress, avoiding 57
Venkat, K. 71n18, **72**
Vermuyden, C. **27**
Vorley, B. 127n13

wartime rationing 201
waste: animal husbandry 72–3, 189–91, 205, **205–6**; controlling waste 200–201; cultural change, need for 185, 198–9, 203, 211; developed and developing countries 185; economics of food waste 210; extent of 182, 183; Falstaffian approach to 182; food processing 96–7, **97**, 98, 191–2, 206–7, **207**; food security, and 183, 184, 185; human health, and 199–200, 209, **209–10**; importance of waste avoidance 5–6, 201–2, 203; kitchen and home waste 196–8, 208, **209**; land waste 186–7, 204, **204**; policy ideas 204–11; retailing and wholesaling 124, **125**, 125, 194–6, 207, **208**; summary of waste in the food food-chain **184**; trade-off between links in the food food-chain 181; transport 192–4, 206, **206**; vegetables 187–9, 204, **205**
Waste Watch 96n18
Watanabe, F. 145n5
water: technological advances in water delivery 39; waste 188; water stress 57; yield on land 37, **38**
weed control 52–4
Weight-control Information Network 163n7, 199n19
Welch, R. 173n27
wetlands: conversion of 27, **27**, 28
wholesaling see retailing and wholesaling
Wilde, O. 11
Wodehouse, P. G. 67, 75, 142, 169
Wohlmeyer, H. 61
Woodham-Smith, C. 54n8
Woodvine, A. 151
World Health Organization 92, 167
World Wildlife Fund for Nature **24**, 69n12, 69n13

yield on land 29; energy and yield 35–7; fertility 31–5; forms of 29–30; increasing agricultural yields 30; land ownership 39; technology to improve productivity 38–9, 61; water and yield 37, **38**
Yoo, S. 122n5
Yudkin, J. 167n17

Zielinski, S. 57n19

Taylor & Francis
eBooks
FOR LIBRARIES

ORDER YOUR FREE 30 DAY INSTITUTIONAL TRIAL TODAY!

Over 22,000 eBook titles in the Humanities, Social Sciences, STM and Law from some of the world's leading imprints.

Choose from a range of subject packages or create your own!

Benefits for you
- ▶ Free MARC records
- ▶ COUNTER-compliant usage statistics
- ▶ Flexible purchase and pricing options

Benefits for your user
- ▶ Off-site, anytime access via Athens or referring URL
- ▶ Print or copy pages or chapters
- ▶ Full content search
- ▶ Bookmark, highlight and annotate text
- ▶ Access to thousands of pages of quality research at the click of a button

For more information, pricing enquiries or to order a free trial, contact your local online sales team.

UK and Rest of World: online.sales@tandf.co.uk
US, Canada and Latin America: e-reference@taylorandfrancis.com

www.ebooksubscriptions.com

A flexible and dynamic resource for teaching, learning and research.